An Unholy Drought

ALSO BY MADHULIKA LIDDLE

The Muzaffar Jang Series

The Englishman's Cameo (2009)
The Eighth Guest & Other Muzaffar Jang Mysteries (2011)
Engraved in Stone (2012)
Crimson City (2015)

The Delhi Quartet Series

The Garden of Heaven (2021)

The Mandala Purana Series (co-authored with Kannan Iyer)

The Pledge: Adventures to Sada (2023)

Short Stories

My Lawfully Wedded Husband & Other Stories (2012)
Woman to Woman: Stories (2017)

An Unholy Drought

A Novel

Madhulika Liddle

SPEAKING
TIGER

SPEAKING TIGER BOOKS LLP
125A, Ground Floor, Shahpur Jat, near Asiad Village,
New Delhi 110049

First published by Speaking Tiger Books in 2024

ISBN: 978-93-5447-769-0
eISBN: 978-93-5447-747-8

10 9 8 7 6 5 4 3 2 1

Typeset in Sabon LT Std by SÜRYA, New Delhi
Printed at Impressions Printing & Packaging Limited

For Dipali Taneja. Thank you.

Contents

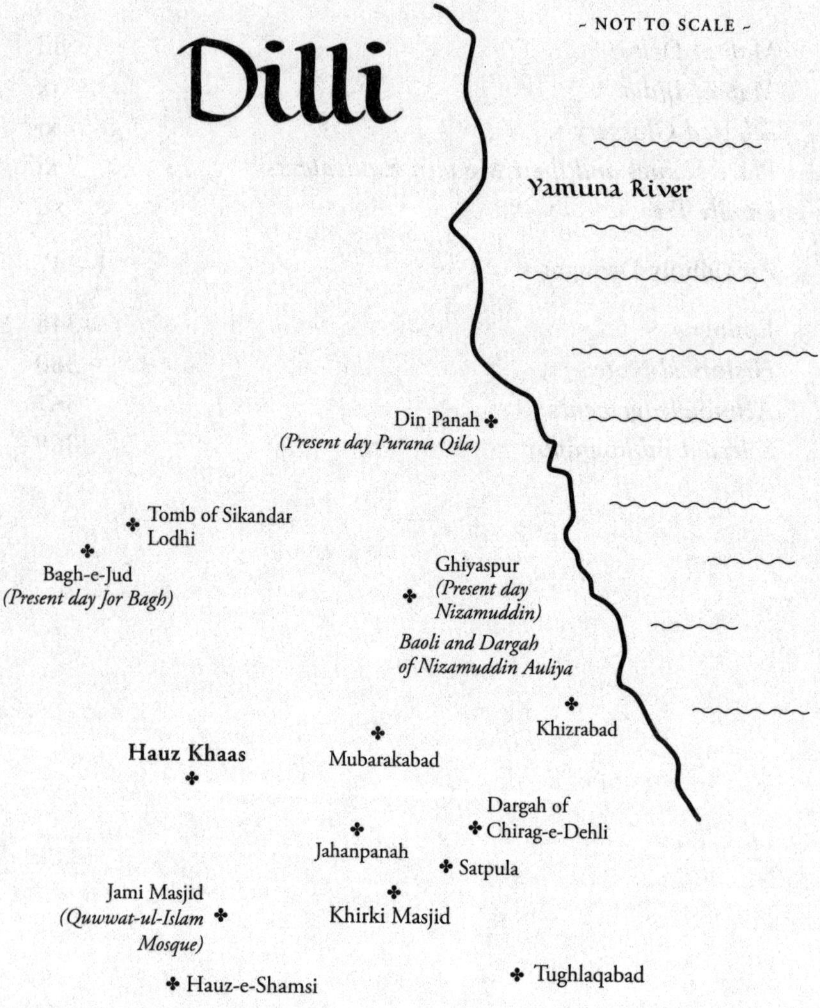

Dilli
- NOT TO SCALE -
Yamuna River
Din Panah
(Present day Purana Qila)
Tomb of Sikandar Lodhi
Bagh-e-Jud
(Present day Jor Bagh)
Ghiyaspur
(Present day Nizamuddin)
Baoli and Dargah of Nizamuddin Auliya
Khizrabad
Mubarakabad
Hauz Khaas
Dargah of Chirag-e-Dehli
Jahanpanah
Satpula
Jami Masjid
(Quwwat-ul-Islam Mosque)
Khirki Masjid
Hauz-e-Shamsi
Tughlaqabad

- NOT TO SCALE -

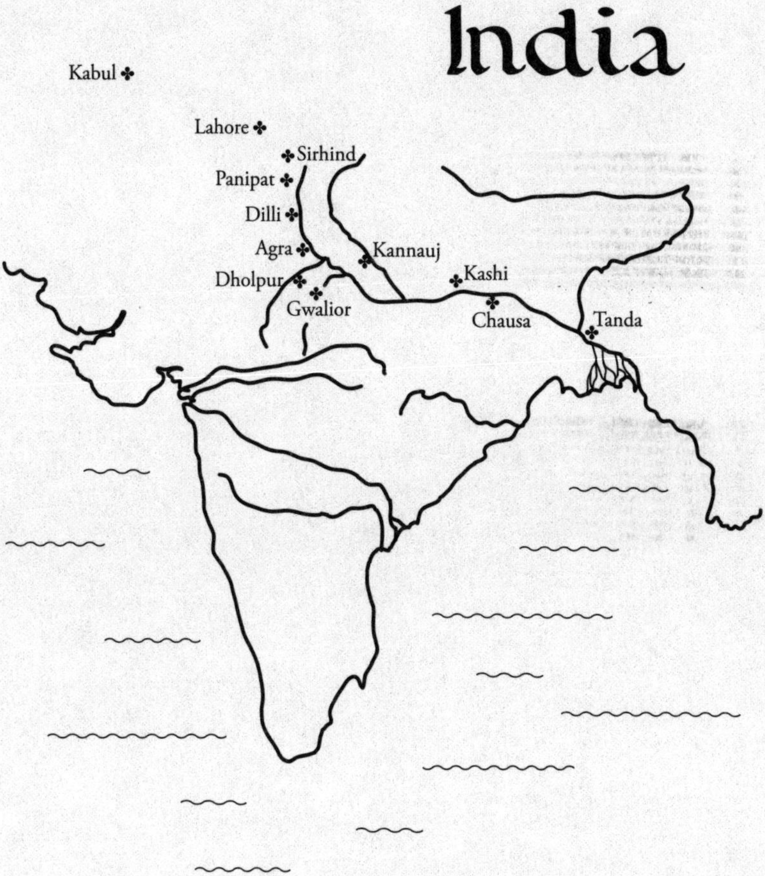
India
Kabul
Lahore
Sirhind
Panipat
Dilli
Agra
Kannauj
Dholpur
Gwalior
Kashi
Chausa
Tanda

Selected Glossary

Angoorshefa	*Atropa belladonna*, or deadly nightshade, a poisonous plant that is also used medicinally
Bakain	*Melia azedarach*, also known as Persian lilac or chinaberry, a tree that looks similar to the neem (to which it is related) and bears bunches of lilac-coloured flowers
Chamrod	*Ehretia laevis*, a small tree native to Delhi
Faraash	*Tamarix aphylla*, a small bushy evergreen tree found mostly along the riverbank in Delhi
Gular	*Ficus racemosa* or cluster fig, one of Delhi's most common fig trees. The gular's figs grow in clusters from the trunk of the tree
Hauz	Water tank, pool
Kaas	Wild sugarcane, *Sachharum spontaneum*. A tall, wild grass with feathery masses of tiny white flowers
Kadamba	*Neolamarckia cadamba*, a common tree across much of India, known for its globe-shaped orange-yellow flowers
Madarsa	In medieval India and elsewhere, a term used for a school of higher education, a university
Maulsari	*Mimusops elengi* or Spanish cherry, a tree native to the Indian sub-continent and common in Delhi
Palash	Flame of the forest, *Butea monosperma*, also known as dhak. One of Delhi's native trees, this is known for its thick leaves, used to make leaf-plates, and for its deep orange flowers, which are shaped like a parrot's beak
Semal	Red silk cotton, *Bombax ceiba*. A tall, handsome tree with a thorny trunk and large, fleshy red or orange flowers

Place Names and their Modern Equivalents (Where Valid)

Ajodhan	Pakpattan, now in Pakistan
Dibalpur	More commonly known as Dipalpur, now in Pakistan
Tanda	Tandah or Khwaspur Tanda, in Bengal. Now vanished; it was inundated by floods circa 1826 CE

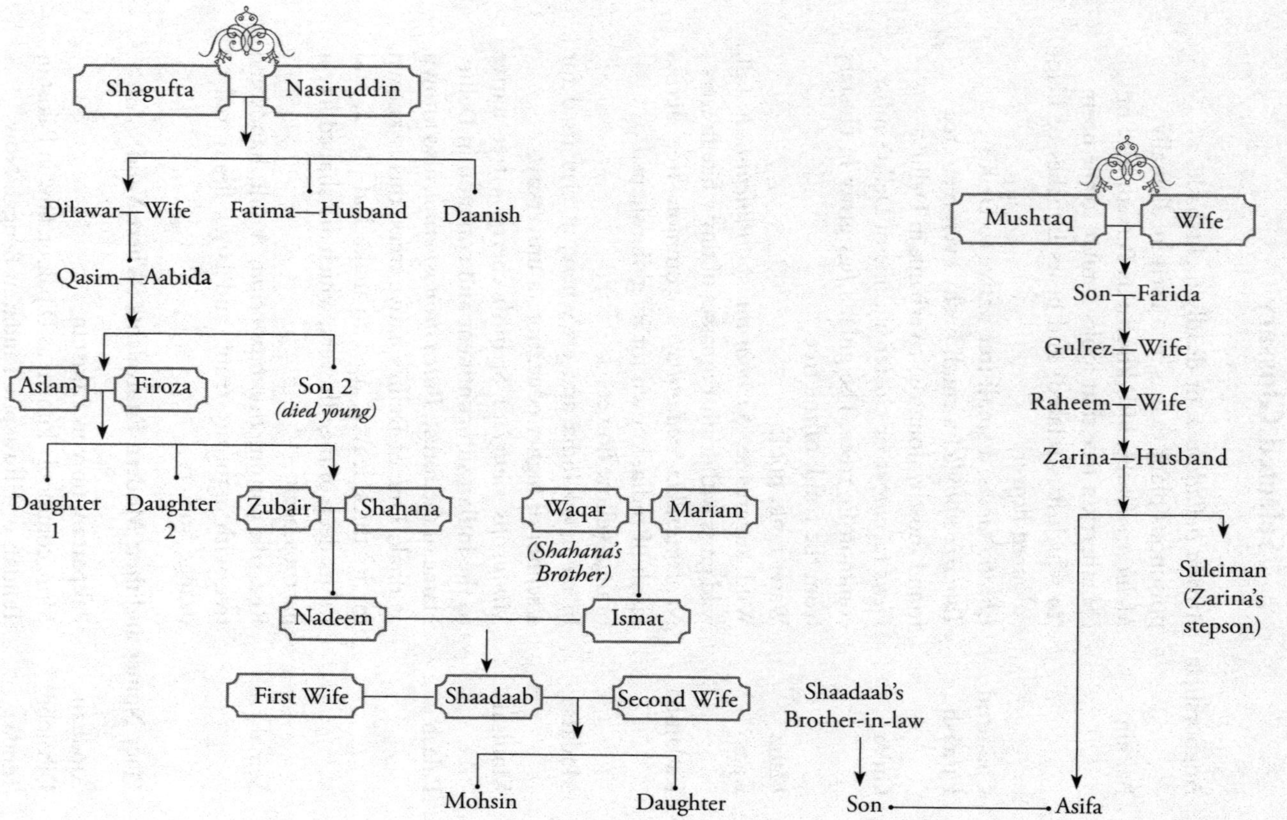
Shagufta
Nasiruddin
Dilawar
Wife
Fatima
Husband
Daanish
Qasim
Aabida
Aslam
Firoza
Son 2
(died young)
Daughter 1
Daughter 2
Zubair
Shahana
Waqar
Mariam
(Shahana's Brother)
Nadeem
Ismat
First Wife
Shaadaab
Second Wife
Mohsin
Daughter
Mushtaq
Wife
Son
Farida
Gulrez
Wife
Raheem
Wife
Zarina
Husband
Suleiman (Zarina's stepson)
Shaadaab's Brother-in-law
Son
Asifa

Prologue

Rabi Al-Awwal 12,
963 Hijri (24th January 1556 CE)

I am sitting on the mattress, one leg folded under, the other bent at the knee. On my bent knee is a thin rectangle of wood, on which rests the page I will write on.

I take a deep breath. This is how my uncle Waqar taught me when I was a child training to be a calligrapher. 'Hold your breath,' I can hear him say, even though more than half a century has passed. 'It will steady your hand.'

I have not needed any artifice to steady my hand these past forty years and more; but now I do. I am failing. My hands tremble, my eyesight is dwindling.

But I have a task to complete. I was given the responsibility of recording this story, not just because I am a calligrapher by training and aptitude, but because I have the requisite reverence for the past that an endeavour like this commands. Those who look only to the future will see little worth in what I am about to begin; but I know it must be done.

In the well of black ink, I dip the nib of my reed pen, the qalam which has been my constant companion since I was four years old. It has been sixty years now: at my last birthday—uncelebrated, unnoticed, forgotten even by me—I turned sixty-four.

The Baadshah, may Allah preserve him, may be dead.

Mohsin, who has been looking over my shoulder as I write this, says it makes no sense. 'If Allah is to preserve the Baadshah,' says my grandson, 'how can the Baadshah be dead?' He is fifteen years old, this boy, and too cocky for his own good.

I try to be patient.

'All lives of true believers are in the safekeeping of Allah,' I reply. 'Whether alive or dead.'

'And the Baadshah may be dead? How?' Mohsin persists. This is another of his traits that I disapprove of: he is too curious to be discreet.

'Keep quiet,' I say.

Suleiman came today, bearing the news. Din Panah, the grand citadel that Sher Shah Suri had begun and which the Baadshah completed, is north of our neighbourhood, Ghiyaspur. It is not all that far, but certainly not next door. But Suleiman, who looks up to me as mentor and teacher, says he did not think twice about travelling all the way.

'Suleiman is a sycophant,' says Mohsin.

'He is not,' I say. 'He is a good man and a wise one, and he acknowledges that I have played an important role in the shaping of his personality.'

Mohsin makes an odd sound, something like a stifled giggle. When I look at him, though, he is merely looking bemused. He shakes his head, as if to deny his amusement, even though I have said nothing by way of jest or admonition.

'Go away, Mohsin,' I say. I love the boy—Allah knows I would give my life for him—but sometimes he can be tedious. I need to return to my work. Work that is not easy, and which will probably take me several months to complete. At my age, several months is not to be assumed as a given.

Come to think of it, in these times, a month or a week or even a day cannot be a given for any of us, not after this famine and the plague that has followed in its wake. Not after the wars and the almost perpetual unrest here in Dilli. It has been almost a year since the Baadshah returned to the throne, but little has changed since his coming. I had thought, I had hoped, that there would be relief, that things would change.

Sher Shah Suri had been a good ruler, and so was his son, Salim Shah Suri. But ever since the death of Salim Shah Suri, the empire has been in such turmoil that if on any day you had asked me who sat on the throne, I would have had to think. When the Baadshah Humayun returned, I thought, as did many, that finally peace had returned as well. And with peace, plenty would return. And health, fullness of life, joy.

Over the past two years, we have seen things go from bad to worse in ways we could never have imagined. Famine has destroyed this land, all the way from Agra west into Gujarat, and it has done more than merely render the earth sterile and sere; it has ravaged our souls, our humanity. That it reduced people to eating wild grasses and cow hides was bad enough; but the whispers that it had turned the more desperate to cannibalism… that sent shivers down my spine the first time I heard of it. Initially, I had dismissed it as a ghoulish rumour flung about by those with a taste for the macabre. Now I know it is true; I have seen bands of men, their limbs stick-thin, the madness bright in their eyes, digging up graves and breaking into houses.

We, my family, are fortunate. We have enough wealth to keep us fed, yet not enough to draw unwanted attention. We are a small family, after all; just the four of us, and since my daughter-in-law had already left for her parents' home in Bengal when this famine set in, it is just my son, Mohsin, and I. We need little, and we have convinced ourselves that we can do with even less than that. We eat one meal a day, and that carefully rationed. My son takes Mohsin every now and then on excursions: along the riverbank, or into the low hills to the west, to forage. Sometimes they bring back pods of Egyptian thorn from which we can harvest seeds. Sometimes there is a tuber, a small wild animal or bird. A fortnight ago, they brought back a bandicoot. It was small, shriveled and starved, but it was a feast for us.

All three of us have become gaunt, dry, older than we are. My years have worked against me, my muscles so weak that I can now barely move. But—oh, the irony of it—in the midst of this scarcity, I have a surfeit of time, paper and ink. The many stacks of paper, from my heyday as one of Dilli's most famous and well-respected calligraphers, are still here. My reed pens, carefully trimmed. My ink slabs. My memories. I have to put them down on paper, for who knows how long this famine will last? If the drought does not kill us, the pestilence will. Or this unrest will, this uncertainty.

I wonder what will happen, if the Baadshah is indeed dead. The young prince Jalaluddin is a mere boy, not even as old as my irritating Mohsin. True, he has already been appointed Governor of the Punjab; and true, too, that he has good advisers, men who are seasoned generals, worthy administrators; but it all boils down, eventually, to the man himself. And he is not yet a man. What can he do? The prospects look grim.

'But if you're writing the history of our family, why begin with the Baadshah's death?' Mohsin asks.

'To set the context,' I say, dipping the nib of my pen in the ink once again and bending back to my work.

He has seen me at work before, enough times to know that I do not like company when I have my qalam in hand. From the corner of my eye, I see him leave the room.

Suleiman, I should explain, is an official at the Imperial Court, and no mere fan-swinger or spittoon-holder, either. He is a scribe, and well-respected. Well-respected enough to be fairly well-fed even in these terrible times.

Suleiman came, and brought with him—besides a small melon—momentous news. This is all hearsay, none of it confirmed, as Suleiman was quick to emphasize.

Four days ago, the Baadshah was in his library at Din Panah. It is an unusual building, a short octagonal tower made of red stone, called Sher Mandal—anyhow, the Baadshah was in Sher Mandal when the aazaan, the call for prayer, rang out from the mosque nearby. In his hurry to offer namaaz, the Baadshah tripped on the staircase and fell. Suleiman told me that some believe the Baadshah had already realized it was time for the namaaz, and had been descending the staircase when he heard the aazaan, and tried, therefore, to kneel on the steps. I doubt that.

The Baadshah, while he had his weaknesses, his too-great generosity and his naïveté among them, was not so foolish. He would not have imagined a steep and narrow step would be a suitable place to offer namaaz.

For four days he lingered. For four days, the Governor of Dilli, Tardi Beg Khan, administered the city and waited for Allah's mercy. Prayers have been offered continuously for the Baadshah's life, and the highest and most powerful in this land have wondered and watched—and feared? They say a message was sent to the Shahzaada Jalaluddin, informing him of the tragedy. The prince turned his forces around and marched towards Kalanaur, where he received further news, optimistic news—for the Baadshah had recovered long enough to assure his son that he was on the mend.

'And today,' said Suleiman, 'the Baadshah has died. I am certain of it. But tell no one yet, Mirza Sahib. Until Tardi Beg Khan Sahib or one of the others makes a proclamation, keep this to yourself.'

That was insulting; I am no tattle-tale. But I let it pass. Suleiman must be overwrought.

When he had taken his leave, I sat down to think.

I am older than the Baadshah was. Death is never far when you are this age. It is the mercy of Allah that has kept me alive and well all these years. But what if an accident should befall me, the way it did the Baadshah? The Baadshah, with all his legions of physicians and well-wishers and slaves, could not stall Azrael, the Angel of Death. What of me, then?

For if I die, my story will die with me.

Not the story of my own life, for that is inconsequential. But the story of my ancestors, of which I am the only one now who knows. Once, many years ago, my grandfather had sat me down and told me about our family, about how we came to be where we are. He had told me then to pay heed, to not forget, and to pass it on. Because future generations need to know, he had said, that they may learn from the mistakes of their forefathers.

I have put it off all these years. Who thinks of death when all is well? In the midst of plenty, when one is healthy and safe and well-fed, who would even imagine that death might come knocking?

But now, it is different. With the way things have been these past two years, I am surprised, sometimes, to find that I still live. It is high time I put pen to paper.

Before I begin, I should explain. Many years ago—more than a hundred and fifty years—an ancestress of mine told a story such as this. She told it to a soldier, a man from an invading army. He was badly wounded, and she (we, in my family, have a long history of taking decisions with our hearts rather than our minds) took him in and tended to him. He went away, back to his own land, after a week or so of listening to her tale, but he returned, two years later. Shagufta—for that was her name, even though she was born a Hindu and perhaps oscillated between the two faiths through much of her life—married him.

Shagufta was well into her thirties by the time she married Nasiruddin. She had been married before and had been widowed after just a few months, with no child to comfort her. With Nasiruddin, though, she was luckier: not only did they spend twenty years as husband and wife, she bore him three children as well.

The eldest of them, Dilawar, was a quiet man of no special significance, who drifted away into mysticism and then into a detachment from the world that none of his family quite understood. Dilawar did not merely distance himself from the mundane and the materialistic; he distanced himself from his friends and family. One day in his youth, with bowed head but defiant eyes, he said goodbye to them all, never to be seen again.

There was a daughter, named Fatima, who went off to Kabul after she was married to a merchant from that mountain town. There was the occasional letter from Fatima—and that too only while her mother, Shagufta, was alive; when Shagufta died, her daughter seemed to consider her last bond with Dilli broken. There had not been a letter from her ever since.

And there was the second son, Daanish. Daanish, who lived on in Dilli. Daanish, whose name meant wisdom. Daanish, who did not seem inclined to live up to the name bestowed on him.

1
Dilli
824 Hijri (1421 CE)

Daanish woke late that morning. His throat had been sore the previous day, and night had brought with it more discomfort: a blocked nose and a dry mouth that made him rise repeatedly to drink from the earthen waterpot in his room.

He blinked in the ray of sunlight streaming in through a crack in the wall, and winced at the headache that throbbed at his temples.

His first thought was to stay in bed, under the thick sheet that covered him. The weather was at that rare point in Dilli's year when it was neither too hot nor too cold, neither too wet nor too dry and dusty. The monsoon had gone, leaving the city cool and refreshed. Diwali was a mere week away, and winter had not yet set in. It was a day when lying in bed and dozing through the day was permissible. Especially if one had slept little the night before, and was feeling unwell. Especially if there was no parent to prod and push and scold.

And no parent to comfort, to provide, to care. Nobody to draw water from the well or cook food. Or earn the money with which to buy food.

Daanish cursed as he sat up, his headache flaring up at the movement.

He had to go to work. If he was not there at the market square, someone else would be. Junaid, for instance, eighteen years to Daanish's fifteen, and envious of the younger man's already established career as a letter writer. Junaid was not well-read; he was literate, that was all. For those who knew what they wanted written, Junaid and the single coin he charged as fees were sufficient. For those who wanted more—to create a good impression, through fine penmanship and accomplished prose—Daanish was the choice.

But if Daanish did not set up his business under the banyan tree well before noon, Junaid would be the one they would go to. Some may never return to Daanish.

As he washed and dressed, Daanish wondered if the man he had replaced a year ago had thought the same way about him: an upstart with little skill, trying to compete with his betters. Daanish had never even learnt the man's name: he had been a small, shrivelled fellow with a penchant for neatness that showed in everything from his carefully trimmed beard to his threadbare but scrupulously clean clothes. A man with a sour face, who had looked contemptuous but unworried when Daanish had first set up shop under the banyan tree.

It had taken less than a fortnight for Daanish to steal away half the customers from the man. Within less than a month, his eyes full of reproach, the old man had gathered up his paper and pens and gone away.

Daanish felt better after he had eaten a handful of the roasted gram that, along with fruit, was his staple diet. Ammi would not have approved. She had known only poverty before she had married Abba, and even though the marriage had brought her happiness and a degree of relative comfort, she had never quite forgotten what it was to be poor. 'You must eat well when you can afford it,' she used to tell her children, filling them with rotis and dal and vegetables and the occasional meat. 'If you are strong, you will last longer. Then even if disaster strikes and you have to go without food, you will not collapse immediately.'

That had not been Ammi's own experience; she had been used to eating whatever she could scrape together. But it had been Abba's experience, and Ammi had seen it. Abba, though he had been a mere soldier, was from a family well-off enough to be able to afford meat and grain in abundance, dried fruit and almonds... Abba, who had suffered a wound that might have been fatal had Ammi not rescued him and nursed him back to life. Feeding him the meagre scraps she herself ate, and whatever she could forage. And he had survived, survived and grown in strength enough to return to his own land. Because of a lifetime of eating well. Or so Ammi would have her children believe.

Daanish could not resist a wry grin. Ammi and her beliefs. Or were they even beliefs? For a woman like her, something had to be deeply felt, down to the very essence of her being—to merit the investment of her trust in it. Abba had passed the test. Fatima had, to some extent: but Ammi would never know that with her death, her daughter's allegiance to her birth family had been withdrawn. Dilawar, of course, had betrayed that trust, leaving Ammi shattered.

What would she have said about Daanish? Would she have thought him still worthy of her trust?

❧

The bazaar hummed in the low, lazy way that characterized the afternoon. The buyers had gone home to their lunches. The shopkeepers were resting, even if that involved nothing more than sitting back against a bolster and staring, glassy-eyed, onto the lane while chewing paan. The Qutb Minar, silhouetted against the cloudless blue of an autumn sky, stood half a kos away, a black kite circling lazily around it.

Daanish had had a busy morning. As he had feared, there were customers who had gone to Junaid as soon as they had discovered Daanish's absence. But there were others who had waited for him. Once he had taken his seat, work had gone on nonstop for the next few hours. When the ink had dried on the last page and it had been handed over to its owner, Daanish stood up and stretched, trying to work the tension out of his muscles. His headache, numbed briefly by breakfast and then half-forgotten by work, howled back into existence. He squeezed his eyes shut.

'Are you the son of Nasiruddin?' asked a voice.

It was a man, a man whose clothing did not fit his

features. That dark complexion, those black eyes and that neatly oiled moustache belonged with a cotton dhoti, not the pajamas and tunic he wore.

'Yes,' Daanish said. 'My father has been dead three years now,' he added.

The man had come closer. There were threads of grey in his moustache and crow's feet at the corners of the eyes. There was something about his skin—a weathered look, a cobweb of fine lines and spots and blemishes—that lent him a timeless look. He could have been thirty years old and prematurely grey; he could have been sixty.

'My name is Devraj,' he said. 'I knew your father in Samarqand.'

'Samarqand?' Daanish frowned. 'But Abba had not been to Samarqand for many years.' And what were you doing in Samarqand, he thought of asking. Because from the looks of you, you belong in Dilli, not in Samarqand. But your clothes fit with Samarqand, perhaps. Or what would pass muster if Samarqand got as hot as Dilli. Did it? Daanish did not know; he had never happened to ask his father that question.

'Well, perhaps that was not accurate,' Devraj conceded. 'It might be more correct to say that I met him on the way to Samarqand. We left Dilli together.'

ơ

That explanation too had given the wrong impression; it had implied that they had been friends, fellow travellers. Fellow travellers, yes; but one of them had been unwilling.

Even as Taimur had plundered Dilli of her honour and her wealth, he had taken note of her beauty, the majesty of her mosques and the elegance of her palaces. When he was done, he had taken prisoner those he thought primarily responsible for the beauty of Dilli, and had carted them off to his own city back in his native land, to make Samarqand as beautiful as Dilli. There had been stone masons among them, carvers, metal workers, architects. Men skilled in stucco and in the hundred other ways in which Indians decorated their buildings.

Devraj, a stone carver, had been one of those thousands of artisans and craftsmen carried off to Samarqand.

'It is not another Dilli,' Devraj said, shaking his head. 'It is a different city, nothing like Dilli at all. All he wanted was our skill, to use as he pleased.'

On the long trek from Dilli to Samarqand, Nasiruddin had been assigned to guard Devraj and a dozen others. 'It took me a few days to realize he was not like the other guards,' Devraj murmured, his eyes softening as they gazed at the past. 'They were under orders to not ill-treat us; after all, we were being taken back to work—it would do no good to have us wounded or crippled. But few of the soldiers heeded that order. We were not marked, but we got kicked and slapped, cursed and spat upon. We were given half the rations allowed, and that too grudgingly.

'Nasiruddin was not like that,' Devraj added. 'He was a good man; he rarely even raised his voice. His comrades mocked him for it. Some went further. There were arguments, blows exchanged. But Nasiruddin did not change.'

Daanish could not afford to leave his place under the banyan tree just yet; there were still several hours of daylight left, the chance of more customers. 'I will sit with you if I may,' Devraj had said, and from that had proceeded the story of Nasiruddin and how Devraj had come to know him.

They had reached Samarqand after a long and arduous journey of several months, with many—soldiers and artisans—succumbing to disease, fatigue and wounds along the way. In Samarqand, Devraj was in Nasiruddin's charge one moment, sent off to a work site another. Devraj was lucky that a few of the other stone carvers who had been with him through the journey were also fellow workers at the same site. They were to build a mosque, and while the architects worked with the masons to erect the structure, the stone carvers, tile-makers and stucco workers sat in vast workshops and did their work.

'I did not see Nasiruddin for many months; I had even forgotten him. Then one day, I was in the bazaar, and there he was, buying dates.'

Suddenly, they found themselves friends. No longer captor and captive, not even just acquaintances, because once you have sheltered under the same makeshift tent with a man, once you have dribbled water into his mouth during a raging fever and he has helped dig an arrow out of your back, you can no longer be mere acquaintances. They had become friends, even though neither of them had noticed that fact when they had parted ways earlier. Now they renewed that acquaintance, and acknowledged it for the friendship it was.

Nasiruddin had told Devraj about the woman he had met in Dilli, about the love he had left behind in the city. He had spoken long and with an aching heart of Shagufta, though not in the way most men spoke of women. Not of her beauty or her virtues, but of other things: her wisdom and strength, her patience. It was as if Shagufta had become, for him, all soul, all heart and all mind. Her body was immaterial.

'And that is true love, isn't it,' Devraj said. Then, looking embarrassed—he was, after all, talking to a fifteen-year-old who was the son of the man and woman he was discussing—he changed the topic somewhat. 'I think the love he bore your mother, and the love she had for Dilli, endeared the city to him, too. That was why he was different from the others. That was why he felt for us.'

It was Devraj who, seeing the yearning in his friend's eyes, had suggested Nasiruddin return to Dilli. 'His heart was here,' he said quietly. 'He was a mere shell in Samarqand. What is the use of living like that? It was not as if his parents had no other sons. It was not as if he had a wife and children. There was nothing there for him, and everything here.'

And now, more than twenty years later, Devraj too had returned to Dilli. 'I was given my freedom,' he said. 'Samarqand is beautiful, and I had become used to it; but one cannot forget one's own home, can one?' He looked about him, past the surrounding huts and modest houses, to the bulk of the Yogmaya Temple nearby; and beyond, to the soaring stone screens of the Jami Masjid, beside the Qutb Minar. His eyes softened, and Daanish was tempted to ask if Devraj, like Daanish's own ancestors, had perhaps once worked on buildings as magnificent as these. Or was it simply Dilli he saw, not the temple or the mosque? Both symbols of a beloved home town?

Perhaps Abba too had yearned for Samarqand, the way Devraj had for Dilli. Abba had not spoken much of his native land, though, from what Daanish recalled. Perhaps he had been too young to notice: twelve when his father died, nearly fourteen when his mother followed.

'I went to where my home used to be,' Devraj explained. 'But my family is all gone. My wife is dead, my children scattered. The gods alone know whether any of them still live.' He forced a smile to his lips. 'I wonder if I even have a right to call them my children anymore; I was not there for more than a few years during their childhood. They would not remember me.' His eyes had filled. A tear seeped, involuntary and unnoticed, from one eye and made its way down one cheek.

Daanish was unnerved by this display of emotion. Emotion unheeded by its sufferer is even more distressing to the onlooker than deliberate, knowing weeping. 'There must be someone who would know,' he said, feeling compelled to speak. 'Neighbours? Would they not know where your children had gone?'

'They do not know. They say that when my wife died of cholera, my eldest son gathered up everything they had, and took the younger ones away. Nobody knows where.'

'Like my brother,' Daanish murmured, half to himself.

'Your brother?'

Daanish told him about Dilawar and his renunciation of the world.

'We should go out together into the big wide world,' said Devraj with a sad smile. 'You to look for your brother, I to look for my children.'

Daanish shook his head. He wanted to say that he barely even remembered his brother, and did not miss him. But that might sound hard-hearted; so he simply said, 'And what if my brother should refuse to come back?'

'What if my children should fail to even recognize me?' He stiffened, suddenly struck by a thought. 'I am likely to not recognize them.'

Customers had started trickling back to the chaupal by then, crowding around Daanish. Devraj moved away, leaving him to his work. The younger man immersed himself in his work, no longer even thinking of the stone carver.

As evening drew in and the customers dwindled, Daanish put away his paper and ink and pen, preparing to go back home. He was getting to his feet when Devraj reappeared, a smile on his face and a small packet, crafted of palash leaves, in his hand. He held it out to Daanish. 'For you,' he said. 'Your father was fond of sweet things; I hope you are, too. Think of it as a gift from him.'

Daanish accepted the sweet hesitantly, murmuring his thanks as he did so.

Devraj shrugged, falling into step beside Daanish as he moved away from the chaupal. 'It's nothing.' There was a silence, and then Devraj chuckled. 'I still cannot get over the fact that there are coins here in the name of Taimur's successor, Shah Rukh. That gave me a shock when I first arrived in Dilli.'

Daanish frowned, puzzled. 'There are also new coins, with the names of the Tughlaq Sultans.'

Devraj shook his head, the expression on his face one of a somewhat sarcastic wonderment. 'The Tughlaqs, long dead. Shah Rukh, so far away.'

Daanish said nothing. Devraj's words were true, even if his tone was mocking. Over twenty years ago, when the Chaghtai invader Taimur had invaded Hindustan, the Governor of Punjab, a man named Khizr Khan, had sided with him. His devotion and loyalty to Taimur were such that when Taimur's forces withdrew, Taimur left Khizr Khan in charge of the territories he had won: Lahore, Multan, Dibalpur and parts of Sindh included. Khizr Khan had held those regions for Taimur till Taimur's death sixteen years earlier, and continued to administer them thereafter in the name of Taimur's son and successor, Shah Rukh.

To those territories, Khizr Khan had added Dilli when the last of the Tughlaqs, Nasiruddin Mahmud Shah, had died eight years ago. Khizr Khan had become Sultan, a man proudly proclaiming that he was a descendant of none other than the Prophet himself: a Sayyid. Equally vociferously, he had announced that Shah Rukh was his liege lord; he, Khizr Khan, was a mere vassal. In Taimur's name he had ruled the western territories, in Shah Rukh's name he continued to rule both them as well as Dilli. On Fridays, when the sermon was read at the Jami Masjid, it was Shah Rukh who was heralded as ruler, not Khizr Khan.

Khizr Khan had died just a few months back, and with his dying breath, he had passed on to his son, Mubarak Shah, the adjunction to be ever loyal, ever subservient, to Shah Rukh.

'He's a new ruler, isn't he, this Mubarak Shah Sayyid?' said Devraj. 'I wonder if he will continue to kowtow to Shah Rukh.' He shook his head, dismissing the topic.

Daanish, never interested in politics, was more than happy to let that subject be. 'What do you mean to do?' he asked, as they walked along. 'Now that your family is gone, what will you do? Will you really go searching for them? Do you have any money?'

'I have some,' Devraj conceded. 'My earnings, whatever I was able to save out of the pittance I got when I was in Samarqand.' He chewed his moustache, his expression worried. 'I had thought it would suffice for a few months. I had not realized just how expensive it is to come from Samarqand to Dilli if you have to pay your way rather than be dragged along on the end of a chain.' He grinned. 'I have enough for a few days yet, and I am looking for work. When I left Dilli, workers in stone were in demand. I hope they still are.'

ɞ

They had parted ways, and Daanish had gone home. The next morning, when he arrived at the banyan tree, Devraj was back. Daanish nodded a greeting at him, though his heart had sunk at the sight of the man. It was not that he disliked Devraj; he was a pleasant enough man, and he had once, many years ago, been Abba's friend. But Daanish could not help but wonder if he would, sooner or later, ask him for money. Or, equally embarrassing, want to be friends with him.

Daanish did not like being pushed into relationships. There were few people he considered friends and with whom he could be himself. He paused, in the midst of pulling out his papers and his reed pens from the small sack in which he carried them. No, not even a few, now that Abba, Ammi, Dilawar and Fatima were all gone. Now there was only Mushtaq. Mushtaq, his childhood friend; Mushtaq, because of whom he had found employment as a letter writer.

It had been six days since he had last seen Mushtaq. Last week, one of the many festive days of the Hindu calendar just before Diwali had meant that everybody had been in a celebratory mood. The shopkeepers were busy, the letter writers jobless. Mushtaq had come by, and seeing Daanish sitting idle, had dragged him off on an impromptu picnic. They had walked through the winding lanes of the settlement, passing the Dargah of Qutbuddin Bakhtiyar Kaki, and on to the Hauz-e-Shamsi.

The story went that almost two hundred years ago the Prophet had appeared in a dream to the Sultan Iltutmish, and had told him to excavate a water tank at the spot where the Prophet's mount, the buraaq, had left its hoofprint. The next morning, Iltutmish had gone out with his courtiers to see if he could identify the area the Prophet had indicated in his dream. It was found, less than a kos from where the Jami Masjid stood—and lo and behold, on that patch of land, as if to confirm Iltutmish's dream, was a stone slab with the hoofprint of the buraaq on it. Iltutmish had given orders to have a lake created here, and it was named for him, for Shamsuddin Iltutmish: Hauz-e-Shamsi, the water tank of Shamsi.

The water was deep and clear, and the small pavilion that held the slab with its hoofprint still stood in the centre of the hauz. Daanish had been content to relax on the grassy bank, but Mushtaq—forever irreverent—had proposed a swim. A panicking Daanish had warned against what would happen if he were caught, but Mushtaq had taken his own sweet time agreeing. But as he had flung himself down on the grass beside Daanish, there had been in his eyes a lazy mischievousness which had made Daanish wonder whether Mushtaq had really meant to swim, or whether it had all been a ploy to tease a reaction out of Daanish.

Mushtaq was perfectly capable of doing something like that: he was a scamp, with no scruples and few morals. But a scamp, too, who knew how to make Daanish laugh, and who, when Ammi had died, had helped him out of the despair that, shroud-like, had wrapped itself around the orphaned boy.

Mushtaq might be an imp, but he was Daanish's friend. A friend Daanish loved dearly.

'Why the smile?' Devraj's voice broke in on his thoughts. 'If there is good news you may wish to share, I would like to hear it. The gods know I would like to hear something cheerful.'

Daanish shook his head. 'Nothing. I was just remembering a friend of mine.' And because it would seem churlish to disregard the woe in Devraj's voice, he added, 'What of you? Were you not able to find any work?' Of course he would not have, he thought. It had been less than twelve hours. It was a stupid question to ask.

Devraj did not seem to think so. 'No. I spoke to a couple of the merchants at the sarai where I am staying, but it was useless.' He heaved a sigh. 'I should not be dejected; it is too early. There will be work. There is bound to be, in a city so busy.'

Daanish had to agree with that: he himself was so busy that he barely got the time to wolf down a quick meal at a roadside vendor's before scurrying back to his place under the banyan tree. Devraj was gone—he had left before noon—but there was another there. A far more welcome face.

'Mushtaq!' Daanish laughed out loud. 'Where have you been?'

Mushtaq organized the waiting people into a queue. While Daanish attended to them, some plodding slowly through what they wanted, Mushtaq spoke to the others. He cracked jokes. He borrowed a stool of woven reed and insisted that a rickety-kneed old merchant sit down. He whispered conspiratorially to a cocky young man about the appalling degeneration of wit in most of the old fogies around. He picked out the ones most unlikely to be generous with their money, and suggested they go to Junaid. 'Too many people in this line,' he muttered. 'The way this is going, your turn will come tomorrow morning. If then.'

Devraj showed up later that evening, while there were three people still waiting to have their letters written for them.

'Go away, go away,' Mushtaq said, stepping forward. 'There can be no more work done today.'

'I don't need a letter written,' Devraj said, and hearing his voice, Daanish looked up.

'Mushtaq, let him be,' he called. 'He's Abba's friend.'

Seeing Daanish busy, Devraj seated himself at a distance, far enough to not impose, close enough to be able to keep an eye out for when Daanish might be free. Mushtaq, lounging about under the banyan tree, watched him with suspicion. Daanish was too engrossed in his work to notice either of them.

By the time the last customer was gone, lamps were flickering in the nearby homes, and a woman had arrived, accompanied by a little girl holding flowers in cupped hands. The woman had placed a small terracotta oil lamp, a diya, at the foot of the banyan tree. The child arranged her flowers around it, and the woman lit the diya. They had stood, heads bowed in prayer, for a moment before they had gone back the way they had come.

Daanish wished Devraj gone. He wanted to be with Mushtaq, not obliged to make small talk with his father's friend. He could not bring himself to say so to Devraj, but perhaps Mushtaq would see the mute appeal in his eyes, and find some clever way to get rid of Devraj. He was skilled at the art of getting people to do precisely as he wished.

But Mushtaq, instead of coming to his friend's rescue, merely rose to his feet, came to Daanish, and clapped a hand to his shoulder. 'A good day's work, wasn't that?' he said. 'How much did you earn?' He peeked at the handful of coins Daanish held out, and pretended a gasp of awe. 'You'll buy off the market place at this rate!' He laughed at his own joke, and gave Daanish another thump on the back, almost sending his friend stumbling. 'Go on, you. Go and enjoy yourself, throw that wealth around.'

'Wait! Mushtaq!'

But Mushtaq was gone, striding away on long legs, a

tuneless whistle his only response to Daanish's anguished cry. Daanish gazed after him, but within moments, the half-dark, half-lamplit streets had swallowed Mushtaq up.

ଓ

'I found work,' Devraj said.

He had walked beside a silently fuming Daanish all the way to the neighbourhood where the boy lived. They had said nothing until they had come in sight of the tiny graveyard in which lay Shagufta and Nasiruddin. Devraj had looked astonished when Daanish had glanced towards the graveyard, and seeing the sudden pain in the boy's face, had asked if that was where his parents were buried. To Daanish's nod, he had nodded too, but not to Daanish: he had stood, silent and with bent head, looking towards that cluster of unknown graves.

And now he had said what he had come to say.

Well, at least if he had found work, he would find means to occupy himself. He would make other friends and not foist his company on a stranger younger than his own sons.

'It's near Hauz Khaas,' Devraj elaborated. 'A nobleman, wanting to build a tomb for himself. It promises to pay well.'

Hauz Khaas. The mention of the royal water tank made Daanish wish for the family he had once been part of. His mother's second husband, Ibrahim, had studied in the madarsa that stood on the bank of the tank. He remembered Ammi's face softening as she spoke of those days.

Spoke, with a smile, of the tank—excavated originally at the orders of the Sultan Alauddin Khalji and rejuvenated, some half a century later, by Firuz Shah Tughlaq, so much a lover of learning that he had insisted on having his mausoleum constructed in the midst of the madarsa's buildings. And spoke of the madarsa itself, respected through all the Islamic world, with its scholars coming from as far afield as Baghdad. Of the trees, the gardens, the birds. The water glittering in the sunlight. And of that man who had been her childhood sweetheart; whom she had grown up with, and eventually married. And who had died, snatched away from her by a cruel fate.

Like the Hauz-e-Shamsi, the Hauz Khaas was still beautiful, filled with clean, fresh water, but Daanish could not remember when he had visited it last. With Ammi, perhaps. When he had been a child and both his parents had been alive and well, his siblings beside him. Those had been happy days.

He pushed the nostalgia away to the back of his mind. 'Where will you live?'

'Somewhere near there, I suppose,' Devraj replied. 'There used to be a village, many years back, next to the madarsa.'

'It's still there.'

'I will find a place to stay there, then. I will go tomorrow morning.' Devraj chewed on his lip. 'I have a favour to ask of you, if I may.'

The urge to say no was strong, but for the sake of his father's memory, Daanish bit it down. 'Yes?'

'I have a few things that are of value to me. I am reluctant to take them to a place where my dwelling is as yet undecided.' He looked a little uncomfortable. 'Would you keep them for me, for a few days? I will take them as soon as I can.'

Daanish frowned. 'My home is small,' he mumbled. 'And what if someone should steal your things while I am away during the day?'

'I hardly think people like you and I need fear thieves,' Devraj said, with an amused twinkle in his eye. 'Don't worry,' he added. 'It is a small bag, nothing that would attract attention. And anyway, its contents are of little value to anybody but me. Just some odds and ends that would not be precious to anyone else.'

So Daanish had, still reluctantly, accepted the onus of keeping Devraj's belongings till the time the stone carver found a home for himself.

2

'Isn't your friend around?' asked Mushtaq, with an unmistakable sneer in his voice. 'How lonely you must feel.'

Daanish scowled. 'He was Abba's friend, not mine. I told you.' He drank down the last sip of buttermilk and licked his lips. 'It's not my fault he turned up that day, at that time.'

'And you didn't have the guts to tell him you were busy?' Mushtaq beckoned to the milkman's boy, indicating another cupful of the drink. 'Why are you so timid? It's not as if your Abba will come charging out of his grave, angry that you ignored his friend.'

Mushtaq snorted and spat into the dust at his feet. He was sitting on a fallen block of stone, his legs apart, elbows resting on his knees. A wiry young man of seventeen, just two years older than Daanish when it came to age, but infinitely older when it came to worldly wisdom. Or unwisdom, Daanish did not quite know what.

He still remembered the first time he met Mushtaq, five years ago. Abba was out and Ammi, along with Fatima, was inside the house, doing the chores. A ten-year old Daanish had been given strict instructions to memorize so-and-so lessons: his parents may not have been scholars, but they were fanatical about learning, Ammi more so than Abba. Daanish was sitting on a reed mat in the mud-floored courtyard in front of the house, rocking to and fro as he learnt his lessons.

He had heard a snigger before he saw anything. A snigger, followed by a guffaw. He had looked up and around, puzzled. It had taken him a while to find the source of the mirth: up in the branches of the great old tamarind tree that cast its shade over the courtyard, was a boy. A couple of years older than Daanish, and dressed in similar clothes, homespun cotton pajamas and a tunic. Except that where Daanish's clothes were clean, the stranger's were grubby. Not just with the twigs and dirt from his ascent of the tree, but deeply dirty: this was the grime that crept into things long neglected.

'If you rock back too far,' the boy had called out with a laugh, 'you'll tip over backwards. Too far in front, and your nose will hit the ground.'

'Mind your own business,' Daanish had shouted back heatedly.

The boy had been sucking a pod of tamarind. His mouth had puckered, and he had spat out a few seeds. They had fallen into the courtyard, and had been followed shortly after by a whole pod. And another. 'Here, take a break,' the boy had called, the derision now replaced by something like condescension. Daanish had not noticed the condescension or taken offence; he had been too busy wondering whether it would be proper for him to pick up the tamarind that the boy had thrown down. Would it not imply a lack of self-respect? Would it make the boy think that Daanish's stomach was more important to him than his dignity?

On the other hand, there was the tamarind, tart-sweet, the very thought of it refreshing. And it was there for the taking: he would not have to climb the tree, risking Ammi's wrath in the process. Also, he had been studying far too long: his back hurt, his legs had gone to sleep, and he was bored.

In the end, Daanish had put aside his lessons, and had gone to stand beneath the branch on which the boy was seated. 'Why aren't you studying?' he had asked.

Mushtaq had sucked on some more tamarind before he answered. 'It's a waste,' he had finally said, his voice muffled by the seeds in his mouth—he had an odd way of juggling them round with his tongue, getting off the very last bit of pulp before spitting out the seeds. 'What do you think you're going to become, with all this learning of yours? A maulvi?'

A derisive glance had been cast across the modest courtyard, the shabby little house beyond.

Daanish had swallowed down the anger that remark elicited. 'At least I won't be an illiterate and ill-mannered lout who goes about stealing fruit from people's trees,' he had retorted.

And that had made Mushtaq laugh so hard that he had fallen off the tree and onto Daanish. The collision had left them both bruised—and Ammi had later added to Daanish's woes by giving him a few slaps for having abandoned his lessons—but it had borne fruit. Daanish had made a new friend that day.

☙

'Must you spend all your time with that boy?' Ammi had said one day, when Daanish had returned from an hour's loitering with Mushtaq. Ammi called it loitering; Daanish called it enjoyment.

'We aren't doing anyone any harm,' Daanish had replied. 'We just sit around and talk.'

Ammi had huffed at that and had muttered something about wasting precious time. She did not approve of Mushtaq, but when a goaded Daanish had finally accused her of disliking his friend simply because he was an orphan, she had burst out laughing. 'An orphan! Why would I look down on an orphan? I never knew my own parents; who am I to point fingers at others?' She had stopped laughing almost immediately, and had placed a gentle, work-roughened hand on her son's head, one calloused finger pushing back a few strands of hair from off his forehead. 'No, my child,' she had murmured. 'No, that is not why I don't like Mushtaq. I don't like him because he is a bad influence on you. He seems to have no morals to speak of, he's impertinent, he's reckless—oh, Daanish, don't be so attached to him. Please.' Her eyes had filled with tears, and Daanish, shaken and thoughtful, had not gone to meet Mushtaq for a few days after that.

But not for long. He had no other friends to speak of. He was too young to know that a woman with a past like Shagufta's, married to a man who had once come as part of an invading army, was not respected in the neighbourhood. They tolerated Shagufta and Nasiruddin; they did not socialize with them. Their children, carefully tutored by wary parents, kept their distance. Daanish saw the neighbourhood boys now and then, at the mosque during namaaz. They crossed paths, at the well or in the bazaar, but not one ever smiled at him or pretended that Daanish was one of them. Daanish, in his turn, was too shy to make any overtures of friendship.

It was therefore a matter of mere days before he was back to spending his time with Mushtaq. He was careful now: he made sure he slipped away for no more than half an hour at a time, and more often than not, on a legitimate errand. Stopping by at the chaupal, the public square around the banyan tree, where he would invariably find Mushtaq lounging about. Lingering just a few minutes after namaaz. Mushtaq teased him about it—'You behave like a young girl going off to meet a lover!'—but Daanish brushed it off. The friendship was important to him.

And when Ammi and Abba passed away, one after the other in the space of less than two years, it was Mushtaq to whom Daanish turned, and Mushtaq who comforted him. 'Look at me,' he had said, an arm slung carelessly about Daanish's shoulders. 'I never even knew my parents! Allah alone knows who they were. Do I weep for them? Do I wish I was dead too? Hah!' Daanish had thought of pointing out that not knowing a parent was a logical reason for not missing them, but he had let it pass. He had recognized the emotion that underlay his friend's words: a clumsy but well-meaning attempt to console.

It was Mushtaq who had prompted Daanish to take up the one employment that seemed most appropriate for him, and which Daanish himself had never thought of. 'Have you seen the crowd waiting for that old man to write their letters for them?' Mushtaq had said one day, as the two of them loitered on the fringes of the chaupal. With a contemptuous flick of a finger, he had indicated the lone letter writer hunched under the tree, pen in hand. 'He's excruciatingly slow. People come to him because there's no one else.' He had shaken his head in disgust, and had gone on to abuse the old letter writer. He was slow and half-witted, his paper was poor quality and his ink worse. He charged the earth for letters that conveyed nothing but the inept and incoherent mutterings of whoever had dictated them. 'Would you want to receive a letter like that?' Mushtaq had snorted.

Daanish had not understood, until Mushtaq had spelled it out for him. 'You may be a tenth his age or whatever,' he had explained, with a touch of that forced patience he often adopted with the younger boy, 'but I'll wager you are better read than him. You should become a letter writer. Put up a stall under the banyan tree, and you can be assured of a good income.'

Daanish had not merely been sceptical; he had been incredulous. Who would come to a fourteen-year-old boy to have their letters written? Not even the most desperate peasant, unable to put a mark on paper, would think of doing so. 'There's nobody else,' Mushtaq had said—Junaid had not put in an appearance back then, would not, in fact, arrive on the scene till many months later. 'This old derelict is the only one around. At least offer customers another option.' Then, brushing aside Daanish's objections, he had added, 'I will help you.'

He had helped Daanish search among Ammi and Abba's things to find whatever clean paper they could: not much. He had taken Daanish to buy some more paper, along with an ink block and a new reed pen. It was Mushtaq, too, who had taken Daanish's clothes to be specially laundered, bringing them back cleaner and smoother than Daanish could ever have got them.

And, on the morning that a nervous and shy Daanish had first taken his seat under the banyan tree, Mushtaq had sent business his way. To a baffled Daanish had come one man after another—at intervals of half an hour or so—asking him to write letters for them. They were poor men: farm labourers, sweepers, unskilled workers of all types. The letters they wanted written were mundane, relaying news that did not need relaying. *I am well. The weather has been good. I hope you are well.* Nothing, really, that could not have gone unsaid, especially if one was obliged to pay for the privilege of having that written out. Even more, if one stopped to consider that the man dictating the letter could ill afford to pay for it.

Daanish had been surprised, but unsettled, too; he had not exactly smelled a rat, but there had been something not quite believable about it all.

At the end of the day, he had found out, when Mushtaq came home and asked for most of his earnings. Daanish, reaching for the coins he had tucked away in his cummerbund, had asked if Mushtaq needed money. 'Not me, you idiot,' Mushtaq had said, even as he had helped himself to the money. 'What, did you really think those poor men would pay you to write useless letters for them?' he had laughed. 'Those were hired customers, my naïve little friend,' he had said, patting Daanish condescendingly on his cheek. It was humiliating, and there was the disturbing feeling that this was most unethical, but the prospect of greater earnings—of coins that he could keep, that he could use however he wished—had been too much. Daanish had held his tongue.

By the next day, two of the people waiting in line in front of the old letter writer had wandered over to Daanish's space and asked him to write letters for them. They had both been hesitant, but the need to have their letters written quickly had overridden the hesitation. The old man had too many letters to write; the boy had only one, a missive he was writing for one of the men Mushtaq had planted in front of him.

Mushtaq had been even more canny on the second day than on the first: he had kept watch from a distance and chosen the moment when the line in front of the old man was at its longest, the people furthest back in the line beginning to grow restive. He had then sent a man, a crippled ex-soldier, to dictate a letter to Daanish. The man had a loud voice—one that carried across the chaupal, all the way to the line waiting in front of the other letter writer. The veteran had insisted on Daanish reading out everything he had written. He seemed to be terribly hard of hearing, too, and Daanish was obliged to raise his voice to read out what he had written.

By the time the old soldier had hobbled away, the man standing last in the line at the old letter writer's had come to Daanish. By the time his letter had been written, another man had joined him.

On the third day, three men had shifted from the old man's stall to Daanish's.

When ten days had passed, Daanish was able to pay all the money Mushtaq had promised his abettors. The old soldier had to be paid especially well; he had put in what he called fine acting.

One day, not long after, the old letter writer came to Daanish's place under the banyan tree. Daanish had just finished packing up for the day, and so, it seemed, had the old man. His papers, wrapped in a worn old piece of cotton, were tucked under one arm, and in his hand was his box of pens.

The man regarded Daanish with distaste. Then, without a word of greeting, he said, 'I know what you did. It was dishonest.'

Daanish, not knowing how to respond to that—and knowing deep down, too, that the old man spoke the truth—kept quiet.

The old letter writer left without saying anything more. Daanish watched him go with mixed feelings. Anger, mostly, at the man's blunt words; but a twinge of conscience too. The old letter writer need not have said what he did; Daanish knew all too well that what Mushtaq had done was dishonest.

But it had been done without Daanish's approval; even, initially, without his knowledge. What he had not known could not be held against him. Perhaps someday, when both he and the old man had settled in, competitors in the same space, he would tell him. He would explain matters.

But the old man was gone. That evening was the first and the last time he spoke to Daanish.

That had been a long time ago, long enough for Daanish's conscience to have been soothed by the passage of time. A few months later, Junaid had turned up, trying to ply his trade as a letter writer. Daanish paid him no heed; Mushtaq went out of his way to heap scorn on the young man.

On this day, an old woman, toothless and bent double, had come to have a letter written. She had mumbled that she would wait; Daanish, concentrating on writing an involved letter for a trader, had merely nodded and gone back to his work. It was Mushtaq who, unnoticed by Daanish, had left his usual place—under the banyan tree, lying on his back—and carefully steered the old woman away, to where Junaid sat.

She was sitting there, leaning in to dictate her letter to an irritated Junaid, when Daanish finally got a few moments to take a breath, to stretch his legs and have a sip from the terracotta suraahi that sat beside him. 'Don't look now,' Mushtaq whispered to him, 'but Junaid is being swindled.' There was an unholy glee in Mushtaq's voice, and Daanish glanced across the few yards that separated him from Junaid.

'What? It's just that old woman. She's harmless.'

'Harmless! Yes, but can she pay?' Mushtaq's voice had sunk to a malicious hiss. 'Wait and see. When Junaid asks her for money, she'll offer him a handful of millet or something. If that.' He scratched absently at his jaw. 'I saved your sorry hide, you fool. She would have been trying to bamboozle you by now if I'd let her keep sitting here.'

Daanish felt ashamed. The old woman looked very poor, very infirm. Even if she had nothing to pay him with, he could afford it. Junaid, who he knew supported a widowed mother and a brood of younger siblings, could not. If he had had any sense, Junaid would demand payment before writing a letter—especially if the customer seemed unable to pay. Mushtaq used to do that for Daanish in the early days, weeding out from the waiting line all those who might not be able to pay. Nowadays, the older boy had become complacent, aware that Daanish earned enough on most days to feed both himself and Mushtaq. Complacent, and lazier, sitting back and enjoying the fun while those around him worked and fretted.

Mushtaq let out a hoot of laughter. Daanish looked up from sharpening his reed pen, surprised. 'Not even a handful of rice!' Mushtaq called out, loud enough for everybody in the chaupal to hear, loud enough for everybody to know that it was meant for Junaid. 'Just a few jaamuns, was it? Junaid, Junaid, how you've been had!' Mushtaq was was holding his sides, shaking with laughter, his amusement exaggerated.

Junaid threw aside his work and came charging, to barrel into Mushtaq and send him sprawling to the ground in a cloud of dust. Mushtaq sprang back up, now shouting abuses, and it turned into a full-blown fight. A few of the men from around the chaupal and the nearby huts came hurrying to separate the two, but not before Mushtaq had given Junaid a split lip and pulled out a handful of his hair, and Junaid had kicked him in the knee. Daanish, who had tried to intervene, was pummeled by both sides and badly bruised.

When the dust had settled and the crowd had dispersed, Daanish and Mushtaq made their way to a quiet little rivulet that flowed near the tomb of the Sultan Balban. A little boy was keeping a sleepy eye on a small herd of goats, but other than that, it was deserted.

They tended their wounds, washed at the rivulet and then settled down on the grass beside the tomb. An unusual tomb, this one, with its beautifully symmetrical arch, and that dome, the likes of which had never been seen in Dilli before. Ghiyasuddin Balban, who had died more than two hundred years earlier, had been a mere slave to his master Iltutmish; but a slave who had done well for himself. Very well indeed, if that imposing if starkly undecorated tomb was anything to go by.

Daanish was not even thinking of the tomb right then.

'I wish you wouldn't needle Junaid,' he said, trying not to sound as agitated as he felt: the slightest hint of unease, and Mushtaq would leap to take advantage of it. He thrived on the unease of other people.

'Why? Do you pity him?'

Daanish shook his head. 'No. But what is the need? There is room enough for two. Customers enough for two.'

'Like there were for you and that old man you displaced?' Mushtaq made no attempt to hide the sneer in his voice. 'And what happens the day Junaid decides there isn't room for two? That he is older than you, and can possibly inspire more confidence than a stripling like you.'

Anger stirred in Daanish at those words. He was thinner and shorter than Mushtaq; thinner and shorter, too, than many other boys of his age. The jibe had hit home, and hard.

Mushtaq heaved a sigh. 'Listen,' he said. 'Grow up. The world isn't a beautiful place, or a soft place, or whatever rubbish those books of yours teach you. It is a hard place, and it's harder for those of us who have to face it on our own. You cannot afford to have compunctions.'

Daanish did not reply then, but he thought over it long into the night. What, he thought, would Ammi have said? It took little to answer that question; Shagufta would not have approved. She would never have said that it was right, for the sake of survival, to put aside all human feeling.

On the other hand, almost all that he had he owed to Mushtaq and to Mushtaq's business acumen. Unethical business acumen, perhaps, but still effective. Had it not been for Mushtaq, Daanish might not have survived so long.

It was all very confusing.

ଓ

It was a day like any other: hot, dull, tedious. The usual people had turned up, asking for the same boring letters to be written. The chaupal and its surroundings were crowded with the same people he saw every day: the hawkers of fruit and vegetables, the devout who came to pray at the foot of the banyan, the old men who slept and chatted and played chaupar under it, and the beggar who hunched nearby, pretending to be blind.

It had been a day like any other, and would have passed unnoticed had it not been for a man who came to Daanish in the sleepiest hour of the afternoon. As there was nothing to distinguish the day, there was nothing to distinguish the man. Middle-aged, his features plain, his clothes neither opulent nor threadbare.

Even the words, brusque and uttered in a gruff voice, were not so very uncommon. 'I know what I want to say,' the man said as he sat down. 'Just write what I say. Do you understand?'

Daanish nodded. There were customers like this. Men who knew their minds and had experience enough to be able to express themselves. All they lacked was the skill of putting pen to paper. Daanish dipped the point of his reed pen in the ink and looked up.

'Whom am I to address it to?'

'Leave that be,' the man said. 'I will deliver it myself, into the man's hands.'

And then he began to dictate the letter.

From the very outset, it was like no other letter Daanish had ever been called upon to write. He had written other letters, even angry and anguished ones, letters full of rage and a sense of ill-usage—but none had been as vitriolic as this. The man hurled abuses at the unnamed one he addressed. He called down the fury of the gods on him, this child of unwed parents, this whoreson who was sleeping with his own mother.

Daanish, too uncomfortable to go on without at least a word of protest, glanced up. 'Are you sure?' he mumbled. 'This—this can have repercussions.' For a moment, fear gripped him as he wondered if the man would take offence at his meddling; but though a cool steeliness came into his eyes, the man only replied, in a brusque tone, 'You write what I tell you to write. That is what I am paying you for. Not for your advice.'

Daanish returned to his work. The letter now proceeded to level specific allegations at the recipient. He was corrupt; it was well-known that he had bribed his way to the post he now occupied. He was constantly licking the boots of anyone he hoped could help further his ambitions, and it was common knowledge that he had sold his own daughter to—Daanish put his pen down. 'I cannot,' he said. Later he was to wonder where he had summoned up the courage to say that, and to rue the fact that he had been unable to summon it up before. 'If this is an official you're writing to, both of us could get into trouble.'

The man gave him a look of contempt. 'I should not have expected a milksop like you to be able to write,' he said. He snatched up the letter, and flinging a couple of cowries—broken ones, too—in Daanish's direction, he left.

Daanish sat back, the breath whooshing out of him. He could only blink and shake his head in amazement, and imagine the reaction of the man who received that letter.

A few minutes later, Kallu, the blacksmith, came by with a request for a letter to his cousin in the hills. It was a prosaic letter, full of everyday things. Kallu's cow had given birth. It was a heifer, and they were so happy. Kallu's eldest son was getting married, and the bride was a beauty. Kallu's wife was very proud of her future daughter-in-law, and even more delighted that there would be another woman in the household. The younger children were well; one of them had just recovered from a fever that had frightened them all.

It helped Daanish forget that strange, venomous letter.

3

The first hint Daanish had of impending doom was the sound of shod feet, thumping purposefully towards the banyan tree. Feet that approached the chaupal, across which a sudden silence had fallen.

Daanish, bent over the letter he was writing, glanced up. Through the hanging roots of the banyan, dense and bedraggled as a witch's hair, he saw three soldiers. They were standing in front of Junaid, and the oldest of them—a pot-bellied man with a grizzled jaw and the shoulders of a wrestler—was questioning the letter writer. Junaid shook his head, then pointed towards Daanish. All three pairs of eyes followed the direction of his finger. Without another word to Junaid, the soldiers made their way to Daanish.

A fist tightened around his heart. What was wrong? Why were soldiers coming to meet him? Was this something to do with Abba—but no, it could not be, could it? Because Abba, even though he had come as part of an invading army, had left that life far behind. It was nearly twenty years since then, and anyway, Abba was dead. Daanish's mind raced, turning corners, searching for reasons, finding none.

By the time they had reached him, he was on his feet, the sweat pouring down his face and his heart thumping painfully inside his chest.

It was over and done with quickly. The pot-bellied man, an officer of the law, was brusque and swift. The questions came flying, one after the other, and with each, Daanish blurted out the truth and damned himself further. Yes, his name was Daanish. Yes, he was a letter writer. No, there was no other Daanish who wrote letters for people here.

When a letter—a letter he recognized the moment he saw it, and which filled him with dread—was produced, he nodded. Yes, he had written this.

But it had been written for another, and the signature at the bottom of the page, his own name, Daanish, was a forgery.

By the time he had got to that part, nobody was listening any more. The officer had tucked the letter into his cummerbund, and the two soldiers had stepped forward and pinned Daanish's arms to his sides.

Nobody spoke up, nobody came forward to say that Daanish could not have done something so wrong.

As he was dragged off, Daanish turned to look at Junaid. In his eyes was a quiet satisfaction, the smugness of triumph. This would now be his territory, and his alone.

On an impulse, Daanish turned to look at the client who still sat, frozen with shock under the tree, his letter half-written. 'Please!' Daanish called. 'Please—will you find Mushtaq and tell him about me? Tell him to come—' he could not complete the sentence; the officer cuffed him so hard he went sprawling, knocked his head against the tree trunk, and lost consciousness.

Mushtaq did not come. Daanish, puzzled at his absence, begged one of the guards to try and find him. The man laughed in his face. Daanish settled back in the small, cramped cell he shared with three other men. The space smelled of urine and sweat and the overpowering stench of fear. It hung in the air, and it served to heighten Daanish's own fear.

'You are a fool,' said one of the men, when the guard had moved away. 'Did you really think he would do anything for you for nothing?' He did not bother to lower his voice.

Daanish stared, confused. It took a while for him to understand. 'You—you mean offer a bribe? But I have nothing.'

The man shrugged. 'Then you will get nothing.'

Night closed in, and Daanish sat, wide awake. The cell

was suffocating, there were too many mosquitoes, and the uncertainty of his future worried him more than anything else. Sometime near dawn he convinced himself that it was just a matter of time before he was free; when Mushtaq heard what had happened, he would come rushing to his rescue.

It was not until well into the fifth day that he was dragged in front of a judge. By then, the squalor of the prison cell and the coarseness of his fellow inmates had stopped having their effect on Daanish. The nausea and disgust were gone; the fear had dulled into a strange sense of hopelessness that mingled with resignation. He did not question the guard, he did not plead for mercy. He said nothing.

Daanish recognized the officer who had arrested him, and heard him testify that this—this scoundrel, this innocent-looking, seemingly educated but dastardly traitor—had had the gall to write a foul letter to none other than the kotwal himself. The incriminating letter was produced and the qazi who sat in judgement looked it over, his face turning sterner with every line he read. The kotwal's servant, who had received the letter, was presented as witness and verified that yes, this was the letter that had come, brought by a boy who said that Daanish had sent it. The boy had left after delivering the letter; at the time nobody had thought there was any need to make him wait.

The officer of the law who had been sent to arrest the perpetrator did not know about any boy. But everything that was needed to condemn the criminal was right here. Daanish's handwriting was there on the sheet the qazi held; he himself had admitted it. And his name was there, at the bottom of the letter.

'I did not put it there, huzoor!' Daanish burst out. 'I did not write my name. Someone is trying to get me into trouble!'

The qazi looked up, irritated. 'Why would anyone want to get you into trouble, boy?' he asked. Someone in the crowd of curious onlookers sniggered. An officer snarled, commanding silence, and the qazi looked at Daanish with one iron-grey eyebrow raised, waiting impatiently for an answer.

Daanish knew. That chance glimpse of Junaid's smug face had told him all. But he had no proof; nothing but a strong suspicion. And if it came to an investigation, it would be his word against Junaid's. If they dug deeper, they might find that Daanish's claim to being the innocent victim of a business rivalry was founded on a shaky base. He had not come by this work through fair means. There was that old letter writer, whose face still appeared in Daanish's dreams, reminding him of his guilt.

In the end, Daanish said nothing about Junaid. He merely insisted that he was innocent, and left it at that.

Perhaps the qazi was truly a wise man, who could see truth where it existed. Perhaps he felt sorry for Daanish. At any rate, he let Daanish off with a fine and an admonition. 'People who write such letters, no matter to whom, make enemies. Even by penning a letter such as this, you invite the wrath of that enemy too.' It did not seem at all logical to Daanish, but then, he was fast realizing, little in this world was logical.

It was the fine that worried him. A hundred jitals could have bought him more than ten maunds of wheat, or double that of barley. Another hundred would suffice for enough ghee, sugar, gram and lentils to last him through the year, with some left over to buy vegetables, paper, ink, and clothing.

The fine was five hundred jitals. Even if he were to sell off every single item he owned—including the clothing on his back—he would not be able to pay the fine.

The qazi knew it, of course, and he added gruffly as he dismissed Daanish, 'You may pay as much as you can right now. The rest will be due within a month.'

Daanish did not ask what might happen if he were

unable to pay the rest of the fine. He did not want to know.

He had a measly two tankas on him, and he handed these over to the clerk of the court, who looked scornful as he entered the details into his ledger. 'At this rate, you will be dead before you pay this fine,' he remarked sourly. Daanish did not argue; he was too tired to do so. Besides, the man spoke nothing but the bitter truth.

Mushtaq was not to be found in any of his usual haunts. Daanish went first to the chaupal, but Mushtaq was neither there nor at any of the shops and stalls in the lanes nearby. Junaid, sitting under the banyan and doing brisk business, looked at him with contempt, but Daanish, though he felt a surge of anger, refrained from saying anything.

He went next to the Dargah of Qutb Sahib—not that he thought the irreligious Mushtaq would be there, but because he needed comfort. There, Daanish fell to his knees and wept silently before, the brief respite having bolstered his courage, he trekked on, taking a zigzag path to Balban's Tomb, the Gandhak ki Baoli, and finally the Jami Masjid and the Qutb Minar.

Along the way he ran into a couple of people he knew, people who stopped and asked him what had happened. News had spread, of course; but rumour, as usual, had outstripped truth. Daanish said little, and asked if they had seen Mushtaq. They had not. Mushtaq had not been seen this past week; perhaps he was out of town?

Why would a man who had never stepped beyond the limits of the circle bounded by the Qutb Minar at one end and the Hauz-e-Shamsi at the other, suddenly take into his head to leave Dilli the very time he was most needed? Why would Mushtaq, Dilli born and bred, with not a soul in the city or outside, leave just as Daanish was arrested?

Daanish went home and spent the next three hours in mundane chores. He swept, he fetched water and washed.

He brooded. The fine would have to be paid; there was no way around it. But even taking into consideration all the money he had carefully hoarded all these months, the shortfall would be enormous.

After he was done with the housework, Daanish went carefully through the house, critically examining every last possession. Most were things left over from his parents' time: useless or broken, but retained out of a sense of loyalty, of filial feeling.

There was little of any worth. Most of it was clothing, threadbare, stained, and moth-eaten. There was a chipped cup, once valuable because it was made of fine porcelain—perhaps Abba had brought it from Samarqand; Daanish could only guess. There were a few odds and ends that might have been of some worth had they been complete: an enamelled pendant, half broken; a large, beautifully wrought key, but without its lock; a comb of tortoise shell, with more than half its teeth missing.

There was a fine dagger, though, and a bow and quiver, which he might be able to sell for a couple of jitals. There was a necklace of red beads. It did not look valuable to him, but it might not hurt to show it around. He set it aside, on top of the quiver, from where it slid off and fell to the floor. The old and rotten string snapped, and beads went bouncing across the room.

Daanish cursed as he got down on his hands and knees to look for the beads. It was as he was peering under the charpai that he saw something he would almost certainly have missed had he not been looking directly at it. It was a large flat package, about three-quarters the size of the door that lay open behind him, letting in a shaft of sunlight so bright, it lit up even the space under the bed.

The package was hard and unyielding, very heavy. Stone. What was a large slab of stone, so carefully wrapped, doing under the bed?

In that same moment, even as he tugged at the package, he

remembered what it was. Years ago—he could not have been more than seven—Ammi had gathered her three children together and shown them an heirloom, the one treasure she possessed. It was a stone frieze, an ethereal work of carving created by a long-ago ancestor. A piece made to honour Razia Sultan, but never given. Priceless beyond belief. They had stared at it, bedazzled by its beauty even though they had been so young.

'But if this is so valuable, why do we live so poorly, Ammi?' his sister Fatima had asked. Dilawar had nudged her in an admonitory way for that, but Ammi had not considered the question either stupid or mercenary.

'It is a matter of pride for our family,' she had said. 'This was your ancestor, this man with so much skill in his hands that the Sultan herself held him in high esteem.'

'Fat lot of good, an heirloom that can't keep you from starving,' Fatima had muttered, only to be cuffed by Dilawar, pompous and full of self-righteousness even at that age.

'If it comes to starvation, we could sell it,' Ammi had said as she had folded the heavy sacking back over the frieze and tied the strings over it. 'But while we can afford to get by, we must keep it safe.'

She had put it under the charpai, and there it had remained, out of sight and out of mind. He had forgotten about it as if it had never been. Perhaps it had slipped out of his memory in the complacency brought on by having parents to feed and clothe him. Later, the sorrow of his parents' deaths, followed by the enthusiasm of earning for himself, had further pushed aside all memories of the frieze.

Now, however, he remembered, and with rising excitement.

Daanish pulled the door shut, before closing the window and securing its latch. Then, in the dim light that filtered through the cracks in the door and window and from between the loose tiles of the roof, he set about his work.

It was far easier to push the charpai aside than to pull

the slab out from under it. The sacking that covered it was furred with dust, and his hands were grimy by the time he finally drew aside the last fold of cloth to look down at what lay before him.

It was beautiful beyond belief. As a child, he realized, he had not recognized its beauty for what it was. Now he saw it, and it made his breath catch, it was so exquisite.

But now that he had seen it, he did not know if he could bear to part with it.

Devraj looked taken aback, as he might well be. 'Daanish!' he said. 'What are you doing here? I was told a boy had come to meet me, but I never thought it would be you.'

The last time they had met was when Devraj, by then settled into a hut in the village beside the Hauz Khaas, had come to collect the bundle he had left in Daanish's safekeeping. They had exchanged perfunctory greetings, had asked after each other, and then gone their respective ways. Nothing had then indicated that Daanish might want to meet the older man again, the man who had once been his father's friend. Not his own, as he had been quick to reassure Mushtaq, unwilling to risk losing Mushtaq's friendship for the sake of Devraj's goodwill. But Mushtaq was gone, vanished like a dream with an awakening. His memory would linger longer than the memory of a dream, but it too would disappear with time. Daanish, smarting at the betrayal, would make sure it did.

'I remembered you said you had found work near the Hauz Khaas,' Daanish explained. 'There was only one other site where there was construction going on, and nobody there had heard of you.' He looked about him, at the tomb which was being built. The walls, made of blocks of rough-cut grey stone bound together by an equally rough mortar, were devoid of any decoration at the moment. But Daanish could see that Devraj's fellow stone carvers, several of them hard at work in the yard beyond, were carving strips of red sandstone. Lotus buds and geometrical shapes, interlocking triangles and diamonds. Devraj himself had been in the midst of carving a medallion of white marble when Daanish had arrived.

Devraj nodded. Then, again, 'What brings you here?' he asked. As if he realized that Daanish would not have come by just to find out how Devraj was.

So Daanish's indifference to him had not gone unnoticed. It made Daanish feel uncomfortable about what he was about to ask.

It had to be done, though; there was no other way. 'I have come to ask a favour of you,' he said. And then, before Devraj could ask any more questions, he blurted out the whole sordid story. Even as he spoke, the pitifulness of it all mortified him. How alone he was, how friendless; and how cocky he had been just a few days earlier. How far he had fallen, how hard he had hit the ground.

Devraj listened until Daanish had finally finished, and then, after a while, he said, 'The first thing would be for me to see this frieze you describe. It will help me try to estimate how much it will fetch. Will you wait for me? I will be free after sunset.'

Daanish nodded, trying to swallow the lump that had appeared out of nowhere in his throat. It refused to go.

'Have you eaten?' Devraj asked, as he stood up. 'You look half-starved. Wait here. Let me get you something to eat. Eat, and rest a while; I'll come as soon as my work is done.'

The lump in Daanish's throat dissolved into a flood of tears that took even him by surprise.

Devraj folded the cloth back over the slab and sat back on his heels. All through the time he had spent examining the frieze, peering intently at it, caressing it with his fingertips, he had not uttered a word. Nothing, even from his expression, had given Daanish a hint of what was going through the man's mind.

'This is worth a fortune,' Devraj said now, his voice hoarse. 'Are you sure you want to sell it?'

Daanish stared. 'A fortune?' What was a fortune, he wondered? For him, five hundred jitals was a fortune.

Devraj shrugged. 'I cannot say exactly. Not less than fifty gold tankas. Possibly more.'

Fifty gold tankas.

Daanish's head swam. It was a sum far beyond his expectations, a sum that would enable him to live his entire life without having to work. Perhaps another generation too might live blissfully thus.

But it would mean giving up all claim to this work of art, this sole reminder that he was descended from a craftsman capable of creating such beauty out of mere stone. He realized, with a painful intensity, what Ammi had meant that long-ago day when she had implied that it was too precious to be sold, because it was a reminder of whom their family had descended from. He had marvelled, then, that Ammi had preferred to go hungry rather than sell the frieze. Now he understood, but it made things no easier for him.

It was a dilemma, and a dilemma too much for one so young. Daanish stared into space, not even trying to think.

Interlude

'What a ninny,' Mohsin says, his voice dripping contempt.

'He was only fifteen,' I point out.

'*I* am fifteen,' Mohsin replies loftily.

'And you don't falter?' I ask him. 'Are you so wise, so unerring, so sure of yourself that you never find yourself at a loss?' I see the arrogance in his face flicker, a moment of conscience—and then he is gone, called away by his father, who is sorting foraged food in the courtyard. I sit back with a sigh, trying to control my annoyance, telling myself that this too shall pass. He will mature, he will become more forgiving of the frailties that plague human beings.

If the Baadshah is indeed dead, then Tardi Beg Khan must have good reason for concealing his death. I can imagine what that could be. With the heir away from Dilli—and an heir, too, who is so young—it would be foolish to let the ambitious know that the throne is vacant. After all, there are those who covet it. For instance, there is that Hemchandra Bhargav, or Hemu, as everybody calls him. It is said that he started off in life as a lowly trader, selling vegetables—or was it saltpetre?—but he has risen to heights few of us can attain, let alone those without wealth or status to help them along the way.

It was about ten years ago, I think, that we first came to know of the ambitious Hemu. That was when Salim Shah Suri, the son and successor of Sher Shah Suri, became the ruler of Dilli. Some say Hemu had been working as a weighman in one of the city's markets back then, when he was appointed superintendent of all of Dilli's markets. Personally, I find that implausible; which mere weighman, competent though he be, can hope for a promotion such as this? There must have been intermediate steps, a logical progression.

I do not know what those steps may have been, and

I will not bother to speculate; speculation, at my age, is a waste of time and energy.

Whatever his antecedents may have been, and however he may have attained an official position at court, Hemu has used these past years to consolidate that position. He is now not just a much respected (and much feared) administrator, but also a very worthy general. Nearly three years ago, Salim Shah died. His twelve-year-old son Firuz had a tragically brief reign, a mere three days: he was killed by his uncle, Adil Shah. And Adil Shah had, by his side, Hemu, whom he appointed chief minister of Dilli.

Today another boy is in danger. Will the Shahzaada Jalaluddin fall, as Firuz did?

'Whatever you may say,' Mohsin says, when we sit down together again for me to write my memoirs and for Mohsin to pass remarks, 'I think Daanish was stupid. And he lacked principles.' He has been out, the sweat has soaked his thin cotton tunic so that it sticks to him like a second skin. He is so thin, I fear for him.

'He lacked principles? And stupid? How so?'

Mohsin looks thoughtful, as if he is thinking this through. I know this boy: he has already thought this through. He would not have said it if he did not know what he was going to say later. He sees ahead. If he could only tame his tendency towards flippancy, he would be a man indeed.

'He knew what Mushtaq did to get rid of the old letter writer, to get Daanish that job. He may not have known at the start,' he concedes, 'but he discovered soon enough. And what did he do? Nothing. Isn't that unprincipled?'

He is looking so indignant, so very upright and proud of his ethics that I cannot bring myself to laugh. It would humiliate him horribly. But I cannot help but feel amused. Ah, the naiveté of youth.

I content myself with a low, indistinct murmur. Mohsin stops his self-righteous preening and looks narrowly at me. 'What? What is it?'

He knows me so well.

'He was fourteen when he became a letter writer,' I point out patiently. 'He was alone, poor, with nobody to turn to. His parents were dead, his siblings gone. He was forced to do whatever he could to survive.'

Mohsin looks horrified. 'He snatched away that old man's livelihood.'

'That was not good,' I agree. I cannot have Mohsin thinking he has the right to put himself ahead of everybody else. But he has to learn, too, that sometimes there is a difference between how one would wish things to be and how things actually turn out. 'But what could he have done, after the deed was done? It was not as if Mushtaq had told him what he was planning to do. If he had, perhaps Daanish would have refused.'

My grandson shakes his head, unconvinced. 'How could he not have noticed?' he insists. 'And how could he have gone on being friends with somebody like that? Somebody so unprincipled?'

'What would you do if you had not a single friend in the world, and somebody came forward, offering you friendship?'

Mohsin shakes his head, still obstinate. 'How can you accept someone like that as a friend,' he repeats. 'This Mushtaq was always taunting Daanish, making fun of him. And he was nowhere to be found when Daanish was in trouble; what sort of friend is that? No,' he finishes, shaking his head even more vigorously. 'I would rather be alone and friendless than be friends with somebody like that.'

Looking at him, the truth strikes me: this is how this boy thinks, and I do not know if I should be proud of him, or despair of him. I have been thinking, through all this conversation, that Mohsin has the habit, so common in the young, of seeing the world as black or white. Now I see that Mohsin, even perhaps an older Mohsin, may well divide the world into good and bad, beautiful and ugly, right and wrong, with none of the blurring that nearly all of us resort to.

It unsettles me. There is comfort in thinking that one's children and grandchildren have been brought up in a moral way, to understand what is good, to follow the path of righteousness. It is disturbing to think that that understanding could be so literal that it leaves no scope for the reality of life.

'Did he grow up?' Mohsin asks, after a while. We have been sitting in silence, both of us lost in our own thoughts. His words startle me and I can only stare stupidly at him. 'Did Daanish grow any wiser,' Mohsin clarifies. 'Did he realize that what he'd done was wrong?'

He has still not understood that Daanish was more gullible and lonely than unprincipled or immoral. Or even that it was a simple case of being naïve. Mohsin has not grasped that, and I doubt if he will, were I to try to explain it all over again. 'He realized he had been a fool to trust Mushtaq,' I concede.

'That's better than nothing.'

I ignore the sanctimonious comment, and go on. 'He did not want to part with the frieze. It was too beautiful; and I suppose it was the one reminder he possessed, of what his family had once been capable of. Whoever had carved the frieze, he was a man to be proud of.'

'Madhav,' Mohsin says. 'I know.'

I am surprised; I cannot stop myself from staring at the boy. 'How do you know?' I ask.

'You told me,' he says patiently. 'Some years ago. When I was ten, I think? You had written down the entire story that Shagufta told Nasiruddin during the days of Taimur's invasion. Don't you remember? I wrote some of it too, which you dictated to me. You said it was a good way for me to practice my letters. Have you forgotten?' His voice drops at the last sentence, suddenly soft, gentle. As if he has realized that I really have forgotten, that my memory is slipping away frighteningly fast.

I do not answer that question of his. Why answer a question to which the questioner has guessed the answer, and the answerer does not wish to acknowledge the truth? Instead, I agree. Yes, it was Madhav. Madhav, who had carved that beautiful piece of stone for a Sultan who did not live to see it.

'Daanish had no choice,' I say. 'The penalty imposed by the qazi was enormous. Even if he worked nonstop till his dying day, he would not be able to pay it off. There was nobody from whom he could borrow money without being charged interest. He had no friends except Devraj—if he could be called a friend, and not just a well-wisher—and Devraj was as poor as Daanish.'

'So he sold the frieze? He must have,' Mohsin adds, thoughtfully. 'You or Abba would have shown it to me if we still had it. In fact, I remember asking Abba about it when you told me the story. And Abba said it was probably all a myth. That no such thing existed.'

My son has never been interested in the history of his family. Perhaps I am to blame for that; it may have been my attitude towards him that inadvertently pushed him away, from the family and from its history. But that is a story for another time, for later.

And I have a confession to make. I too was never really interested. The present was always so much more enticing than the past. It is only now that I feel my life ebbing away, melding into history itself, that I realize the worth of the past.

'It did exist,' I tell Mohsin. 'I can assure you of that.' In the lane outside, I hear the flurry of footsteps, of bare feet racing along the packed earth. There is a thud, and someone begins to scream. The sound is so strident, it makes my ears hurt. Mohsin has gone pale, his eyes wide with fear. We cannot tell what has happened outside, and we cannot step out. Not to offer help, not to risk endangering ourselves.

This famine has made abject cowards of us all.

Mohsin and I wait until the screaming has died out, ending in a rattling cry that dwindles until it has become part of the silence.

Then, as if nothing had interrupted me, I go on. 'Daanish had to sell it,' I continue. 'Devraj had suggested offering it as surety for a loan, but that idea died a swift death; Daanish would never be able to redeem it, not at the exorbitant rates charged by the money-lenders. So he ended up selling it, to a wealthy merchant who had commissioned Devraj to do some carvings for a dharamshala he was building.'

'Did he get a lot of money for it?' The fear has vanished from Mohsin's eyes, now alight with curiosity. 'Was it enough for him to pay the penalty and live comfortably for the rest of his life?'

It would have been if Daanish was indolent. Or if his conscience had not weighed so heavily on him. 'He had a debt to pay,' I say. 'He had to apologize to the old man he had displaced. He had to beg forgiveness, and offer him some part of the money as compensation.'

Mohsin's eyes widen. 'He did that?' I can hear the respect in his tone. 'I would never have been able to do it. I would have run away.'

'Daanish too could not bring himself to stay in Dilli after that,' I say. 'But he did go to the old man. Faced him, and all of his recriminations and complaints. But after that was done, and the old man had accepted the sum Daanish offered as compensation, Daanish decided it was time to move on. He had had enough of Dilli. The tomb Devraj had been working on was nearly complete, and the dharamshala for which he had agreed to work was in another town. Devraj intended to accept the work, because somewhere within him there lurked the hope that perhaps someday, by some unimagined coincidence, he would stumble across his long-lost family again. In some far-away town, some forgotten corner of the land.

'With Devraj gone from Dilli, Daanish would be left

with not a soul to take his side. So he chose to accompany the older man. They travelled to the town of Sirhind, in the land of the five rivers. Fifty kos from Dilli, and what Daanish hoped would be distance enough to help him get over his past. To help him, at any rate, atone for his foolishness.'

4

Sirhind

Twenty-two years later
847 Hijri (1443 CE)

The vanguard of Bahlol Lodhi's army, such as it was, had re-entered the city in the dead of night. Perhaps they had arrived late on the outskirts of Sirhind, and all that Bahlol Lodhi, who was also the Governor of Sirhind, had wanted was to be back in his own palace. Perhaps the Lodhi, who had traded horses for a living in his youth and may still harbour a love for the animals, wanted to see the cavalry safely home, the horses fed, watered and stabled. It had been an exhausting campaign, and defeat is infinitely more tiring than victory.

Most probably, though, it was a simple case of trying to escape public humiliation. Bahlol Lodhi, after all, came from a long line of Pashtun warriors. Afghans all, hard-bitten men who were used to ruling. Bahlol's uncle, also his father-in-law, had been appointed Governor of Sirhind in the time of the Dilli Sultan Khizr Khan, whom he had served well; after his death, Bahlol had inherited the post—but was not content to remain sequestered at Sirhind. He aimed high. For nothing less than the throne of Dilli.

He had led his troops to Dilli, but had been repelled by Mohammad Shah Sayyid. The Sayyid still remained Sultan, and Bahlol Lodhi had retreated to Sirhind, empty-handed and humiliated. No wonder he had slunk home in the convenient anonymity of the dark.

The bulk of the army, though, had camped outside the city walls. With daybreak and the opening of the city gates, they had begun to trickle in. Some marched through, stoic, their faces like granite: men pretending indifference to the defeat they had suffered. Others crept in, keeping to the shadows. Some were brought in, more dead than alive. There hung in the air the rank smell of blood and ignominy.

'We will bring back cartloads of gold coins from Dilli!' guffawed a man, scruffy-haired and ragged, who was hanging around at the first well along the main street. Several soldiers had stopped at the well, and they turned to look at him, their faces blank. 'Gold and silver and women,' the man continued, his guffaw now a sneer. 'Let's see your gold, eh? Where's the gold?'

One of the soldiers, less tired than the others, or more quick-tempered, reached for the dagger at his hip. Before he could pull it out, though, the jeerer had been pulled away. A man, about forty years of age, had grasped him firmly by the elbow and turned him around.

'Buland Baba?' said the scoffer, his eyes widening in alarm. 'Wh—when did you come here? How long—?' He shut his mouth and looked down.

The man named Buland Baba, his eyes sombre, nodded at the soldiers. 'Go on,' he said, 'Drink.' Then, turning to the one who had been taunting them, he said, 'Come along, Abdul. You've made enough of a fool of yourself.' He turned around and walked away. After a moment, Abdul followed.

'If only they had not boasted so much,' Abdul said in a surly voice a while later, when the two of them were sitting on the mud platform outside the little mosque where Buland Baba spent his day. 'But they were so cocksure. As if there was no doubt about their victory.' He shook his head in disgust.

'Do you think they are happy to have returned defeated?' asked Buland Baba gently. 'Do you not think that they would be even more downhearted than you are?'

Abdul looked sheepish, but he was not willing to accept his mistake yet. 'Why boast of something you may never be able to achieve?' he said. 'Any fool knows that is tempting fate.' He clucked his tongue. 'Stupid.'

Buland Baba sighed. His fingers tightened briefly around Abdul's shoulder before his hand dropped. 'No more stupid than all who are born, who make friends, who get married, who sow crops. Every time we do something, we proclaim intent, do we not? And not everything we are so confident of achieving happens. Our crops fail, our marriages bring us neither happiness nor offspring. Our friends let us down. If each of us was to be mocked for all we could not achieve though the world knew of it: that would not be pleasant, would it?'

Abdul laughed, a rueful sound. As if in an exaggerated and distorted echo of the sound, there was a whoop of excitement, followed by gleeful laughter, from the direction of the well. 'Someone is happy, at least.'

'Of course. There will be anxious families who have been fearing they would never see their menfolk again. For them, it does not matter who won. All that matters is that their men are back.'

The noise crescendoed even as he spoke, and now it was broken by a wild scream of grief, as if someone, unable to contain their sorrow any more in the face of such exultation, had lost their hold on it. The laughter stopped, and the scream turned to a mad keening. A woman was shouting a name, its syllables blurred in her mourning, but a name nonetheless. A loved husband, a father. Even if not truly loved, at least needed.

Buland Baba bit his lip, his troubled expression reflecting some of the grief of that unseen, unknown woman.

'Someone hasn't come back,' Abdul observed laconically.

Through the rest of the day, the noise rose and fell, changed and changed again. There was laughter one moment, weeping the next. Shouts of joy, screams of anguish. Shrieks of sheer despair, and once an outburst of anger so scorching it made Buland Baba rise to his feet, laying aside his work. The fury was as short-lived as it had been strident, and even before he could get off the mud platform on which he sat, the anger had subsided and someone was crying, a low hiccupping that made Buland Baba sit down again, his head bowed.

Sirhind, 'the Head of Hind', was the gateway to India, one of the most favoured stops on the road from Dilli to Lahore. An important town, a vital junction along the highway connecting two of the biggest cities in this part of the world, and it had been hit by its governor's ill-advised and possibly ill-timed attack on Dilli. It was not a blow so deep, though, as to ruin Sirhind forever. Those businesses that catered to the travellers along the highway continued their work as always; the sarais, the smithies, the suppliers of fodder and grain to the caravans—for these it was a day as any other. Those who did not depend upon the trade passing through the town might lick their wounds for a day or so, but even they would return to their routines soon.

Abdul, who needed a letter to be written for him by Buland Baba, returned later that evening. The jeering anger was gone, replaced by a gravity brought on by witnessing the pain the town had seen all through the day. With the gravity had come a resignation too, a bitterness. 'We will bounce back,' he said in a sombre voice. 'These widows will cry now, and in a few years' time, when their sons are old enough to march into battle, Bahlol Lodhi or his son will lead them in place of their fathers.'

Buland Baba, blowing on the still-wet ink on the sheet of paper before him, nodded. 'Yes. He is an ambitious man, Bahlol Lodhi. To have come such a long way, from horse trader to Khan-e-Khanan, the noblest of the noble: that is no mean feat. I have a feeling he will not rest until he has made another swipe at Dilli.

'Or,' he added, with a wistful smile, 'until he is dead.'

Abdul took his letter from the older man and handed over the single coin which was the fee for this service. 'And do you think he will succeed in taking Dilli, Buland Baba?' he asked.

'Whom am I to say, Abdul?' Buland Baba shook his head. 'I am the last person you should turn to when it comes to matters of wisdom. The name my parents gave me never did fit, and it does not fit me now.'

'The town reveres you,' Abdul protested. 'Even if you do not call yourself Daanish anymore.'

'They call me Buland. Am I lofty? I think not. Neither lofty nor wise.' Buland Baba smiled, his eyes crinkling at the corners.

'Then what am I to call you? Daanish?'

'Call me nothing. I am nothing, and I do not deserve to be addressed as something more than I am. And,' he added, 'no. I do not know whether Bahlol Lodhi will conquer Dilli.'

It was perhaps a week before the last tattered remains of the army had returned and settled back in. Perhaps in the palace of Bahlol Lodhi the first cautious plans were already being made to avenge the defeat he had suffered at the hands of the Sultan in Dilli; perhaps those of his generals who had survived were already preparing for a chance at vengeance.

For most of Sirhind, life returned to normal. Caravans came and caravans went. Goods were bartered, strange tales heard when travellers from faraway lands stopped long enough to tell them. Faces came, some foreign and some familiar, and vanished with the following morning.

And then one day there arrived a man in his early twenties, who was directed to Buland Baba. He came, somewhat hesitantly, to where the older man sat, under the neem tree that cast its cool shadow across half of the mud platform in front of the small mosque. Buland Baba was at work, writing a letter for a shopkeeper. When the newcomer's shadow fell across the paper, Buland Baba looked up.

'Are you the one they call Buland Baba?' The young man asked. He licked his lips nervously, and his gaze skittered between the man he was addressing, the paper, the tree, and the shopkeeper who sat in front of Buland Baba.

'I am he.'

'A letter writer,' the young man said needlessly. And because that was no question but merely an observation, he added a question. 'Pardon me, but—but were you once called Daanish, and did you come here from Dilli?'

Buland Baba nodded. He was looking now more closely at this visitor, who was obviously not just another seeker of his services. The young man possessed nothing in his face or demeanour that would make anybody remember him. A thin, plain face, somewhat scarred and pockmarked; a thin but wiry body; clothes of the type that were worn by thousands of others. Unadorned, plain, poor but not ragged.

'Why do you ask?' Buland Baba said.

The young man swallowed, his Adam's apple moving visibly against the cords of his throat. He looked embarrassed, perhaps even caught in some dilemma.

When he said nothing, Buland Baba turned back to the letter he was writing for the shopkeeper. 'Sit down,' he said, addressing the newcomer over his shoulder. 'There is water in the water pot there; help yourself. If you're hungry, there is food in the bundle beside it. I will talk to you once I have finished this work.'

The young man sat down obediently enough, but neither ate nor drank anything. He waited patiently, and half an hour passed. The shopkeeper's letter was a difficult one, with some sensitive matters to be conveyed in language that would alert the receiver, but not offend; would demand reparation but not in a way that would cut off all future communication.

Finally, when it was done to the shopkeeper's satisfaction and the man had gone his way, Buland Baba turned to his visitor. 'And who might you be?' he asked, reaching for the bundle and opening it to take out the food: some chapatis, a double handful of chickpeas cooked dry, and a few dates. Without even asking the young man if he would eat any, Buland Baba shared the food out equally, piling the chickpeas on top of the two chapatis he handed over. 'Eat, then you can tell me.'

The young man pushed away the food. 'No, not yet. Please. Let me ask you first.' He paused, swallowed—it was a nervous tic, this swallowing when he was agitated or nervous—and then asked, in a voice so low as to be near inaudible, 'Will you let me stay with you and be your servant?'

Buland Baba put the food down and looked at the young man with narrowed eyes. 'My servant?' He asked. 'What makes you think I need a servant? Or don't already have one? Or, indeed, that I can afford one?'

The young man was shaking his head vigorously even as Buland Baba spoke. 'No, no,' he burst out as soon as the older man had fallen silent, 'I do not ask to be paid. And I know you do not already have a servant.' He must have noticed the sudden dawning of suspicion in Buland Baba's eyes, because he added hurriedly, 'Everybody in Sirhind knows about you. Everybody I asked said the same: that you are a holy man, that you live on your own, and that you make whatever money you need by writing letters. You live frugally, and no one has ever seen you do anything that was not good or right.'

The words had come spilling out without pause; the young man stopped, out of breath. He looked up at Buland Baba from under long thick eyelashes that were almost girlish in their beauty, but there was the nervousness of a timid colt in those wary eyes of his.

'You have been confusing me with Sadna Qasaai,' Buland Baba said. 'I may have to work for a living, as he did, but that is where the resemblance ends.'

'Sadna Qasaai?' There was outright puzzlement in the young man's face and in his voice. 'Who—who is that?'

It was Buland Baba's turn to look puzzled. His bewilderment, however, lasted only for a moment; then his brow cleared and he said, 'You are new to Sirhind, is it not?

Where have you come from, and what is your name?'

His name was Qasim, and he was from Multan. Not from the city itself, but a village close enough for it to make no difference. His mother had belonged to the village, and his father, after marrying her, had settled down there too. His mother had died several years ago, and his father a few months back.

'And so I came here.'

Buland Baba frowned, an expression of deepening bewilderment. 'So you are here? Where is the "so" in that? Was your coming to Sirhind a consequence of your father's death?'

Qasim had paled. He shook his head violently. 'No, that was not what I meant. I mean, there was nothing else for me to do, so I decided to travel. And when I arrived in Sirhind, I liked the look of the town so much that I decided I would like to live here.'

'And offer yourself to me as a servant? Why that, when you do not even know me? Do you have no other trade? Did you not have lands or any occupation to fall back on in your village near Multan? Do you not have any relatives to call your own?'

Qasim looked taken aback by this barrage of questions. He took a while to respond, and when he did, it was in fits and starts. He rambled, he half-answered a question and then veered off at a tangent. He had to be prodded, he gave evasive answers, he seemed to become confused.

His father had not belonged to Multan; Qasim had never met that side of the family. There were some relatives on the distaff side, but he did not get along with them. There was land, but so little, it made no sense to hold onto it, especially in the teeth of stiff opposition from those same greedy relatives of his mother's. He had no siblings, nobody to hold him back. That little village on the bank of the Chenab was one he had been happy, nay, relieved to leave. 'It is not home any more,' he said.

'But you must have been trained for some occupation,' Buland Baba said, doggedly. 'You must have been working, back in your village. You should have been married by now, you are old enough to be a father several times over.'

'And you are old enough to be a grandfather,' said Qasim unexpectedly. 'Yet you are not.'

Buland Baba's eyes flashed, in a brief and surprising display of anger. 'No, I am not,' he agreed. 'But I am not the one trying to persuade a complete stranger to take me on as servant.' He pursed his lips, looking away from Qasim and towards the small, single-domed mosque that stood behind them. 'You seem to know a lot about me,' he said after a while. His voice and his face had regained their composure. 'For someone who is so new to Sirhind that he does not even know of Sadna Qasaai, you seem to know a lot about me. You even know what my name actually is, not this epithet the people here have conferred on me. You know where I came from, which not many here do. Why? Why this curiosity about me, Qasim?'

It looked as if Qasim would not answer. His face took on a shuttered look, the look of a man who was trying to grapple with a question he did not even begin to understand. Finally, he said, 'I was in the marketplace, and heard about you. You sounded so kind, so benevolent—I wanted to be your disciple.' He rubbed his forehead. 'Then I heard that you are not that sort of a holy man: not the type to take on disciples.'

'So you thought you would offer yourself as a servant?'

Qasim nodded. 'If that is the only way I can get to be with you, Baba.' His voice shook, and all of a sudden, he broke down, tears flowing down his cheeks. 'Have pity on me. I am exhausted, I have nobody in the world to show me the way. I ask nothing except that you allow me to be with you. I will not ask for food, I will not ask for shelter or money or anything except to be with you. Please.' Tears trickled down his face.

For a long time, Buland Baba looked at the young man, his face expressionless. When Qasim had finally quietened down, he said, 'I feel for you, but while I know this will pain you, I must refuse. No. I do not need a servant; I do not even want one. Please do not mention this again: it will only cause both of us further pain.' Qasim opened his mouth to say something, but Buland Baba held up a hand. 'No, do not waste your breath. I do not understand why you are so insistent, but I am sorry, I cannot agree to this.'

And, rising to his feet, he went away towards his home, a small hut behind the mosque. The food, abandoned, lay where he had left it, but Qasim, sitting beside it for the next few hours, did not even look towards it. Eventually, the squirrels and the birds, emboldened by his indifference, came exploring. They ate some of it there and then; most they carried away.

Qasim continued to sit there, and Buland Baba, going to the mosque for the evening namaaz, glanced at him with pity in his eyes. Qasim did not notice him.

Qasim was still there the next morning, his eyes now bloodshot, his thin cheeks covered with stubble.

Buland Baba, sitting down and unwrapping the package in which he carried the tools of his trade, said in a conversational tone, 'Till when will you continue this? Are you hoping to force me into accepting you by being constantly before me?'

The reprimand was so gentle that at first Qasim did not recognize it for what it was. When he did, he reddened. 'I only wish to be with you,' he said stubbornly. 'If you will not have me as a servant, let me be your disciple, your chela. Surely that will not hinder you in any way.'

'My child,' Buland Baba said, 'though why I call you "child" I do not know, given that you are perhaps barely fifteen years younger than I am, if that—well, my child, my dear young man, my Qasim: have you heard about the Hindu concept of the four ashrams, the four stages of a man's life? At this time of your life, you should be entering the life of a grahast, a householder. I do not agree with the philosophy of the ashrams in its entirety; after all, a man should not be obliged to leave his family and go off into the forest just because he's grown old—but I do agree that a man should experience life as a householder. He should know what responsibility is, he should savour the joys and the sorrows of family life before he gives it all up for something higher. If he decides to do that.'

He heaved a sigh. He had been working as he spoke, spreading out his paper and his pens, wetting the ink block, working it into ink.

'Yes,' continued Buland Baba, 'I am hardly one to speak. I have not been husband or father. But that was because I decided I could not burden others with my sins. I have too much on my conscience for a wife or children, who would needlessly suffer too.'

Qasim looked up at this, eyes alive with interest.

'Yes, that intrigues you, does it not?' Buland Baba chuckled, a rueful sound that contained not a trace of genuine amusement. 'I was foolish. Extremely foolish and extremely gullible. I did some stupid things, heartless things. I ruined myself, and by the time I realized and tried to make amends, it was too late. There are some sins that, no matter how hard you try to atone for them, will haunt you for the rest of your life.'

He was looking not merely rueful now, but distressed. He fell silent, and in the silence Qasim spoke up. 'But don't you think it is important to at least try to atone? What if one should sin, and then never be given the chance to atone? If someone were to snatch away another's chance at atonement, would not that be a sin too?'

Buland Baba looked up and nodded, slowly. 'Yes. Why do you ask?'

'Because,' said Qasim, 'I must atone for a sin. And that I can do only by being near you. I do not ask for anything, Baba. I promise you, on the graves of my parents, on the blood of my ancestors—on whatever you wish—that I will not ask for anything. I will help you, I will serve you, no more. Please, just let me do this. Please do not block my one attempt at redemption.'

From somewhere far away, there came, floating on the breeze, the call of a lapwing, its distinctive did-you-do-it, did-you-do-it cry rising higher and higher. It rose, then fell into silence, and then rose again, this time joined by another. Buland Baba squinted up into the sky, as if looking to heaven for guidance. Shading his eyes with one hand, he watched as the birds appeared in the blue above, circling and swooping, their flight and their strident calls aimed at some predator—dog, cat, kite, inquisitive child, who knew what—coming too close to their nest. 'Go away,' he muttered under his breath. 'Go away, and let them live in peace.'

He lowered his hand and looked at Qasim. 'Not you,' he said. 'Mind you, it's not as if I welcome you with open arms. But I see your predicament, and I see that simple humanity demands something of me. Yes, you may stay.'

5

Qasim was true to his word: he did not accept any payment from Buland Baba. Instead, to pay for his food and other necessities, Qasim took to looking around for any small jobs that came his way. At the many sarais along the highway, he groomed and fed horses, acted as porter, and performed errands for the rare merchant travelling without a servant. Sometimes he offered his services to others in Sirhind who had work which needed nothing more than a strong pair of shoulders. Hauling bricks at a construction site, lifting loads, cleaning, sweeping: Qasim did not turn away from any task, did not refuse even an hour's work.

What he liked most of all, though, was to go out to the fields, where there was always work to be found. He would weed, water, and help chase away the birds and the squirrels. While the most lucrative work was with the few farmers who owned large stretches of land, the most fulfilling work was at the sort of small, poor farm where he had grown up. The rhythmic creak of the turning water wheel, the fragrance of new-cut hay, the deep blue of the sky above a field of bright green wheat waving in a breeze: it filled his soul. Paradoxically enough, it both heightened the ache he felt for the home he had left behind, and helped dull the pain of it.

Sometimes he brought work home. Weaving rope, cleaning seed or grain—'women's work,' several said jokingly, but Qasim paid them no heed, and neither did his master.

Buland Baba did not let Qasim do much in the way of work at home. 'I am not decrepit, you know,' he said, the very first day that Qasim had turned up at his hut. 'I am perfectly capable of looking after myself.' In any case, the man lived such an austere life, there was little to be done.

His food was often no more than fruit or parched grain, or a porridge of millet. Some milk or yoghurt, and only occasionally something more substantial, like chapatis or cooked vegetables. He possessed only three sets of clothing, which he washed himself, when he went to the nearby pond every morning for his bath.

'What will you do?' he asked Qasim, his eyes twinkling with a faintly triumphant amusement.

ཆ

But Buland Baba had not reckoned with Qasim's tenacity, or his urge to be of service. Before long, he was doing chores and running errands not just in exchange for money, but to be paid in kind. He would bring home a melon one day, a fistful of barley another. Some beans, some millet. All of these he would insist on sharing with Buland Baba, and his distress the first time his reluctant mentor refused made Buland Baba relent. 'Very well, Qasim,' he had said. 'To please you, I will eat. But for no other reason.' Qasim's delight at this favour seemed absurd to him, but oddly touching as well.

After they had eaten, Qasim had gone outside the little hut they shared. From a friendly neighbour he had borrowed a hoe, and had used it to dig furrows in the ground outside. Buland Baba, stepping out of the hut, had watched with a somewhat benevolent amusement as Qasim had pressed down into the furrows the seeds of the melon, and whatever he had saved of the beans and grain. 'Is the weather right?' Buland Baba had asked.

Qasim, sitting on his haunches, had looked up, grinning through the sweat streaming down his face. 'The rains will come soon. Till then, I will fetch water.'

'And they will grow.'

'If Allah is merciful,' Qasim replied.

'And what will we do with the crop, if there is one?'

'Eat it?'

'We have enough to eat,' Buland Baba pointed out, his

voice patient, as if he were merely reminding Qasim of the fact.

Qasim smiled, blithe and innocent, back at Buland Baba. 'Then we will give it to those in need. So many who come to you, Baba, need help. We will give it to them.'

Buland Baba, a lump in his throat, nodded, but could not bring himself to say anything.

That had been several months back, and since then, Qasim had proved that his confidence in his own ability to turn Buland Baba's yard into a kitchen garden had not been misplaced. Some of what he had planted had never even sprouted; some had been nibbled away by squirrels or birds before it had grown enough to be of any use. Some had been stolen, possibly by passers-by who had little reverence for Buland Baba: but neither Qasim nor his master thought of putting up a fence around the patch.

But some had survived, and it was enough: enough to give them a respite from the usual, and enough to give away. More often than not, the small harvest of vegetables from the patch was donated quietly away to someone who looked in need of it.

Today, for instance, to a young woman, newly widowed, who had come to Buland Baba to seek his wisdom. Her children played nearby, while their mother wept silently and Buland Baba murmured consolation to her. She was grieving, of course, for the husband who had died so young; but she was scared, too, for there was little to eat, and she did not know what to do. She needed sympathy, but also advice.

Qasim did not know what their conversation was about. He made it a point to sit far enough away to not even inadvertently overhear the conversations between Buland Baba and those who came to him. Those who dictated letters merited privacy, but those who searched for advice and comfort were perhaps in even greater need of solitude.

The woman's older child, bored of trying to entertain his younger sibling, left the toddler in his mother's lap and wandered over to where Qasim was sitting. Qasim did not have much work that day, and so was busy picking over some seeds he had harvested from the last crop. There were bitter gourds here, ripened till they were fire-red, their seeds thick and woody. There were orange-yellow cucumbers with wrinkled skins, and some knobby, fibrous okra. Beside him, wrapped loosely in a cloth, were some vegetables at their best and brightest: a few bitter gourds, a dozen eggplants, a couple of cucumbers. And, knotted into one corner, a handful of glossy purple jaamuns.

The little boy stared, his eyes wide. Qasim smiled at him. 'Have some jaamuns?' he asked, pushing forward the cloth, unknotting it from around the fruit.

The child stole a glance at his mother, half-hidden behind the trunk of the neem tree. 'I don't think you should disturb your Amma while she's talking to Buland Baba,' Qasim murmured. 'Why don't you take the jaamuns—and here, these too; these cucumbers are good. Do you like bitter gourd? No? Eggplants, then?' As he spoke, he made up a separate little bundle from a clean rag tucked in at his waist. 'There you are. This is for you and your little brother. Take them with you when you go, and if your Amma says yes, you can eat the jaamuns, all right?' He grinned, and the little boy grinned back.

❧

'That was a kind thing to do,' Buland Baba said later. The woman was gone, her toddler in her arms. The older child had walked beside her, his hand clutching Qasim's gift of vegetables. 'Had you not said, this morning, that you would try to barter those vegetables?'

Qasim shrugged. 'Let us say I used them for the advancement of my own soul.' He smiled. 'You would approve of that, wouldn't you, Baba?'

Buland Baba looked levelly at Qasim. 'You know,' he said, 'when you first came here, intent on being my servant, I was certain you had an ulterior motive.' He had been sharpening the nib of his reed pen, and blew gently at it, clearing it of the particles of wood and fibre. 'I trust you now, but I must admit I still do not understand you... Why do you help me? Why do you help others? Why are you not like the other young men of your age, who live for their families and for themselves?'

Qasim looked away. He did not avoid the question, or deny Buland Baba's observation about him. Instead, after a few moments, he murmured, 'I will tell you someday, Baba. But not now. Now is not the time. But just let me be with you. That is all I ask.' His eyes crinkled as he smiled. 'Like the shaligram stone.'

'What?' Buland Baba stared in puzzlement. 'What on earth do you mean?'

'When I first came here, you told me that I was probably mistaking you for Sadna Qasaai,' Qasim replied. 'Don't you know the story of Sadna Qasaai and the shaligram?'

'I only know of Sadna Qasaai because of his poetry and his philosophy,' Buland Baba said. 'Who in Sirhind does not know of Sadna Qasaai? He is the greatest of the local gurus, the one revered saint that Sirhind can claim as its own.' He had started sharpening the second of his reed pens. 'But you know, don't you, that I came late to Sirhind? So, no; I know nothing of this shaligram. Tell me. I can see you want to.'

'I have heard several versions of this story,' Qasim said, settling back with a sigh of contentment. 'He was really a qasaai, you know, before he saw the light and became a mystic, three hundred-odd years ago. A butcher. Every day he would kill goats and chickens and cut them up to sell in his shop. One day, Sadna Qasaai was walking along the riverbank when he stumbled across a shaligram. You know what that is, I suppose?' He paused.

Buland Baba shook his head. 'The Hindus consider it sacred, do they not?'

'Those who worship Vishnu revere the shaligram. They say that shaligram stones are an embodiment of Vishnu. I was told by one man that there are many shaligrams to be found in the eastern mountains. They look like spirals, like the shells you sometimes see on seashores. But they're black stone, not shell at all.' He shook his head in awe, as if unable to believe that the elements, or an unfathomable divinity, could shape stones to resemble shells.

'Sadna Qasaai found this shaligram in the sand of the riverbank, and he thought it so beautiful, he brought it back to his shop. It proved to be the perfect measure for his weighing scales: whether he needed to weigh out a ser or a maund, it made no difference: he merely had to think how much he wanted to weigh, and the shaligram would make itself heavier or lighter. That doesn't seem to make sense, does it, Baba?'

Buland Baba shook his head. 'Folklore rarely does,' he remarked.

'At any rate, the shaligram was very useful, and Sadna Qasaai could not imagine how he had managed before he had found it. Then one day, a Vaishnav monk passed by Sadna Qasaai's shop, and he saw the butcher using the shaligram as a weight. The monk was furious: this was his god! And Sadna Qasaai was using it for something not just mundane, but something blasphemous as well: to weigh, of all things, meat!' He drew in a deep breath. 'The monk got very angry, and demanded that Sadna Qasaai give him the stone. Sadna Qasaai was surprised, but when the monk had calmed down and explained matters, Sadna Qasaai readily gave the stone to the monk. The monk took it home, and carried out various rituals and ceremonies to purify the shaligram, after which he installed it in his pooja ghar, giving it pride of place beside all the other idols there.

'In the middle of the night, the monk heard a voice calling plaintively to him from the pooja ghar. It was the shaligram, wailing to be taken back to Sadna Qasaai. It told the surprised monk that it had been happy beyond compare in Sadna Qasaai's shop. It did not want to be in the monk's pooja ghar, to be forgotten amidst the other idols, the conch shells and flowers and other items of worship. It just wanted to be in Sadna Qasaai's shop, where it was loved and cherished. Where, every day, many times a day, Sadna Qasaai would use it to earn his livelihood. Where, after every transaction was made, Sadna Qasaai would wipe it clean, would caress it and look at it lovingly. It felt wanted in Sadna Qasaai's shop.'

He was looking sheepish now. 'That, too, is folklore. Things like that don't happen.'

Buland Baba nodded sagely, though if Qasim had looked closely, he would have seen the twinkle in the man's eyes. 'Very true,' he said.

'Let us just say, then, that the monk realized his mistake,' Qasim said hurriedly. 'Next morning he came, and with great humility, he returned the shaligram to Sadna Qasaai. He told Sadna Qasaai that the shaligram's place was where it had come to rest on its own.'

There was silence. The sun had risen high in the sky, and it was getting uncomfortably hot. From an unseen well nearby came the creak of the pulley, followed by the clank of a bucket being placed on the stone lip of the well.

'So you are the shaligram to my Sadna Qasaai?' asked Buland Baba, with a smile. 'This is where you want to be, and I am not to question that?'

Qasim merely ducked his head in acknowledgement. 'Let us go, Baba,' he said, getting to his feet and gathering up the seeds he had picked and cleaned. 'I have enough to plant another crop of vegetables,' he said, with a contented smile. 'Perhaps we may even have enough to sell this time, not just give away.'

'And what will you do with the money?' Buland Baba asked conversationally.

Qasim shook his head. 'I don't know. Keep it aside, for

when it is needed? Is there anything you need? Anything you want?'

For a moment, a cloud seemed to pass over Buland Baba's face. For a brief spell, a few heartbeats, no more, there was deep regret, an intense sorrow written across his features. He heaved a sigh. 'Not anything that I can get by using another man's money, because what I lost was as a result of my own foolishness. I was too naïve, too stupid, and too ready to look the other way when wrong was being done, because I benefited from that wrong.'

'I cannot believe you could do any wrong,' Qasim mumbled, obviously uncomfortable.

'I am no saint,' Buland Baba replied bluntly. 'Those who have known me since I first set foot in Sirhind know that I am as ordinary a man as anyone else.' From up above, in the canopy of the tree, there came a sudden barrage of squawks and angry cheeps. Buland Baba squinted up, smiled fleetingly, and said, still looking up, 'I lost a family heirloom because of my foolishness, and every day since I have spent atoning for it. I do not know whether I will ever be able to bring back what I lost, but I try. Every coin I save goes towards paying for my sin. Every sleepless moment of the night is passed in cursing myself.'

Because he had been looking up, he had not seen the way Qasim's eyes had suddenly widened, or the consternation that had come into his expression. When Buland Baba looked again at Qasim, the younger man's face had regained an expression of somewhat bland curiosity. 'Is that why you live the way you do, Baba?' he asked gently. 'Without wife or children, without anybody on whom you may need to spend money?'

'Perhaps,' Buland Baba agreed. 'Perhaps also because I am obsessed with my past. I have never had the peace of mind to think of anything else, or anyone else.'

He forced a smile to his lips and patted the younger man's shoulder affectionately. 'No, there is nothing I need.

And if I did, I would buy it. I earn money from my letter writing, do I not? Keep your earnings, Qasim. Keep them for when you have tired of this selfless life of sacrifice and austerity. Someday, you will get married and you will have a wife and children to look after; keep it for then.'

Buland Baba was always up, his ablutions done and his mind prepared, long before the muezzin's call for the fajr namaaz, the morning namaaz, had woken the neighbourhood. He never insisted that Qasim accompany him to the little mosque next door, and on some days, an especially lazy or bleary-eyed Qasim stayed back. On this day, though, Qasim had gone with Buland Baba. Nobody was at home when a visitor arrived.

A visitor, though, who seemed to have made himself at home. When they returned from the mosque, Qasim was taken aback to see that the charpai had been pulled down from where it used to stand, leaning against the mud wall of the hut. An old man, his luxuriant moustache startlingly white, was sitting cross-legged on it, calmly chewing paan.

'Daanish,' the old man said, on catching sight of Buland Baba. 'Have you suddenly turned gardener?'—he gestured at the plants growing in front of the hut.

On Buland Baba's face blossomed a smile of rare joy. 'Devraj,' he said, bending to touch the older man's feet in a gesture of respect that surprised Qasim. 'You are looking well, I am glad to see.'

Devraj, though at least sixty years old, if not more, was indeed looking well: his eyes were bright, his teeth all intact, and when he stood up from the charpai, his movements were brisk, fluid. Buland Baba introduced him to Qasim, fetched a terracotta tumbler and poured water into it from the suraahi they kept just inside the hut. Devraj gulped greedily, asked for more, and when he had had his fill, sat back and asked for all the news. All that had happened since he had last come by, a little before Bahlol Lodhi's abortive swipe at Dilli.

It had been a few months, but an eventful few months those had been. Qasim, busying himself in the kitchen garden, overheard much of the conversation, since the two men made no attempt to lower their voices. Devraj, he gathered, had a reputation as a stone carver of exceptional worth—'See, being picked by Taimur to drag off to Samarqand had its advantages!' Devraj chuckled. The conversation revealed more: that Devraj was much in demand, invited every now and then to some distant part of the realm, for a commission. A wealthy merchant might employ him to work on the building of a mansion; a provincial prince might send for him to carve something for a palace or a tomb or a mosque. He was a master, acclaimed far and wide.

To a gently murmured question by Buland Baba, Devraj shook his head. 'No. I have given up, even though I still wander the length and breadth of this land. Who knows, perhaps my children too are dead and gone by now; I am the only one, perhaps, who is doomed to live on.' He drew in a deep breath, steadying himself. 'But tell me, what does Bahlol Lodhi plan to do now? One attack on Dilli failed; what do they say of the chances of another?'

Buland Baba chuckled. 'You think Bahlol Lodhi is my bosom friend, that he will tell me?' Devraj did not react, and after a moment, Buland Baba shrugged. 'They say he won't give up so easily. There will be another campaign, if only for the sake of his reputation.'

Devraj nodded, his lips pursed thoughtfully under his moustache. 'In Dilli, they fear another assault any day. Not that the Sultan seems bothered; he cannot seem to understand the gravity of the situation.'

'Or he's got too much on his platter,' Buland Baba pointed out, but Devraj was not to be mollified so easily. He shook his head. 'Dilli is in a mess,' he said. 'Every minor princeling within twenty kos of the city is rearing his head and declaring his independence. Chaos rules. Lawlessness rules. Nobody knows what is happening, the Sultan least of all!' He snorted, so loud that it brought on a cough that had to be soothed with much water.

'But I must tell you,' Devraj said, when he had recovered his composure. 'Whom do you think I saw in Dilli when I was there this time? Mushtaq.'

If Devraj had expected a dramatic reaction to this pronouncement, he was bound to be disappointed; Buland Baba said nothing.

'He lives very close to the Hauz-e-Shamsi,' Devraj offered after an uncomfortable silence. 'He has a shop. A small one, which his son looks after. They sell odds and ends, mostly pots and pans and baskets.'

Buland Baba still said nothing.

'I met Mushtaq, sitting by the hauz,' Devraj added. 'He didn't recognize me, even though I told him about meeting him at the chaupal, when you used to sit there.' He cleared his throat, and took a sip from the terracotta tumbler sitting on the ground beside his feet. 'He's aged beyond his years. Drinks, I think; I could smell the liquor on his breath, and his eyes were bloodshot.' He paused. 'I'll admit I was shocked. But what is to be done, eh?'

Qasim, bent over a row of okra plants, pinching away dead leaves, did not catch Buland Baba's almost inaudible reply to that; all he heard was a snatch of something that sounded like 'my fault. I cannot blame Mushtaq.'

Then Buland Baba was getting to his feet and telling both Qasim and Devraj that he was hungry, and that perhaps a good breakfast was in order. After all, they had company. They could surely offer him something beyond the mundane millet gruel they usually had.

Long after Devraj had gone his way, after a fond farewell to Buland Baba and a polite nod to Qasim, Qasim asked, 'Who is Mushtaq?'

A shuttered look came into the eyes of the older man. 'A friend,' he said finally, reluctantly. 'From a long time back.'

Qasim could sense that Buland Baba did not wish to speak of this Mushtaq, whoever he was. 'And Devraj?' he asked, certain that here, at any rate, there may be some eagerness to talk: it had been clear to him that the camaraderie between the two men was of long standing, despite the difference in their ages.

Crow's feet appeared at the corners of Buland Baba's eyes. 'Also a friend,' he said. 'A friend I did not recognize as one until I travelled with him.' He shook his head, smiling absently as he looked down at the millets he had been sifting through and picked out a bit of chaff. 'He had once travelled with my father, and become his friend. When I met Devraj, I was a callow teenager, and too full of myself to see his worth. He's a good man, that one.'

6
Sirhind

Four years later

851 Hijri (1447 CE)

Buland Baba, his eyes brimming with joy and his smile wider than Qasim had ever seen it, stood back and looked admiringly at his handiwork. He was the one who had insisted on helping finish the new home for Qasim and his bride-to-be. It was not a hut like Buland Baba's, but a proper house. 'Because I doubt your wife will be able to live in a hut,' Buland Baba had said. The smile on his face was genuine, so full of joy, one might have imagined he was the one getting married. But since he had had a hand in finding a bride for Qasim, perhaps that somewhat proprietary happiness was valid.

As it was for Devraj, who, too, claimed a part in the making of this match. For it was Devraj who had first made the acquaintance of Badruddin Mirza, a brocade worker in a village a few kos from Sirhind. Devraj had met Badruddin in a sarai on the way to Sirhind, where both had happened to stop for a breather, and had quickly struck up a friendship. It was Devraj who had brought a distraught Badruddin to Buland Baba after Badruddin had suffered a severe setback in his business—his warehouse had burnt down, taking with it many months of work. It was Devraj who had offered practical advice while Buland Baba had offered a shoulder to cry on, and words of solace to comfort the man. Qasim, gentle and concerned, had hovered nearby, offering cool water, buttermilk, fruit, a massaging of Badruddin's aching head.

It was Devraj who nurtured this relationship, and who pointed out to Badruddin the suitability of Qasim as an employee. Badruddin needed a man who could read and write, a man dependable and honest, whom he could rely on to get the warehouse rebuilt, while Badruddin focused his energies on weaving the brocades to fill it. Badruddin's other workers were either weavers or naqshbands—the men who drew the detailed and intricate naqshas or patterns for the brocades—and all unlettered. Besides, all were needed to do extra work now that there had been this sudden shortfall.

Badruddin, already approving of Qasim, had agreed. Qasim, initially hesitant and unsure of his own capability, had finally acquiesced. He had gone to Badruddin's village with him, and had stayed there for the next several months. He may have known nothing of what to do, or how to do it; but he was eager to learn. And, as Devraj had told Badruddin, he was both honest and reliable. The warehouse was rebuilt without Badruddin having had to expend any of his own precious time and energy supervising the work.

It was Qasim who stood, from dawn to dusk, making sure that each brick was laid just so, that each batch of mortar was mixed in the correct proportions of stone dust, yoghurt, lentils, cow dung, fenugreek seeds and the pulp of hard-shelled wood apples. He had not known all these strange and unexpected things went into mortar, but Qasim, when he took on something, flung himself into it completely. He learnt quickly, and he was unrelenting in making sure everything was done exactly as he had been told it should be. Badruddin was there, beside him, for all of the first day; after that, Qasim handled it all on his own.

Badruddin was impressed. Not just impressed, but beyond. A little in awe, perhaps; touched, grateful, even charmed. Qasim had an intensity about him that was beguiling. And, combined with his innate goodness of heart, his kindness and gentle nature, it was a potent combination.

Badruddin Mirza had one daughter. Sixteen years of age, Aabida was the apple of her father's eye: so dear to him that no man so far had proved worthy of being chosen to marry her. Now, having seen Qasim at close quarters, Badruddin decided: this earnest young man would be Aabida's husband.

Qasim, taken aback to the extent of being distressed, had protested. He did not wish to marry; who would look after Buland Baba if he went away?

It had taken the combined efforts of Buland Baba, Badruddin, Devraj, and several others who had come to know Qasim over the years, to break down his resistance. They reasoned with him: would his parents have approved if they knew their son was doing nothing to continue the family line? Would they want him to devote his life to someone who did not even want or need the care Qasim was so intent on offering?

It was Badruddin who had finally drawn Qasim aside and said, 'Have it as you wish. I beg your forgiveness for having put you through this.' Qasim, horrified and acutely embarrassed, had opened his mouth to speak. Shut it without speaking, opened it again. And then, at his wits' end and unable to think straight, he had run away. The rest of that evening and the night he spent under the huge mango tree that overlooked the fields beyond the little cluster of houses. The next morning, bleary-eyed and stubble-chinned, he had come to Buland Baba and expressed his willingness to marry Aabida. 'But I will not move away,' he had added stubbornly. 'Into another house, yes. But no further. Not to Badruddin Sahib's village. Please.'

☙

They would have to travel the two kos from Sirhind to Badruddin's village for the wedding, which Qasim had gently begged would be a small one. Though he had looked disappointed, Badruddin had agreed.

Qasim, Buland Baba and a small group of their closest friends set out early in the morning for the bride's village, a quartet of palanquin-bearers with them, taking the palanquin to fetch the bride later in the day. The womenfolk of the neighbourhood had decorated it: garlands of jasmine hung down the sides, and a paste of rice flour had been used, along with vermilion and turmeric, to form a pattern of dots and stripes along the edges of the litter.

As they neared the village, Buland Baba squinted up at the sky, iron-grey and heavy, even though the sun had risen a couple of hours earlier. 'I hope it does not begin to rain during the ceremony,' he said. Then, with a forced chuckle, he added, 'My mother used to say that if it rained at a wedding, it meant the bride had licked too many pots during her girlhood.'

Aabida, it appeared, had been guilty of that bit of gluttony. The clouds had darkened by the time the little marriage party had entered the village. Even as the qazi was taking the consent of the bride and groom to the marriage contract, there was lightning and thunder, and by the time lunch was served, it was pouring cats and dogs. Arrangements had initially been made to serve food to the men in the courtyard of the house, but at the first ominous signs of rain, Badruddin took the decision to shift the feast inside the house. It was a tight squeeze, and they had to improvise. There was discomfort, yes, but it was shared discomfort, and it served to lighten the mood, to make friends out of acquaintances. They looked out at the pouring rain, they laughed at a sodden latecomer who had mud up to his knees. They joked about swimming home after the feast.

Badruddin wept when it was time for Aabida to leave her paternal home. Her mother and sundry female relatives had already said their farewells inside the confines of the zenana. The downpour had dwindled into a drizzle, but the after-effects of the storm would remain for some hours at least. The rain had soaked deep into the earth, leaving huge puddles everywhere; the road to Sirhind would be more mud than firm ground. 'Do you think it would not be better to stay the night here?' Badruddin suggested, a little hesitantly.

Buland Baba, to whom he had addressed the question, shrugged. 'Qasim? It is your decision to make.'

But Qasim was intent on getting back. A storm such as this could not possibly have been so localized as to have passed over Sirhind. Surely Sirhind had been hit equally ferociously, and if that had happened, he wanted to get back to see what damage it had caused to the little kitchen garden he had so carefully nurtured. 'I would prefer to go back,' he said. 'As it is, the rain has stopped.'

So they set off, the men on foot and Aabida inside the palanquin, which had been carefully shielded from the rain so that it shone bright and colourful even now. It was not an easy journey, for the road was muddy, and a stream near the village had overflowed enough to become a raging creek, bringing with it debris that lay all across their path. There were twigs and leaves, mud, stones, a few small dead animals. The wedding party picked its way carefully across it all. Aabida's palanquin swayed frighteningly, but the kahaars were sure-footed and steady.

Not so Buland Baba. Crossing the creek, he slipped. One moment he was on two feet; the next instant, with a sharp cry, he had fallen, his feet slipping out from under him as he went down on his spine onto the rocky bed of the stream. Qasim, a few steps behind, sprang forward with a yell of alarm and despair. The water, swift-flowing even if not deep, had caught Buland Baba unawares: the current had already begun to carry him away when Qasim, half-wading, half-swimming, hampered by his wedding finery, finally caught up with him.

The men accompanying them back to Sirhind had stopped in their tracks. The younger and more able-bodied came rushing after the rescued and his rescuer, and helped them out onto the bank. Buland Baba hung, seemingly lifeless, between Qasim and the others when they put him down under a big kadamba tree nearby. One of the men, a former soldier who knew the rudiments of medicine, noticed the blood dripping halfway down Buland Baba's back, and remarked on the odd angle at which Buland Baba's back bent when they lay him down. He turned away, and with a face like granite, went to where his companions stood. He said nothing to them, and they, looking at his face, said nothing. Instead, they stepped back, giving Qasim space beside the man who had been mentor, master, and father to him these past few years.

'Baba!' Qasim said, his voice urgent, bordering on panic. 'Baba, are you all right?' Behind him, the kahaars had put down the palanquin. Aabida, unmindful of purdah, had flung aside the curtain and was looking out. Only for a moment; when she saw the scene before her, she scrambled up and out of the palanquin, to come to the side of her new husband as he knelt beside his dying mentor.

Buland Baba's eyes fluttered open and gazed at Qasim with a mix of agony and affection. 'Qasim,' he whispered. 'Qasim.'

Qasim was blabbering, saying that nothing was wrong, all it needed was good medicine and a little rest, and Buland Baba would be all right. He said it to the dying man, he said it to himself, repeating it mindlessly, ceaselessly, as if his saying it again and again would somehow make it come true. He looked up into the grey skies and shouted it out loud, until the birds rose fluttering up in a panic from the branches of the nearby trees and flew away.

'No,' said Buland Baba, tersely. 'I am going, Qasim. I know it. I wanted to thank you for all—'

But Qasim cut him off. 'No! No, you cannot. Not like this, not until I've told you!' His voice was high with panic.

Buland Baba frowned. A spasm of pain wracked his body; one of the men came forward with a small earthen cupful of water. Buland Baba shook his head, and winced at the pain that small movement caused. 'Told me what, child,' he whispered.

'I am your brother Dilawar's son, Baba,' Qasim said.

And, even as a bewildered Buland Baba looked on through eyes clouded with pain, Qasim blurted it all out.

How Dilawar, the quiet young man who had left home and family and forsaken it all for mysticism—had changed his mind less than a year after he had left Dilli. Near Multan, to be precise, where he had met the girl who was to go on to become his wife and Qasim's mother.

'Abbu was too ashamed to go back to Dilli,' Qasim said. There was an urgency in his tone now, a frantic rush to tell all.

Dilawar had not known how to go back and face the family he had left so unceremoniously—and, though Qasim did not say it—with so much self-righteousness. Qasim perhaps did not know the truth of his father's separation from the rest of his family, how Dilawar had quietly mocked what he called the worldliness of his folk. But Dilawar had remembered it with shame, and that shame had kept him from returning to Dilli.

'But when he was dying, he told me to go and seek them out, my grandparents, my uncle and aunt. I went to Dilli, but you were gone, and the neighbours told me what had happened.' It was known that Daanish had made his way to Sirhind, and so to Sirhind Qasim had followed the trail.

'It was my fault,' Buland Baba said, grimacing. 'I was so foolish, so naïve.'

'No, never.' A sob escaped Qasim's lips. 'Forgive me, Uncle. Forgive my father.' He was kneeling now, his head bent to Buland Baba's chest. Buland Baba made as if to lift a hand, but it fluttered uselessly. His gaze skittered about and settled on Aabida, who was standing a few paces away. Her head was covered, but her face was unveiled, and when her eyes met Buland Baba's, she seemed to understand what he wanted. Without a word, she moved forward and gently but firmly clasped her husband by his shoulders and raised him. Qasim, confused and disoriented, turned to look up at her, but she tilted her chin, indicating Buland Baba. 'Listen to him,' she whispered.

She retreated, and Buland Baba smiled, a tired and worn

smile. For her, in gratitude. For Qasim, with affection. 'I thought you looked like him,' he said. His voice was a mere thread now. 'I thought it coincidence. But you—you are his son. Yes, so much like him. My nephew.' The smile wavered, and a stray tear made its way from the corner of his eye, down the side of his face and into his greying hair. 'Go to Dilli, Qasim,' he said. 'Take the money I have saved. Go to Dilli. Buy back the heirloom I sold as a boy. It's a frieze. The Garden of Heaven.' He was gasping, each word a shuddering, laboured effort.

Qasim made as if to say something, but his uncle did not let him. 'No,' he insisted. 'Let me speak. Ask Devraj. He knows whom we sold it to. Buy it back. Or note his name. Someday, perhaps your son will redeem it.'

A few stilted sentences only, and they had sapped what little strength he had. The last words were spoken haltingly, with great gasps in between. Qasim placed an arm below Buland Baba's shoulders and tried to lift him, but his uncle shook his head. 'No. Let me keep lying—it is—easier. My son.' He smiled, a fading smile, but one full of pleased pride. 'My son.' Then, by way of farewell, he chuckled. 'Imagine. Daanish became the mystic, not Dilawar. Imagine.'

And, with that, he was gone. Qasim lowered his head over his uncle's dead body and wept.

The general consensus was that Buland Baba would have liked to be buried in Sirhind, the town he had adopted as his own. Qasim was too shaken to go all the way back to Badruddin's village; a few men who had been accompanying him did so, therefore, to inform the family. The rest proceeded towards Sirhind. Four of the men, Qasim at their head, made a makeshift bier out of branches and carried Buland Baba's corpse. Two of the pall-bearers had taken off their turbans and spread them out over the body, but Qasim insisted on adding his turban too. It was incongruous, with its fine brocade edging, woven by none other than Badruddin himself. But it was a sign of deep affection, and no one spoke up against it being draped over Buland Baba.

The next morning, after Buland Baba had been buried, Badruddin accompanied Qasim from the graveyard to the small house Buland Baba had helped build. Qasim had left Aabida here the previous evening, and when her parents had arrived, with a maid and a couple of Aabida's younger siblings, he had brought them there as well. He had not apologized for the poorness of the house; new though it was, it was still far below Badruddin's level. But Badruddin knew his circumstances, and neither he nor his family made any demur.

Qasim was silent as they walked back from the graveyard. It was only when they were within sight of his new home that he turned to Badruddin and said, 'Mirza Sahib—Abba—I do not know how to say this to you, not after all that you have done for me, all your many generosities—'

'Don't say it, then,' said Badruddin, his voice gentle. 'If it pains you, hold your peace, Qasim.'

But Qasim could not do that; he was too distraught, too restless. It had to be said.

After what Buland Baba had told him, he could not rest easy until he had found the Garden of Heaven. 'How can I quietly go back to life as I knew it?' he exclaimed, his voice cracking with emotion.

'What, then, do you intend to do?' asked his father-in-law.

Qasim could only think of one thing: to get to Dilli, to find that merchant to whom a desperate Daanish had sold the frieze he called the Garden of Heaven.

'But you need to talk to Devraj first,' Badruddin pointed out. 'He is in Jaunpur, I think, you said? Which is why he could not make it for the wedding?'

Qasim nodded. 'Yes, yes. Jaunpur. I will go to him—no, should I write? That might be easier. I can go to Dilli in the meantime, and tell him to send me his answer there. It will save time.'

They had reached Qasim's home by then, and he halted outside it, looking at the mud-plastered walls of it. In an outpouring of affection, Buland Baba had used red ochre and kaolin to paint an inept but charming pattern of peepal leaves and five-petalled flowers all along the edges of the walls. For a few moments, Qasim stared, as if uncertain whose house he had come to; then, straightening his shoulders, he said, 'Let us sit outside.'

Badruddin looked askance at Qasim, but before he could say anything, the door of the house opened, and there was Aabida. The tunic and loose pyjamas she wore were simple, unadorned cotton, and the voluminous odhni draped about her shoulders and over her head was similarly plain. A new bride, the henna on her hands a deep crimson, but a bride in a house that had seen a death.

Qasim froze, unsure. This was his wife, but he had not spoken a word to her yet. His wife, and this was actually the first time he was seeing her face. Pleasant-looking, if not classically beautiful, but with deep, liquid brown eyes that drew him in.

'Aabida,' said her father. 'This is your home, remember.' A gentle nudge to remind her of her duty: to offer water for them to wash, to bring refreshment.

She was quick, and efficient. The men were soon sitting on a charpai under a small maulsari tree beside the house. Aabida had brought them earthen tumblers full of spiced buttermilk, before going back into the house to bring them some roasted chickpeas. As she placed the copper plate on the charpai, she said, 'I will sit here, if you please. We have something to discuss, I think.'

'Allah preserve us, daughter,' Badruddin snapped. 'How brazen can you be! Get back into the house. This is men's business, none of yours.'

'This is my husband, Abba,' Aabida said quietly. 'I have

vowed, just yesterday, to be a faithful wife. Is it not right that I should know what I must do to keep that promise?'

Those few words had been enough to show Qasim something of what his bride was like. Badruddin had soon proved that the brusque way in which he had tried to dismiss Aabida was nothing more than bluster: his daughter was precious to him, he could not deny her her way.

Qasim, too gentle, too naïve and just too overwrought at this moment, could speak only haltingly. A word here, a phrase there: no more would emerge.

'I see no reason to go to Dilli until you definitely know whom you should seek there,' Aabida said. Her voice was soft, but there was steel in it, decision, hard practicality. 'And until you have some idea of how much money you will need to even think of redeeming the frieze.'

'All my life's savings,' interrupted Badruddin in fervent tones, 'I will give you, if you need them.'

Qasim shook his head. 'No. Thank you, but I cannot.' His head continued to wag, his distress so deep that it distanced him from a realization of what he was doing. 'My family is responsible. My father, for deserting his parents and his little brother. Had he been there, had he looked after my uncle, the frieze might never have been sold.' He looked up, determination written all across his face. 'No; I will pay.'

Badruddin looked doubtful. A frieze created for a Sultan was not to be dismissed so lightly.

'We will discuss that when we come to it,' Aabida said. 'Let us find the merchant first. That is priority. How many years have passed? Twenty-five? More? Who knows where the man is now.'

It was she, too, who suggested that it might be more practical to write to Devraj in Jaunpur than to travel there. Jaunpur was halfway across the breadth of Hindustan from Sirhind, a mind-boggling five hundred kos or so. 'You can be employed more profitably here, earning money and saving it for when we finally travel to Dilli,' she said.

Qasim did not miss her implication that she would accompany him to Dilli. It surprised him, but it also gave him some comfort: he would not be alone in what promised to be a daunting quest.

The sun had set. Aabida's parents and siblings were inside the house with her. The smell of woodsmoke and of cooking food drifted out to where Qasim sat cross-legged on the ground, his back against a wall. Fleetingly, the thought had crossed his mind that this solid wall, not flimsy wattle-and-daub, was of *his* house. His in name.

What would he do with it when he went away to Dilli? Could he hope that everything would fall into place quickly and easily, that all it would need would be a month's trip to and from Dilli, and the frieze would be back in his hands?

He had no way of knowing how much money the frieze would cost, but a despairing intuition said no.

A little while later, Aabida came, summoning him for dinner. 'Eat something,' she said. 'You have to keep your strength up.'

'I'm not hungry.'

'I know. But you must eat. I will bring out a thali for you, if you will not come inside.'

'I was told Buland Baba helped you build this home,' Aabida said when she had brought the food out to him. On a kaansa thali, made of gleaming bronze, were rotis, a little heap of cooked vegetables, a small bowl of dal. Aabida waited while Qasim washed his hands from the water pot beside the door, and having handed him the thali, she settled herself down beside him.

She watched silently as Qasim picked at his food, pushing it around on the thali. From a nearby home, they heard the muffled crying of a colicky baby, replaced after a while by the soothing tones of a woman singing a lullaby. Crickets sang in the bushes, and somewhere in the trees an owl hooted.

'Shall I remove that thali? Do you think you might want to have a tumbler full of milk instead?'

Qasim had eaten one morsel of food. The rest lay as it was, the roti shredded, the vegetables mushed and scattered across the thali. He blinked, looking down in dismay at the ruins of his food.

'I—I'll eat it,' he mumbled, and hurriedly began to make morsels. Aabida did not stop him; perhaps she knew, as well as he, that he could not afford to waste food.

When he had finished—an undignified, unashamed gobbling up of food—Aabida rose to her feet to pour water onto his hands. As she set the water pot back in its place, she said, 'You are my husband now. Why not accept it?'

Before he could react to that, she added, 'I do not know what pressure Abba put on you to get us married, but this is not how I had expected things to be.' Her voice was low, but there was a restrained sort of irritation in it: as if she were holding her anger in with difficulty. Her patience was wearing thin.

'No, no,' he hurried to say, but she was already speaking, her voice now sharp and brittle. 'But whatever it may be, we are married now, and we had better make the best of it.'

The moon had come up even as he had toiled over his dinner. Scudding clouds, silvered by the moonlight, plunged her face into darkness one moment and lit it up the next.

'Your father,' he said, his voice sounding, to his own ears, like a harsh croak in the stillness of the night. He cleared his throat, spoke lower, slower. 'He didn't put pressure—it's not—not as if I didn't want to marry.' A lie, of course, because he had, after all, allowed himself to be browbeaten into this; but he would not be so cruel as to admit that. 'I—I really don't know women. I had no sisters, no cousins.' He licked his dry lips, wishing his breath would not flutter so, his voice not tremble.

'A mother?' There was, to his surprise, a hint of amusement in her voice. Qasim stole a look at Aabida's face, but the clouds had suddenly blotted out the moon, and he saw only a vague shape there before him. He could not tell if she was still annoyed. He did not think so.

'A mother is a mother,' he replied, now feeling a little bolder. Her amusement—he assumed it had been amusement, surely he had not mistaken that emotion—had emboldened him like her gentleness and patience could not.

'And no woman,' Aabida agreed dryly.

'And you are a woman.'

She laughed at that, a chuckle which made his heart skip a beat. It was an odd sensation: new, unfamiliar, unexpectedly pleasant. 'Indeed I am,' she agreed. 'And I am your wife.'

Later, as she lay back in the thick, lush grass of the fields into which they had wandered, Aabida smiled a smile of contentment. 'Abba used to talk about you, you know,' she murmured. 'He always said how good you were. Good. Not brave, not dashing, not ambitious.' She reached up and trailed her fingers down Qasim's cheek. 'And do you know, when Abba told me he wanted me to marry you, I was happy. Because a good man is more important than anything else.'

The clouds had vanished long ago, as if they had never been. The moon shone down on her face, and Qasim thought he saw the stars reflected in her eyes.

'I don't think I'm good,' Qasim said, embarrassed. 'What is good about me?'

He had meant it as a protestation, to refute a claim he thought flattering; but she seemed to think it a genuine question.

'For one,' Aabida said, 'you are earnest, and honest. Reliable.' Her hand, caressing his jaw, meandered slowly down and back, behind his ear and into the hair curling about his neck. 'Then, there is your shyness. You *are* shy,' she repeated, her fingers tightening on the hair at his nape.

'There you go, turning away. Why will you not look at me? Don't shy away from me.'

He smiled at that, and was still smiling when she added, 'And there is your conscience. It made you devote your life to trying to atone for your father's mistake.' She tugged at the neck of his tunic, loosening it, though she continued to speak, as if her actions did not affect her words, or her words her actions. As if her seduction of her bridegroom were disconnected from the sombre truth she spoke.

'And now, you are ready to go off and devote the rest of it to atoning for your uncle's mistakes. That,' she finished, pulling him down to her, 'is conscience.'

Qasim was too intoxicated by then, his mind too muddled and his senses too aflutter, to be listening to her. He breathed in the fragrance of crushed grass and jasmine, the whiff of sandalwood, as he buried his face in Aabida's tresses.

7

It was winter by the time a letter arrived from Devraj, in faraway Jaunpur. He wrote of his sorrow at hearing of Buland Baba's death, and rued the fact that his work, and the distance from Sirhind, had not allowed him to attend Qasim's wedding. Had he been there, he might have had the chance to say farewell to the man he had once known as Daanish.

Fortunately for Qasim, Devraj remembered well the name of the merchant to whom he had helped Daanish sell the frieze. Sudarshan, a man who traded in grain. His business spread from Dilli in the west into the Punjab, and east far into the Doab, bringing barley and millet, wheat and rice into the imperial capital. A shrewd businessman, and one who could afford the price a work of art like the Garden of Heaven could command.

I must warn you, though, wrote Devraj, *on one of my trips to Dilli—this might have been eight years ago, perhaps a year or so here and there—I heard someone say that Sudarshan had suffered a terrible setback in trade. He had lost almost all his wealth, and it was said that he was considering leaving the city. He may not be in Dilli any more. And if he lost his wealth, it may be that he sold off the frieze.*

'He says "may",' said Qasim doggedly. 'There is a chance it didn't happen.'

Aabida's first child was in her belly, but so far showing its presence only by making its mother feel queasy now and then. She did not look up from the lentils she was picking through, but simply said, 'What will you do, then? If he isn't in Dilli?'

'At least I should go to Dilli and check.'

'I will come with you,' she said, as she set aside the lentils, now clean. She got up from the charpai where she was sitting, and walked the few steps to the kitchen garden that Qasim had already worked into existence. The bits of chaff, clods of earth and other debris she had picked out of the lentils, she now scattered across furrows already green with eggplant and coriander, the shoots of onions, and the curling tendrils of beans that would not ripen, perhaps, till spring. Aabida plucked a handful of coriander, held it to her nose and breathed in deeply of its powerful scent.

'The child is not a sickness,' she said, looking up at her husband, who had followed her into the kitchen garden. 'Nothing will happen.'

But Qasim would not agree. On this matter he was adamant; he would not risk anything happening to Aabida or their baby. Perhaps Aabida saw in his obstinacy his love for her, so she did not pursue the matter.

'We will have to find a solution,' she reminded him that night, after the lamp had been extinguished. 'I cannot live here alone, and I will not go to my mother's home, not until it is time for my confinement.'

Aabida's mother came to stay with her daughter, and she was there with Aabida a little over a month later when Qasim's letter arrived from Dilli.

'The merchant is not in Dilli,' Aabida said with a sigh when she had read the letter. 'My husband has asked around, among those who knew him. But nobody knows where he went.'

'He must have sold the frieze, then?' her mother asked. Badruddin's wife was busy making gudaris, little padded blankets, for the grandchild that was coming. She had gathered together scraps of soft old cotton cloth, and spent a few hours every day on her handiwork, putting one neat stitch after another into the cloth. Without looking up, she added, 'Something like that, people would know when it exchanged hands.'

'Or not.' Aabida frowned as she re-read parts of Qasim's letter. 'Nobody seems to know about it. This Sudarshan might have been embarrassed about having had to sell it off.'

'In that case, it might even be that he did not.'

Aabida sat, the letter still clutched in her hand, her mouth pursed.

'What will you do now, daughter? Does your husband say when he will be back?'

Aabida laughed, a bitter and unhappy laugh. 'He will not come home, Amma,' she said. 'If I know him, he will not give up so easily.' She set the letter aside. 'I will have to go to Dilli; there is nothing else to do.'

Qasim arrived, dejected and weary, a few days later, following in the wake of his letter. He came late in the evening, when Aabida and her mother had already eaten. Her mother had retired to bed, too, but Aabida welcomed her husband home, wrapping her arms about him with a long sigh of relief. Qasim held her close, before drawing away, murmuring that he was dirty and sweaty, that he needed to wash.

By the time he had cleaned himself up, Aabida was pounding ginger and green coriander in a small mortar. She mixed the coarse paste into a tumblerful of buttermilk along with a pinch of salt, and held it out to Qasim. He sat himself down on the charpai and took a deep, grateful swallow of the drink. Aabida settled herself beside him. Qasim watched her for a while, then murmured, apropos of nothing, 'If that Sudarshan sold the frieze before he left Dilli, chances are it is still within the city. In the home of some wealthy merchant, perhaps, or a powerful nobleman…'

His voice trailed away, overcome with the enormity of the task that lay before him.

'You cannot just barge into the homes of the wealthy and powerful of Dilli and demand to know if they bought the frieze from Sudarshan,' Aabida said. 'And anyway,' she added, 'how long ago was that, twenty-five years? A man who bought it back then might conceivably have left Dilli himself.'

She was being the devil's advocate, but it pained her to see his pain. 'Look,' she said, her voice softening. 'You know I want your happiness. If your happiness rests in finding this frieze, so be it. But if you're to fulfill your uncle's mission, you must think carefully. Plan.'

ଓ

It was Aabida's father, Badruddin, who came up with the closest thing to a solution. Among the men he knew in high places was a goldsmith: a man whom Badruddin had become acquainted with because of their shared work in precious metals. The man was a Hindu, a well-respected craftsman. But it was because of his daughter, Hema, that Badruddin now remembered the man: for Hema was the beloved of Bahlol Lodhi. It was said that he had been entranced by her exceptional beauty from the moment he saw her, and that he intended to marry her soon.

'Mind you, I do not say that the goldsmith will necessarily have any say in the matter,' said Badruddin, outlining his plan, 'but it just may be. Hema, I believe, has a good deal of influence with the Lodhi. And Bahlol Lodhi is bound to have men in Dilli, working to help him achieve his ambitions. One more man in that group will hardly make a difference, but it might mean a lot for you.'

After that disappointing first campaign against Dilli, in the year that Qasim had arrived at Buland Baba's doorstep, Bahlol Lodhi had bided his time. Had plotted, planned, recouped his losses. Then, in the year that Buland Baba died, Bahlol Lodhi had struck again at Dilli, and had once again been repelled.

A lesser man, or a more superstitious one, might have taken that as an omen. But Bahlol Lodhi's ambitions were not so flimsy that they could be so summarily crushed by defeat. Perhaps, too, he saw that the only way to wipe out the stain of humiliation from two defeats was to make certain the third time was a victory, a resounding one that everybody would remember long after they had forgotten his two unsuccessful attempts at being Sultan.

In Dilli, anyway, the situation was veering towards collapse. By the time Bahlol Lodhi began flexing his muscles for the third time, the throne at Dilli had been deserted by its Sultan, Alauddin Alam Shah. Alauddin had decided he had no taste for kingship and had retired to the sleepy town of Badayun. His throne and his city had been left in charge of his right-hand man, Hamid Khan.

Hamid Khan was a canny man, who realized that Alauddin Alam Khan had no intention of coming back to Dilli and his rightful throne. He knew too that a vacant throne—even if in the charge of a designated caretaker—was a temptation, an open invitation. Just as a band of greedy monkeys will lay a mango orchard to waste when the fruit ripens, so it was with Dilli: the city was too tempting for would-be invaders to ignore it. And like the monkeys that would mindlessly pull off leaves, ripe fruit and raw fruit—everything—in their mad desire to feast on the fruit, so would they decimate the city. Dilli could ill afford another attack.

Or perhaps the mundane truth was that Hamid Khan had no wish to be the Sultan himself; he was content with being the power behind the throne.

And he seemed to have set his sights on Bahlol Lodhi as a possible candidate for the role of puppet Sultan in Dilli. There was gossip in the bazaars that Hamid Khan was already making overtures to Bahlol Lodhi, egging him on to come and occupy the vacant throne.

'I can talk to Hema's father,' Badruddin said, 'and request him to put in a word. Maybe, if Allah is willing, some method may be found by which Qasim may be able to get access to some of the wealthier homes in Dilli. Perhaps even as a servitor accompanying an official about? I don't know; let me ask.'

The goldsmith, who lived in Sirhind, was welcoming and attentive. He listened with a sympathetic ear to Badruddin's account, and finally suggested that it would be better if Aabida spoke to Hema personally. 'I could tell my daughter,' he said, 'but that would be only my word. Not my emotions, not my own plea. But if your daughter were to speak, I am sure she could present her husband's case far better than I could.'

Aabida was initially reluctant. 'Me, and meet the lady?' she gasped, when Badruddin told her. 'I would not know what to say!'

'You, of all people,' said her father gently, 'would be able to speak. Do it, daughter. If you want the stars, you have to reach for them, you know.'

Aabida had finally agreed. On the appointed day, dressed in her finest clothing, and bearing a gift—a length of brocade, the best her father's workshop could produce—Aabida went to the home of the goldsmith, where Hema lived with her family until such time as Bahlol Lodhi married her and took her away to his own palace. Badruddin had offered her a palanquin but Aabida had flatly refused. 'How will I ever climb out of it without disgracing myself?' she had said, indicating her belly, big with child. 'I will go in the bullock cart, Abbu. That will suit me far better.'

Hema, she was relieved to discover, had few of the airs one would have expected of a lady of her standing. The chamber in which she sat was not overly opulent, and, besides the lady herself, contained only two others: a maid who was fanning the lady with a large handheld fan made of cloth, and another who was reading, in a low, mellifluous voice, from a stack of birchbark sheets. Hema looked up when Aabida was ushered in, and with a soft word, dismissed the reader.

She was an exquisitely beautiful woman, but more than her features, there was about her a self-assurance, an elusive charm. A goldsmith's daughter, not the obvious choice as wife for an ambitious man like Bahlol Lodhi, who might have been expected to marry only for political reasons. But a woman with so arresting a presence that Aabida could understand why, even without the clout an influential family might offer, Bahlol Lodhi might wish to marry Hema. Unless, of course, she wondered with a twinge of cynicism, if the goldsmith's money might have been a consideration.

Hema heard her out, regarding her watchfully throughout. When Aabida fell silent, the lady did not reply immediately. She was looking down at her hands in her lap, resting on the embroidered lehenga that spread about her. On her wrists were intricately worked gold bracelets, a filigree depicting lotuses; Hema traced the flowers absently with a fingertip.

'You must be very devoted to your husband,' she said finally, looking into Aabida's face. 'But I fear your husband is equally devoted to this quest of his. He will abandon you for it.'

Aabida was sitting on a sheet-covered mattress in front of Hema, who was seated on a low divan. She had to lift her head to look up into the lady's face, and when she did so, she surprised a look of compassion on Hema's face.

'I know, my lady,' Aabida admitted. 'But if I try to thwart him, it will serve no purpose. He will find other means to carry out his search.' She shook her head. 'It will make him unhappy, and bring me no joy. It is better to adapt to change than to fight it.'

Hema could spare no more than a quarter of an hour, and Aabida soon found herself being gently dismissed. 'I shall see what can be done,' the lady told her. 'Mind you, there may be nothing very enviable about the work he will get; perhaps as a mere servant—but it might allow him a glance into the houses of some of Dilli's leading citizens.'

'That is all I ask for, my lady,' Aabida said, bending awkwardly to offer a salaam. 'I will be ever grateful to you.'

Hema smiled. She glanced at the brocade Aabida had gifted her, silver threadwork decorating a turquoise background. 'If someday your husband is able to find and redeem the frieze, you can bring me another brocade,' she said, the teasing amusement in her voice betraying the fact that this was simply her way of offering a compliment.

The goldsmith's daughter was true to her word. Less than a week later, a message was brought by one of her maids: employment had been found for Qasim at the office of Hamid Khan, the chief minister in Dilli. Qasim would be one of the many minions in the service of Dilli's most important man, and his duties could be anything, from fetching and carrying to running errands, waiting on the master, doing whatever Hamid Khan or one of his officers required him to do.

'It is more than I could have hoped for,' Qasim said with a sigh of relief. 'If I am to run errands, or perhaps to wait on Hamid Khan when he visits the nobility or the big traders...' he let the sentence trail off.

'And,' added Badruddin, ever pragmatic, 'you will be paid.'

Within a day of receiving the message, Qasim had packed up his few belongings and made arrangements to travel to Dilli with a caravan that had stopped for a couple of days at Sirhind en route to the imperial capital. The night before he was to leave, he held Aabida close, even though her big belly made it difficult.

'Pray,' he whispered. 'Pray that I will find it soon. So that I can come back to you, to our child.'

'I will come to Dilli,' Aabida said, 'as soon as the child is old enough for the journey.'

Qasim nodded, his palm pressed tenderly against the tautness of her stomach under the thin tunic she wore.

'I will be there,' she repeated. 'Find me a comfortable

house. It need not be large, just one room will be enough. But there must be space for a garden.' She smiled at him, her eyes full of affection. 'You will have time for that, will you not? To plant a few seeds, so that I can nurture them while you are away searching for your own garden?'

Qasim's eyes filled with tears as he gazed at her. 'My Aabida,' he whispered, his voice husky with emotion. 'You—you know I love you, don't you? This, all this,'—he gestured vaguely, indicating nothing and yet everything—'this is all nothing. This I have to do,' he added lamely, unable to say what he had to, hoping she would understand.

'I know,' Aabida said, reaching up to brush the tears away from his cheeks. 'This is duty, and duty must come before love, isn't it?'

He stared miserably at her, her face pale in the dim light from the single diya which flickered in a niche beside her. Slowly, so slowly that it seemed he did not even realize what he was doing, he withdrew his hand from where it had rested so proprietorially on her belly.

'You are hurt,' Aabida observed. 'Because I spoke what I feel. But that is the truth, isn't it? Why deny it? If you had thought love more important than duty, you might have realized that you harbour a futile hope, that you will ever find the frieze. Or it might have struck you that you have a duty towards your wife and child.

'You have chosen your path. And I have not come in the way of it,' she finished. 'But do not tell me that I cannot resent it.'

A few hours later, even before the first bulbuls and sparrows had begun to chirp in the tree outside their window, Aabida stood at the front door, bidding farewell to Qasim. She had cooked for him rotis and some dry spiced lentils. With a lump of jaggery as a sweet, she had wrapped it all up in dried palash leaves and then put it in a clean napkin which she now placed in his hands. 'Go with Allah,' she said.

Qasim nodded, and went his way without turning to look back.

ଓ

It was almost a year before Aabida was able to leave Sirhind and come to Dilli. Her firstborn, Aslam, was a sickly baby, weak and prone, from his first week, to the gamut of infant ailments. If he was not colicky, he was coughing; if he was not coughing, his delicate skin had broken out into a rash. His mother and grandmother and all their maids, friends, neighbours and distant relatives pampered the baby, cosseting him and surrounding him with every old wives' tale they could think up between themselves.

All the milk, ghee and dry fruit, the prayers and votive threads tied at dargahs, mosques, and temples in and around Sirhind, worked their magic—or perhaps Aslam simply outgrew the frailties of his early babyhood. Once Aabida was assured that the journey to Dilli would not be too strenuous for her child, preparations were swiftly made. Qasim was summoned to fetch them to Dilli, and the house was sold to a shopkeeper newly arrived in Sirhind. On her last day in Sirhind, Aabida went one last time around her now bare home, silently bidding farewell to it, to the memories it held.

The thought of that house came to Aabida when she stepped over the threshold into the cramped dwelling in Dilli, which she would now call home. Qasim was outside, taking down her bundles from the bullock cart. Aabida, Aslam asleep on her shoulder, looked about the room. Its mud-plastered walls were cobwebbed and sooty, the thick reeds underlying the mud showing through in places. A musty smell hung about it all.

She was shaking her head when Qasim re-entered, bringing with him her luggage.

'I'm sorry,' he mumbled. 'This is paltry, isn't it? I am almost never at home; I haven't had the time to even clean up a bit—'

Aabida made him put the bedding down and placed her baby on it. 'I will clean up,' she said. 'It won't take long.' She was still looking about, searching for a twig broom, a rag, something with which to begin. 'It's not the dirt that is the problem,' she finally said, opening one of her bundles and pulling out one of the many clean rags she had brought along to use for the baby. 'It's the place. It's just'—she shook her head, trying to find an appropriate word for it—'just so dilapidated. As if somebody forgot about it a long time ago.'

Before he could reply to that, she was shaking her head. 'We'll talk later. Can you get me some water? Is there a well nearby? Where do you get water from?'

Instead of a well, there was a large lake.

'It's called the Hauz-e-Shamsi,' Qasim said.

'You did not choose this house simply so that you could be close to the Hauz-e-Shamsi,' Aabida said, later that evening. It had taken her less time than she had imagined to clean the house, simply because it was so small. Qasim had minded his son in the meantime, and when Aabida was ready to finally rest a bit, he had brought his wife and child to the bank of the pool. The water glittered in the last rays of the setting sun, and the pavilion in the distance, holding the slab with its sacred hoofprint, looked almost burnished. It was tranquil, beautiful. Aabida did not notice any of it.

'It is not so very far from Hamid Khan's mansion,' Qasim countered.

'As are many other homes. We passed several on our way into the city.' Aabida waited, not saying anything, aware that the silence would draw forth what her questions might not.

Her tactic worked. 'Our landlord is a man in need,' Qasim said finally, when the silence became too awkward. 'I feel so sorry for him.'

'Charity is all very well, but surely it is more appropriate to leave the giving of it to those who can afford it?' Aabida raised a hand to stall the protests she could foresee. 'Yes, I know. We are bidden to give, especially when we can least afford to. But all this while, we have been saving so that, if you find the frieze, we have some hope of buying it back. What of that, then?'

Aslam, crawling about, stumbled over a tussock and fell flat on his face. He had to be picked up, brushed off, kissed and played with, before the conversation could continue. Qasim was inclined to let the matter drop, but Aabida, irritable and exhausted from the journey and from the hours of housework and childcare, would not rest without an answer. 'Tell me,' she said. 'Tell me why you are doing this.'

Qasim dithered, but was forced, finally, to give in. 'Some years back,' he said, 'I overheard a conversation between Devraj and Buland Baba. Devraj spoke of this house, this man, Mushtaq. Mushtaq had once been a friend of Buland Baba's—of Daanish's—and Devraj said he now lived here. Buland Baba said then that he, my uncle, was the one at fault. He had wronged Mushtaq. How, I do not know; but it has preyed on my mind ever since.'

Even before he had shown up at Hamid Khan's office, bearing with him the letter of reference from Bahlol Lodhi's palace, Qasim had gone looking for Mushtaq. He had remembered Devraj's description: that Mushtaq owned a small shop near the Hauz-e-Shamsi, run now by his son, where they sold odds and ends, including baskets. It was a good description, and precise; Qasim had no difficulty finding the place.

'And I did not hide my identity,' he said. 'I told him straightaway who I was. The nephew of Daanish, who had wronged him.' The old man, Mushtaq, had looked taken aback, confused; but that too Qasim had been prepared for. Devraj, after all, had mentioned it, had said that Mushtaq had aged beyond his years.

But Mushtaq had eventually explained the whole story to Qasim. How he and Daanish had been friends, how Mushtaq had helped him set up his business as a letter writer, and had loaned him the capital to begin the work. 'But then, when Daanish got into trouble and was arrested, I discovered just what a rascal he was,' the old man had said.

He had gone on to explain how, once Daanish had emerged from prison, he had come to Mushtaq, asking for money to pay the penalty imposed on him. Mushtaq, horrified at how his old friend had behaved, had told him to leave, but instead of quietly going away, Daanish had assaulted him. He had beaten Mushtaq, knocking him unconscious. When Mushtaq came to a while later, it was to find that Daanish had run away with every single thing Mushtaq owned. 'He told me nothing was left,' remembered Qasim. 'Not a coin, not a shred of clothing. Daanish took away everything. How could I have not offered anything by way of reparation? My uncle, and such a shameful act.' So he had taken over the little shed behind Mushtaq's home, and was paying Mushtaq a goodly sum for it.

Aslam, bored and now sleepy, had crawled into Aabida's lap. She patted him absently, cooing a few snatches of a lullaby to him.

'He is an old man, Aabida,' Qasim said, as they walked back to their home a while later. 'Old, getting a bit senile. Frail. They have the shop, but it is poor, and his son is worthless. He spends most of the day gallivanting with his friends, locking up the shop or leaving it with one of his children to tend as best as they can.' He shook his head. 'It pains my heart to see the state of affairs in their family. Mushtaq's daughter-in-law cries every night, late into the night. You'll hear her; she's the only woman in the house.'

And she did. Aabida heard those muffled sobs long after the rest of the settlement had fallen asleep. As she tossed and turned, bitten by bedbugs and mosquitoes, and tormented by her thoughts, Aabida wondered about that household, separated from theirs by just the width of a brick wall. A pitiable old man, a ne'er-do-well son, a household to be run on a pittance. One woman to try and make ends meet. She could not blame Mushtaq's daughter-in-law for weeping.

But how she wished it was not they, so poor themselves, who had to provide.

8
Dilli

Two years later
855 Hijri (1451 CE)

'Mmm.' Farida's fingertips wandered over the piece of embroidered silk, light as a whisper across its surface. As if her coarse, work-roughened fingers might mar the beauty of those luminous silk threads. 'Mmm.'

For someone who wept so uninhibitedly in the dark of the night, Farida was very taciturn in her conversations, very sparing with her words. Not unemotional; by no means—just reluctant to put those emotions into words. Everything she felt, her pain, her joy, her anger, her fear, was reflected in her eyes. Little of it ever made its way to her lips.

'Thank you.' Aabida smiled, first at Farida and then at Farida's ten-year-old son, Gulrez, who was sitting cross-legged next to his mother, drawing on a sheet of paper Aabida had given him. 'You know, don't you, that Gulrez drew the design for this embroidery?' Aabida reached out to pat the boy on the head, and he grinned back at her. 'A child to be proud of.'

In response Farida raised her eyes, nodded imperceptibly, and then made a swift gesture, her fingers drawing away from Gulrez's temples, to knuckle at her own. Indeed a child to be thankful for, and a child from whom one would wish the evil eye well and truly away.

Gulrez had returned to the drawing he was making, a pleasing one of butterflies, large and small, flitting amidst tiny buds. Aabida, setting aside the piece she had been embroidering, leaned across to the cradle, a heavy shawl slung from a beam, that held her baby son. He was clean and dry, fast asleep.

'You go,' Farida said. 'I'll manage.'

Of course she would. During the day, she was calm and able to cope with all the many domestic crises that came her way, from falls to minor squabbles between siblings, from the cracks and cobwebs in the walls of her home to those in her relationships. It was only at night, when the last diya had been extinguished and the rest of the city had fallen asleep, that Farida set aside the cloak of stoicism she had been wearing all through the day. Her children, like young ones everywhere, were able to sleep through her weeping, but how her husband and her father-in-law bore it was a mystery. Or why they did nothing about it.

'Life is hard,' she had told Aabida soon after they first met. She had said no more. Aabida had been puzzled, and not knowing Farida, had tried to probe. Nothing had come of it.

Within a day of arriving in Dilli, Aabida had come face to face with her neighbour. Both women had initially been cautious, neither of them overly outgoing. Aabida had been resentful of the fact that Qasim was giving away money uselessly to someone no poorer than himself; Farida was suspicious of the newcomer.

But the children had helped break the ice. Farida's brood had quickly discovered the baby Aslam next door, and had taken him to their collective bosom. Aabida, a young mother left to fend for herself in a strange and intimidating new city, had reached out to the more seasoned mother who lived next door. They had, gradually, become friends of a sort.

Farida's eldest daughter's twelfth birthday had prompted Aabida, by then expecting her second child, to take out her embroidery silks and a length of muslin from one of the bundles she had brought with her from Sirhind. An odhni, she had thought. Or something less ambitious? A handkerchief, or perhaps a length of kinari, an intricate bit of embroidered edging that could be added to whatever piece of clothing it might suit.

She had used a stouter piece of cotton than the fine

muslin, and had made a kinari. Two fingers wide, it had been a confection of little knots along the edges, holding in a pattern of fruit: green grapes, paisley-shaped mangoes and glossy purple jaamuns, a tribute to the girl's fondness for raiding the mango orchards nearby.

'You could sell these,' Farida had said, her eyes widening when she saw the gift Aabida had given her daughter.

It was not as though Aabida was oblivious to the merit of her own talent and training, but it had never occurred to her, until Farida commented on it, that she might earn something from her work.

She thought over it long, pondering deep into the night, weighing the pros and cons. She would need time to create embroideries, and with one toddler and a baby on the way, besides all her daily housework, she had little time in which to do embroidery. On the other hand, some extra money would be welcome; Qasim did not merely pay Mushtaq for the use of the shed they called home, he also gave the old man gifts now and then. A little package of dates, a small pouch of crystal sugar: nothing extravagant. But little gifts, over time, cost more money than they could afford to spend, especially with a growing family.

For the sake of her children, Aabida decided to take the plunge. She had pieces of cloth and silk threads aplenty among the things she had brought from Sirhind. And she could take her time, working as and when she could snatch a few minutes. In any case, with Qasim gone all day and Aslam playing with Farida's children, Aabida had some time every day to herself. If she hurried through her chores, she might be able to do some embroidering.

By the time her new baby had arrived and was able to turn over, Aabida had a sizeable number of embroideries in a bundle she had set aside for that purpose. Odhnis and kinaris, handkerchiefs and even a coverlet embroidered on thick cotton. Even to her critical eye, they looked good.

Qasim, all along unaware of his wife's enterprise, was

taken aback when she asked him for references, for wealthy homes where the ladies might wish to buy her work. His eyes widened when Aabida spread out the embroideries before him, but he did not probe: did not ask how she had done it, and when. More importantly, why. Perhaps he could guess. He was, in his way, an astute man; perhaps he realized that—though Aabida's management of the household hid the fact that she ran it on a minuscule budget. He had looked guilty, but he had suggested a few names: wealthy families, the rich and powerful of Dilli.

'But how will you go there? What of the baby?'

Aabida had folded away her embroideries, wrapping them carefully in unbleached cotton. 'I will make arrangements,' she had said.

Gulrez accompanied her in the bullock cart, a stolid little assistant, proud of the responsibility that was his. He held a bundle of the smaller embroideries, the handkerchiefs and scarves, while beside Aabida was a larger package, wrapped first in thick cotton, then in jute. This time most of what she was carrying was commissioned: part of the trousseau for a bride; a gift for a first-time mother; other presents for other people with achievements to celebrate, milestones to be marked.

This would be a long trip, taking up most of the day. Aslam and his baby brother had been handed over into the care of Farida that morning, and Gulrez, excited and eager to start, had hired a bullock cart. This he had been doing from the first time, several months back, that Aabida had asked for his help and his escort. 'Go so far, alone?' Farida had said, but she had summoned Gulrez, and ever since then, Gulrez had had this responsibility added to the other tasks he did as Aabida's assistant.

In his lap, besides the package of embroideries, was a ledger and a pen case. He was her clerk too, now.

But still a child, his eyes wide with interest as they travelled eastward from the vicinity of the Hauz-e-Shamsi. Past the ruined stone walls of Lal Kot, the fort built by the Tomar Rajputs long before Mohammad of Ghur had invaded the city and put paid to the Rajput dominance of Dilli. Between the walls of Lal Kot on the west and Siri on the east spread the city of Jahanpanah, built by Mohammad bin Tughlaq a little over a century earlier.

'Look, look,' said Gulrez, leaning out. 'Those domes. That is Khirki Masjid, isn't it?'

Aabida, still new to the city, and bound to one corner of it by her circumstances, shrugged. 'We came by here two months back,' she reminded him. 'You asked, then too, what it was.'

Gulrez nodded eagerly. 'I asked the maulvi sahib, when we got back. He said it's the Khirki Masjid. It was built by a great minister, many decades ago.' He squinted, the bright sunlight shone so harsh on the forbidding stone walls of the mosque that looked more like a fortress than a place of worship, complete with rounded turrets at its corners, its gate high, the steps leading up to it steep. Were it not for the many domes—there were probably a hundred there, or near about, thought Aabida—she would never have imagined it was a mosque.

Just a little beyond the mosque, and clearly visible from it, was a structure that rather more obviously revealed its purpose: a weir, three of its seven wooden gates right now raised to let the water through. 'Satpula,' said Gulrez sagely, smug in newfound knowledge. 'Maulvi Sahib told me. Mohammad bin Tughlaq built it, so that his city could get water for their fields.'

He was a good child, eager to learn, vivacious and guileless in the way of children. He knew when to be silent, and would watch carefully and with concentration when she worked; but he knew, too, when it was acceptable to be chatty. Right now, travelling beyond his usual haunts, seeing the sights, he was more garrulous than usual.

There was something soothing about his chatter. Aabida settled against the woven reed covering that curved over the cart. The road was too rough for the ride to be comfortable, but it could not be helped. And she enjoyed listening to Gulrez, his enthusiasm infectious as he told her all he had been told. 'Also,' he was saying now, pointing to the weir, its walls diminishing as the cart drew away from it, 'do you see how high those walls are, how solid? That was meant so that if anybody attacked Jahanpanah from the south, those walls would stop them. So that's not just a dam, it's also a fort! How clever, eh?'

Just after the weir, the cart turned left and wended its way slowly northward, past the Dargah of Hazrat Khwaja Nasiruddin Mahmood Chiragh-e-Dehli, the poet and mystic. Aabida had been here once, when she had first arrived in Dilli. Qasim, out of a sense of duty, had thought it fit to show her the sights of the city, and this was the one place he had brought her. A little over a century ago, Dilli, it was said, was in the depths of darkness and decrepitude. Lawlessness, governmental apathy, poverty, fear: all of these, and more, caused Dilli to be derided and scorned far and wide, as far abroad as Baghdad. 'But Dilli is not utterly dark,' a man in Baghdad was supposed to have remarked to another who was debating the point. 'As long as there is, in that city, Nasiruddin Mahmood Roshan Chiragh-e-Dehli, the "illuminated lamp of Dilli", as they say. While he lives, Dilli is not wholly lost.'

Chiragh-e-Dehli, as the saint was referred to affectionately by hundreds of the faithful, was destined to be the last of the great mystics of Dilli. He had been dead these past hundred years, and his resting place was a quiet, calm oasis of cool shady trees and the sleepy cooing of pigeons. They could not spare the time to stop, so Aabida shut her eyes briefly, while still sitting in the cart, and offered up a silent prayer.

They ate the food Aabida had packed for them sitting in the cart as it travelled north-east towards the river. By the time they had finished, they were nearing the Yamuna.

Near the riverbank, the first of the Sayyid rulers, Khizr Khan, had built his palace and laid out a city around it. The city had been named Khizrabad, and in it, outside the gateway to a large, single-storeyed mansion, the bullock cart came to a stop.

It was a beautiful building, the red sandstone carved sparingly but with taste. The three-arched dalaan into which visiting menfolk would be ushered could not be glimpsed, since Aabida was taken straightway into the zenana, leaving Gulrez in the cart. Not an infant who could go into the women's quarters, yet not a man who might be taken into the dalaan and entertained, he was obliged to wait while Aabida completed her work.

ᴓ

'They say Bahlol Lodhi will arrive in Dilli any day now,' said Gulrukh Begum when she had examined the pile of embroideries Aabida had brought, had paid for them, and had had them put away by her maid. Gulrukh Begum was a plump, placid woman, surrounded by three daughters-in-law, a couple of daughters, and a small horde of granddaughters, ranging in age from two months to ten years: all of them had crowded around while Aabida had spread out the embroideries before them. Now that the business of examining and admiring the wares had been completed, the matriarch had sat back, eager to chat and to glean gossip. The little girls ran off, back to their play, but their mothers stayed back, clustering around.

'Hamid Khan will regret inviting him,' said a daughter-in-law. 'Bahlol Lodhi is not a pony, that he will be led by the bridle wherever the wazir wishes.'

Gulrukh Begum nodded eagerly. 'Hamid Khan will get a rude shock.' She turned to Aabida, remembering why she had introduced the topic of Dilli's politics in the first place. 'Your husband is in Hamid Khan's employ; what does he say?'

Aabida shook her head and denied that Qasim said anything about his work. Which was true; by the time he came home, he was too tired to do much more than eat, wash, and go to sleep. And from all that Aabida knew of her husband, he was probably too preoccupied with trying to find the long-lost frieze to eavesdrop on conversations or listen to bazaar gossip.

'Hmm.' Gulrukh Begum made a face, her pink rosebud of a mouth pursing up in dissatisfaction. 'What a pity. But I hope it will be well for your husband, if Hamid Khan is forced out of Dilli by Bahlol Lodhi. It would be a shame if you had to leave. Where would we find work so fine, eh?'

'Do you think Bahlol Lodhi will make himself a new city when he takes over Dilli?' Gulrez asked a few hours later. From Khizrabad, they had travelled southwards, to yet another city built by yet another Dilli Sultan with a thirst to assert his power: Mubarakabad, built by Khizr Khan's successor, Mubarak Shah Sayyid. Here, not too far from Mubarak Shah's fortress-like domed tomb, Kotla Mubarakpur, was another household where Aabida had to deliver her work. A wealthy home, not as grand as Gulrukh Begum's, but well able to afford fine things.

They were finally headed back, exhausted but pleased, too. The long and tiring day had not lessened Gulrez's enthusiasm or his talkativeness; he was as ebullient as ever.

'Let Bahlol Lodhi take over Dilli first,' Aabida said. 'Then we will see.'

'We've been through three cities today,' Gulrez said, and began to count them off on his fingertips. 'Khizrabad. Mubarakabad. Jahanpanah. And of course, there's back home. Mehrauli is another city, isn't it? Why does every ruler build a city? Not every,' he corrected himself, 'but most?'

Aabida shook her head. 'Who knows? Perhaps it's just a way of showing off.'

'But to build a city to show off? And, anyway, who lives in these places anymore? Not Jahanpanah, of course; but the others. Khizrabad and Mubarakabad are like a wilderness compared to Jahanpanah.' He chuckled, his mind skipping ahead, to other thoughts. 'I wonder what Bahlol Lodhi will name his city? Bahlolabad? And where will he situate it? Beside the Yamuna? But the best spots are already taken, aren't they, with Khizrabad to the south and Firuz Shah Tughlaq's kotla north of that. Maybe he should try building in the upland areas, that would be a good stronghold if an enemy attacked.'

He prattled on, his voice melding pleasantly with the sounds of the dusk: the twittering of the birds, the tinkling of cow bells as the cattle were brought in from their day's grazing, the rhythmic clack-clack of the cart's wheels. Aabida listened, half her mind on his words, but the rest wandering.

She did wonder what would happen if and when Bahlol Lodhi arrived in Dilli. Not even if; *when*. He was certainly coming, it was only a matter of when.

As they went past the Khirki Masjid and the stretch of the Jahanpanah city wall around it, the somnolence of the evening was pierced—though gently, melodiously—by a low, musical piping. No bird, this, but a human. It was joined right after by a twanging sound, and then an exuberant drumming. All three joined together into a tune of joy: vibrant, infectious, so emphatically inviting that Gulrez, taking advantage of the slow pace of the tired bullocks, jumped down from the cart and ran off in the direction of the music.

He was back before the bullocks had covered a hundred yards. 'Mirasis,' he said, grinning from ear to ear as he climbed back up into the cart. 'Wandering minstrels, and they said they will try to come to our area too! Won't that be good?'

☙

The mirasis did not come to Mehrauli after all, not the next day or the day after; or ever, as far as anyone could tell. But the next day, when the city woke, it was to the sight of a huge army approaching Dilli. Bahlol Lodhi had returned, once again, to the city he had been trying to capture these past eight years. Bazaar gossip had it that the mirasis were no real minstrels at all, but Bahlol Lodhi's soldiers in disguise. The elite of his force, men who had entered Dilli incognito and sneaked into the palace to capture it for their master.

Bahlol Lodhi, coming at the head of his troops, made straight for the city of Jahanpanah. Other cities—the Sayyid settlements of Khizrabad and Mubarakabad among them, Firuz Shah Tughlaq's Firuzabad—had been established after Jahanpanah, but none had the lasting power of Mohammad bin Tughlaq's Jahanpanah. The city still thrived, Dilli's recent rulers preferring it as a stronghold.

People went out in droves to watch the army enter the city. Many, who remembered Bahlol Lodhi's two previous attempts at the throne of Dilli, four years ago and eight years ago, were apprehensive. There was no knowing what would happen. Bloodshed seemed a real possibility; turmoil at the very least. A change in ruler was a disturbance; a change in dynasty could be an upheaval.

'Of course it was expected,' Qasim said that night, when he was home. It had been a day like none other at Hamid Khan's palace; the uncertainty, the chaos, the excitement of it all had thrown the entire household into a state of agitated nervousness. Qasim had received conflicting instructions from several different men, had been sent off on one errand after the other, and then recalled hurriedly from half those errands.

'But you still don't know what Bahlol Lodhi has in mind,' Aabida said. She had put Qasim's thali in front of him and sat beside him, wielding a hand fan in such a way that its gentle breeze swung between the two of them equally. On the charpai beside them, the children lay fast asleep, Aslam's arm curled protectively across his baby brother's chest.

Qasim shook his head. 'Who knows? Perhaps there have

been talks between him and Hamid Khan; perhaps not.'

Aabida let him eat a few more morsels before she spoke up again, asking the question that had been nagging at her ever since she had heard that Bahlol Lodhi was approaching Dilli.

'And what will happen of you?'

Qasim looked up. 'What do you mean?'

'Hamid Khan's days are numbered in Dilli. If he leaves, what will you do?'

Qasim chewed absently, a pensive look in his eyes. 'I've been into dozens of homes, wealthy homes, these past years. You know. And not a sign of the frieze.'

Aabida shook her head. 'It's not in Dilli anymore. And the world lies outside Dilli.'

A heavy silence hung in the little room, broken only by the noisy breathing of the baby, who had a cold.

Qasim pushed away the thali. He looked at Aabida, misery written in the lines of his face. 'It is my duty to find it,' he whispered. 'My uncle entrusted the task to me on his deathbed, Aabida. I will not be able to rest if I know that somewhere out there is a man from whom I might get the frieze back.'

A few weeks went by, and the city was all abuzz with rumours flying left, right and centre. Hamid Khan would stay on as wazir; no, he was angling to be sultan. Bahlol Lodhi had told Hamid Khan that he would not sit on a throne that was not rightfully his, since the true sultan was Alauddin Alam Shah, now living quietly in Badayun. Bahlol Lodhi had written to Badayun, inviting Alauddin Alam Shah to come back to Dilli, but had received a courteous refusal. No; no courteous refusal, a frightened one; Alauddin Alam Shah knew this was mere eyewash, and if he so much as approached the throne of Dilli, he would be put to death.

All the rumours died a swift death when Bahlol Lodhi

had the khutba—the Friday sermon at the Jami Masjid—read in his name, proclaiming the Lodhi as the Sultan of Dilli. The next thing they knew, Hamid Khan was taken prisoner and handed over to Bahlol Lodhi's cousin, who was the Governor of Samana, near Sirhind. Hamid Khan was taken away to Samana and oblivion.

Meanwhile, a message had been delivered at Hamid Khan's palace for Qasim. Devraj had sent word that he had come to Dilli.

I have been unwell, he wrote. *Age is catching up with me, and I would gladly have breathed my last in Jaunpur, where I was comfortable, had it not been for you. You are to me like the son who was separated from me a lifetime ago. Come and meet me, if you can; I am too weak to move any more.*

He had given directions to a sarai just outside the city gates of Jahanpanah, and Qasim decided to go that very day.

'I will make laddoos,' Aabida said. 'Take them with you, and give them with my regards. He is a good man.'

When she was handing Qasim the small bundle a while later, she said, 'Ask his advice. He has lived long, he knows the world.'

☙

Aslam and the baby were napping and Aabida was mending a small pile of garments when Qasim returned. She heard the creak as he pushed aside the makeshift gate he had made, slung on a rope hinge, to fit on the thorn fence around their hut. She heard the sound of his footsteps and then a shadow fell across her work. He said nothing, just stood there.

Aabida looked up, concerned. The look on Qasim's face was one of utter devastation. Eyes staring into space, face drawn, mouth downturned. Ashen complexion.

She hurried forward, offering water, helping him to settle himself comfortably. Cooing softly until he had regained some semblance of composure.

He had had a shock, that was all. No; it was not Devraj, who was still surprisingly spry, given his age. Tired from the long journey from Jaunpur, but that was all.

'Then? What is the matter?'

Devraj had asked about Qasim's family, Aabida, the children. Where they lived, how they liked Dilli. Qasim had told him, not just of where they lived, but how that had happened. How he was making reparations for the long-ago wrong Daanish had done Mushtaq. Mushtaq was dead, felled by a weak heart the previous month, but Qasim had no intention of ending the relationship between the two families. Daanish's misdeeds were a debt that had to be repaid, with interest many times over, into the next generation.

'He told me it was nothing of the sort,' Qasim said, with a shudder. 'I had misunderstood it. Daanish had said it was his fault, not because he had wronged Mushtaq, but because he had been gullible, and because he had turned a blind eye to all Mushtaq did.'

He recounted to Aabida all that Devraj had told him, of what had taken place years ago when Daanish was a letter writer in Dilli. Of how Mushtaq had helped set him up as a letter writer, and how, when Daanish was accused of slandering a high official, Mushtaq simply vanished.

'He was never wronged,' Qasim whispered, his throat choked with anger: anger at Mushtaq, of course, but also anger at himself, for having been so pitifully naïve. 'How he must have laughed, when I turned up here, begging to be allowed to make reparations! He must think us a family of idiots.'

Aabida heaved a sigh. 'You realize, do you not,' she said, 'that there is only so much you can do by way of duty? You have done what you could, all these years. Now let go of it.'

She caressed his hand, the veins standing out on it, the skin leathery and deeply tanned, old before its time. 'Come back,' she whispered. 'Come back to those who have loved you all these years. Be with your family, Qasim. We need you.'

A long, winding cavalcade had come into town, following the route Bahlol Lodhi had traced some weeks back as he had entered Dilli. This entourage, however, was very different from Bahlol Lodhi's, though the cavalry and foot soldiers were in evidence here too. Instead, the bulk of the retinue consisted of bullock carts, a few women mounted on horses, and many servants and slaves who went on foot. They moved at a sedate pace, slow and stately. The aim was not to hurry forward and lay claim to a throne that might slip out of reach, but to show the watching populace the grandeur and self-assurance of the Sultan. For this was his new bride, born Hema, now titled Bibi Ambha, coming to join Bahlol Lodhi.

The carts, not just the one in which she rode, but those which accompanied her too, were splendidly decorated. The horses' coats were glossy, the maids decorously veiled. Even the sweepers and water carriers who went ahead, clearing the road for Her Highness, were better dressed than most of the onlookers. Every now and then a couple of maids would be handed out baskets from inside the second cart, and from these they would distribute largesse: copper and silver coins, dry fruit, rice, wheat, lumps of jaggery.

For once, Aabida had set aside her work and come to watch the pomp and the show. Qasim, who had found employment at the home of a noblemen he had visited often with Hamid Khan, was at work. Aabida had brought Gulrez with her, and it was he who held Aslam's hand while Aabida held her baby.

'It is all so very fine,' Gulrez said in a voice filled with awe. 'And you have met her? How is she, to look at? Is she very beautiful? Does she talk like a queen? Nose in the air?'

Aabida smiled. 'It's been several years,' she said. 'She

wasn't married to Bahlol Lodhi then, and was quite approachable. Now?' She shrugged. 'I don't know, I will have to see for myself, I suppose.'

That evening, she opened the small wooden chest she had bought for her best embroideries, and from it she drew out a length of thick beige-gold silk, two yards across and one wide.

When Aabida had begun working on this, with the spectre of Bahlol Lodhi hanging on the horizon, Qasim was still Hamid Khan's servant. Every night he would return, exhausted and downhearted after a long day of work and of fruitless searching for the frieze. In the depths of the night, she would hear him muttering in his sleep, describing the Garden of Heaven to himself.

That frieze had become Qasim's mistress, and Aabida had embroidered that mistress onto the silk she had hoped one day to give to Bibi Ambha. In silk thread dyed with indigo, she had worked a stream, its ripples picked out in silver thread. Turmeric, madder, lac, powdered tamarind seed, pomegranate peels: dyed with these, the threads she wove into flowers and leaves, stems and birds. Butterflies. Dragonflies. Fish, their scales picked out in silver, swimming in the stream. The Garden of Heaven, interpreted by Aabida's needle.

'It is beautiful,' Qasim said when she showed it to him. 'It is appropriate that you chose this motif. The Garden of Heaven was meant for a Sultan; this too deserves no less than a Sultana.'

Aabida smiled, pleased at his words.

'You do not mind, do you,' she said later, when she was wrapping the embroidery in a fine new length of unbleached cotton, 'that I made you stop? Does it hurt too much?'

Qasim stared at her for a moment or two, his gaze unwavering. 'I do mind,' he acknowledged. 'A little. At times I feel restless, and I wonder where the frieze might be.' He shook his head. 'But you were right; how long would

I wander? And where?' He took her hand in his. 'I think, really, that I don't mind. I have made my peace with it.'

'Excellent.' Aabida had taken out another length of cotton, thick and embroidered with a simple, basic edging of a line of red curlicues. She wrapped it around the embroidered garden, and patted it. 'Tomorrow, then, I will set out. Let us see what happens.'

When they were lying on the thin mattress that made up their bed later that night, Qasim—emboldened by their conversation earlier that evening—said, 'I had thought you would want to move out of this hut once you heard about how we—I—had been fooled by Mushtaq. I thought you would be furious.'

Aabida shook her head. 'There was no use.' There was a pause. 'What would it help anyone to be angry? Would we rave and rant at Farida? At Gulrez? Mushtaq is dead, and his worthless son rarely around. Even if those two men were here, it would be like water off a duck's back. The ones who would be hurt would be Farida and her children.'

She paused, 'I like them, Gulrez most of all, but the others too. And I don't think Farida ever knew how her father-in-law was deceiving us; she's asked me countless times why we paid him so much for this place.

'Let us put it behind us,' she finished, turning onto her side, facing him. 'What's done is done, and we should move on.'

'Move out?' Qasim's voice was a startled whisper.

'That too, but later. For now, let me seek an audience with Bibi Ambha.'

Interlude

'Stupidity runs in our family,' Mohsin says in a gloomy voice.

I have been a little under the weather these past few days. It has forced me to ask for help; I have had to get Mohsin to write it all down, for I cannot bring myself to lift my pen.

Since he has been keeping abreast of this history of ours, it is befitting that he contribute in documenting it. Also, his calligraphy needs work. At his age, I was a full-fledged qaatib, a calligrapher of considerable repute. Each letter, each stroke I made on paper was perfect, even though I say so myself.

'Why so?' I ask. 'Why stupid?' My throat hurts from all the speaking I am having to do as I dictate. Once upon a time, I would have had servants bringing me, at regular intervals, cups of a soothing decoction of licorice and ginger, gently heated to calm the sorest throats. There would have been a lad to massage oil into fingers stiff from work, and to pour cool water while I splashed my eyes.

No longer; all our servants are long gone, dead or driven to desperation by this drought. Those not yet dead and not yet run away to their villages, we have had to let go; we could not possibly have fed them anymore.

Mohsin, with the self-centred obliviousness of the young, has not even noticed my discomfort. He has been too busy thinking over my question. 'Look at Daanish,' he says. 'I told you my opinion of him, didn't I? So naïve. And then Dilawar. Why leave home and run off to become a mystic, only to give it all up immediately after? And if he decided to not be an ascetic after all,' Mohsin concedes, 'then why the shyness about returning to his family? That is stupid. Didn't he trust his family to forgive him?'

He is precocious, but there is some wisdom in that last

sentence of his. Mohsin has more to him, I realize, than this surface impatience. If only he would cultivate those depths.

'And what about Qasim?' he says, his voice rising in indignation. 'Why this coyness about telling Buland Baba who he was? Also foolish.' He grimaces. 'Imagine, if he had told Buland Baba right at the beginning who he was, they would have had so much time together, to get to know each other. Perhaps, even to find the frieze together.'

'It is difficult to go to a stranger and say you're actually a close relative,' I explain. 'Especially for someone like Qasim, who was quiet and shy. And burdened with the guilt his father had passed on to him.'

But Mohsin is in no mood to accept what I suspect he labels platitudes. He shakes his head stubbornly. 'How can anybody pass on guilt to another? It is the mind of a slave, to accept thoughts like that—to think you are in any way a part of another's failings. Not that Dilawar failed, I don't think so. But even if Dilawar thought he failed, why should Dilawar's son share the blame?'

I give up. It is pointless to argue, and I have no time to waste in pointless arguments.

'As it is,' I tell him, 'the person who really mattered, as far as we are concerned, was neither of these. Aabida was the one on whom this part of the story hinged, I think.'

It took patience and perseverance for Aabida to meet Bibi Ambha. After some thought, Aabida had decided against taking the embroidery of the garden the first time she approached the lady: there would be countless guards, servants, maids and ladies-in-waiting along the way, and a priceless gift handed over to one of them for Bibi Ambha might go astray. Perhaps even intentionally. No; the first thing to do was to make an overture, to attract the attention of none other than Bibi Ambha herself.

Aabida therefore returned her embroidery of the Garden of Heaven to its place in her wooden chest, and took out a simpler, smaller, yet beautiful piece. This she wrapped and took, along with a note, to the palace. It took several visits, several more notes, several pieces of embroidery, before one day Aabida was ushered into the presence of Bibi Ambha herself.

Bahlol Lodhi's wife had not remembered Aabida, but the embroideries she had been gifted had impressed her; and when Aabida was ushered into her presence, Bibi Ambha recalled her too. More importantly, she praised Aabida's embroidery in front of all her ladies, drawing attention to its finesse, the aesthetics of it as well as the talent and the skill. 'Come tomorrow,' she said, as Aabida's audience with her drew to a close. 'There is something I wish to commission.'

In gratitude for that benevolence, and now assured that she would indeed meet none other than the lady, Aabida took the embroidered garden along the next day. It was the day that was to mark her entrée into the world of the court.

Within a few months' time, she had begun to train a couple of promising young girls from the neighbourhood. By the end of the year, Gulrez had been appointed a full-fledged apprentice. Aabida had realized, early on, that his forte lay in the creation of patterns for her embroideries; she knew, too, that more than the embroidery, it was woven brocade that was likely to succeed. When it came to weaves, a skilled artist could be trained as a naqshband, a creator of the designs or naqshas that were used as the basis for each brocade. Gulrez, she thought, would make an excellent naqshband, and it was not yet too late for him to be trained.

Taking her children and Gulrez with her, Aabida travelled to her father in Sirhind. There, she handed over Gulrez to be trained; and when she returned to Dilli a few months later, she brought with her the detailed design for a loom.

A loom, of course, could never fit in the cramped confines of their little home. Besides, some of her best clients—people like Gulrukh Begum, who had expressed an interest in the brocades she had described—lived in Khizrabad and Mubarakabad, both a good way away from the Hauz-e-

Shamsi. To move north-east, somewhere near the river, was the obvious solution. Aabida chose Ghiyaspur, where Dilli's most revered mystic, Hazrat Nizamuddin Auliya, was buried. Ghiyaspur was conveniently located, and she found there a house which suited her needs: it was just the right size for a small but prosperous family, and nearby, within a few minutes' walk, was a large, single-storeyed building that stood in a secluded garden. This had once been a warehouse for a trader who had since moved away to another city; now Aabida saw in it the perfect workshop. She could house here not just the one loom she had intended, but more.

When he was fifteen years old, and a passably good naqshband, Gulrez returned to Dilli and to what was now Aabida's brocade workshop. Aslam was an apprentice by now, and Aabida looked to him to continue the legacy she had established. Her younger son had been frail and sickly ever since he was a toddler, and even if he lived to adulthood, there was little hope that he would be able to handle the hard work the workshop demanded. Sadly, he did not live to see his tenth birthday; one summer, he was stricken with a fever that did not go away, no matter what Aabida did.

Aslam, thus, became Aabida's only hope: the heir of all her dreams.

Two weeks after Aslam's sixteenth birthday, he was married. His bride, Firoza, was two years younger than him, a sturdy young woman with clear eyes and a way of lifting her chin that Aabida liked.

'She is a good girl,' Aabida said to Qasim, her eyes shining with happiness. 'She will bear Aslam many sons, and we will never have to worry about the fate of our workshop.'

Mohsin remarks that she was quite a woman, an ancestor to be proud of; but barely has he begun speaking than he is interrupted. There is someone in the street outside, calling for me.

'Suleiman Sahib had sent a messenger,' Mohsin says when he returns from answering the door. 'There is news that Hemu has set off from the eastern provinces towards Dilli.'

This is unsettling news: what if the young Baadshah—or rather, his men—fail to hold back Hemu? Hemu is not to be lightly dismissed; he is a canny man, and an ambitious one. The Baadshah's commanders and advisors would be well advised to take measures to face up to him. For if he succeeds, who knows what will be the result? Is Dilli capable of suffering more turmoil, or will another change of guard prove to be the straw that breaks the camel's back?

I think not.

Dilli is too durable to fall thus. She has borne many attacks. Again and again, over the years, from men lusting after power. Other cities have fallen, other cities will continue to fall, unable to bear the knocks of ambition, greed, and sheer hatred. Dilli, to me, is immortal. Even if she falls, she will recover herself. She will rise from the ashes.

9

Dilli

Twenty-six years later
895 Hijri (1490 CE)

'What do you think?' Aslam said, holding out the length of turban fabric to Gulrez. 'Would Ammi have approved?'

Gulrez frowned, bushy eyebrows drawing together in concentration as he examined the silk, its edge woven in a pattern of peepal leaves. He turned it over and peered at the reverse side.

'The weaving isn't bad,' he conceded. 'What is wrong is the basic naqsha. Look,'—he stabbed at the cloth with a forefinger, pointing here, there, here again. 'There is nothing to relieve this empty space, here. And here, do you see? That leaf is drawn with straight edges. Which leaf have you ever seen in nature that had a straight edge? Eh?' He was getting annoyed now, his iron-grey moustache fluffing out because of his agitated breathing. 'And this stalk here, and this one: they're not stylized, but it's not as if they're mirroring nature, either. Where are the little knobby bits, where are the quirks and curves? Whose handiwork is this—'

Aslam interrupted with a chuckle. 'At least,' he said, 'We can safely say this is none of our doing. We had no hand in making the brocade Zubair's father-in-law has chosen to gift him.'

Gulrez, his temper settling back into its usual placidity as quickly as it had flared up, grinned. 'The verses from the Quran that he's penned for the occasion could not have been more beautifully written,' he said. 'I suppose each of us has his place in the world, as my Ammi used to say.'

Both Farida and Aabida were dead. Farida had died six years back, a contented but still taciturn woman, satisfied that Gulrez, her eldest son, had done well for himself. Aabida, who used to visit her old friend and neighbour at least every month, braving the journey from Ghiyaspur to the Hauz-e-Shamsi, had always brushed away Farida's words of gratitude. 'As you always say, Farida, "each of us has his place in the world". This is Gulrez's place, and he fits it well.'

Aabida had died the previous year, following in the wake of Qasim, who had succumbed to a fever.

Now Aslam ran the workshop, with Gulrez somewhere between naqshband and head clerk and primary advisor. His training as a naqshband meant he knew more about the work, and had a love for it beyond the business-like interest that Aslam could boast of. Gulrez's son, Raheem, having been trained as a naqshband since he was a child, had joined the workshop almost as soon as he could hold the naqshband's pen in his chubby hand.

Aslam's son Zubair, now twenty years old, had been working at the workshop too for half his life. Like his father, he lacked the innate talent of people like Gulrez and Raheem; but, like Aslam, he was content to supervise work, meet clients, manage the accounts, and to make sure that work proceeded unhindered.

For the moment, though, there was a brief lull in work. Zubair was to be married to his betrothed, Shahana, in two days' time, and as the only son of the family—he had an elder sister and two younger ones, all married and mothers by now—the home and the workshop was in the grip of an excitement so intense that even Aslam, not usually so indulgent, had smiled and forgiven any temporary laxity in work.

Zubair's future in-laws were descendants of the Gulrukh Begum whose patronage Aabida had won in her early years as embroiderer. The Begum's family still lived in their grand old mansion in Khizrabad, and they still patronized the workshop Aabida had established. Little embroidery was done at what was now a brocade workshop, but the family remained loyal customers. Loyal, and wealthy. In Gulrukh Begum's time, they had been courtiers, their wealth drawn from lands granted to them by those they had succeeded in pleasing. Those lands were still in their possession, and still brought in a fat income; but one of Gulrukh Begum's grandsons had proved to be a worthy calligrapher. He had been skilled enough for his work, distributed as gifts to other noblemen, to be soon requested in exchange for money. All unplanned, all unbidden even, the calligraphy had evolved into a profession. And that had, in turn, become a hereditary profession over the next couple of generations.

Shahana's father was a calligrapher, as was her brother Waqar. They were, of course, minor noblemen too, and therefore, Shahana's marrying Zubair was a step down for them in status. But perhaps Waqar—a canny man, two years older than Zubair—had reasoned that by earning money from their calligraphy, they were in any case a little lowered in the esteem of most of their peers. Also, there was the very real fact that Zubair was the sole heir to an extremely lucrative business. As wife to Zubair, Shahana would be well off.

ଓ

The wedding was a glittering, happy occasion, as weddings invariably are. Even in the midst of chaos, of differences and bickering over trifles—there is something about weddings and birthdays and naming-ceremonies that is innately joyous. The auspiciousness of the occasion overrides everything else.

But here, amidst the joyful folk songs, the dholak and shehnai, the smiles and flowers, there was a discordance. A face that bore no smiles, eyes that were empty.

'What on earth is the matter with Zubair?' Gulrez whispered to Aslam. 'He looks so down in the mouth.'

Aslam harrumphed.

'He's not been as jubilant as I'd have expected a

bridegroom to be, actually,' Gulrez added, after a pause in which he realized that Aslam was not going to answer his question—or could not. 'I remember, when I was getting married, I was hopping about with glee! Not, of course,' he said, 'that all men are like that. But you expect a little more enthusiasm.'

And Zubair certainly did not look enthusiastic about his role as bridegroom. His expression was not that of an embarrassed young man, as many bridegrooms are. Nor was it the bored look of one exhausted by the ebullience all around. It was pure and simple unhappiness.

Aslam heaved a sigh. 'Who knows what the matter is,' he said. 'Perhaps he is just sick of all this ceremony and whatnot.' He glanced towards Zubair. The young man's sehra, a curtain of fragrant white jasmine hanging from the front of his turban, had been pushed aside and folded back now that the ceremony was over and the festivities beginning. There was a faint smile on his fine-featured face as he accepted the congratulations of the weavers who had come from the workshop. He smiled, he nodded. And, as soon as they had gone, his smile was gone too.

'His begum will bring back his smiles,' Gulrez said, with a chuckle. 'Depend on it.'

Gulrez, it appeared, had been overly optimistic.

The days went by, the household settled back into its routine, and all the friends and relatives who had come for the wedding returned to their homes. Firoza's neighbours came by to meet her new daughter-in-law at their leisure, lingering to see her trousseau, and offering comments on each piece of jewellery, each item of clothing. The gifts—the money, the jewels, the fine silks and brocades—were put away or put to use. The men went back to the workshop, leaving the house once more in charge of Firoza and her minions, except that now the new bride was there too.

Shahana looked impossibly fragile. Her skin was like the finest porcelain, her bones so narrow that Firoza wondered that she could lift a full water pot without wincing. Not just a fragile-looking woman, an emphatically silent, shy one as well.

'But the problem is,' Firoza said to Aslam one day, as they sat by themselves after the evening meal, 'I am not sure she says anything to Zubair either.' She settled herself against a bolster, and reached for a paan from those arranged on a tiny silver salver beside her. 'Zubair is a straightforward soul; he will not be charmed by these graces, this whimsy. As it is, he has never really shown an interest in women, anyway.'

'I should hope not,' Aslam grunted, helping himself to a paan. 'Running about after women, indeed!'

Firoza made a soothing sound and patted her husband's hand. 'That isn't what I'm saying. Just that he hasn't even shown an interest. Not even in Shahana. It's as if he doesn't want to have anything to do with her.'

'He's probably uncertain, nervous,' Aslam offered. 'Remember, since he was about ten, he's spent most of his life in the confines of the workshop. To him, your tribe is mostly an enigma. Give it time, Firoza; it will all resolve itself.'

Now that Zubair was married and there was an interesting new inhabitant of the zenana, the ladies of the neighbourhood came calling more frequently. They found Shahana fascinating: she was so fragile, so exquisite, like a 'delicate rosebud', as one effusive woman put it. They were eager to ask her questions, to learn more about her family. Who else was there in her natal home? How many siblings? How old?

Shahana, tongue-tied and terrified, mumbled barely audible responses to their persistent questions. Firoza, sitting beside her, grew increasingly irritated, though she did a good job of hiding her impatience. It was only when they were alone by themselves that she spoke up.

'My child,' she said, 'I know that you have been brought up—and rightly so—to be lady-like, self-effacing and gentle. You may be inherently shy, but you must get over at least some of that shyness. You're a married woman, Shahana; don't tell me you are so shy with Zubair as well!'

She had laughed as she said that, hoping for her assumed light-heartedness to take away any hurt her words may have caused. But Shahana's cheeks flared into colour, a rosiness spreading down to her neck as she suddenly lowered her eyelids and turned her face away, still silent.

'Allah,' Firoza whispered. 'Don't tell me you are so painfully shy with Zubair, too?' She persevered, probing, questioning, wheedling, until Shahana suddenly said, in a strangled little voice: 'He doesn't love me.'

Firoza stared for a moment, before her eyebrows snapped together. 'What nonsense!' she said sharply. 'Love you, indeed! What, do you want to be the Shireen to his Khusro? Is this a fairy tale?' She was too annoyed to pay attention to Shahana, who was now looking at her mother-in-law with confusion. 'Love is not what marriages are made of, not in the real world. Marriage is simply a contract, a bond that you will live together, bear children, and bring them up. If you can be happy doing so, that is excellent. But love? Hah!'

Firoza did not find out till much later what her daughter-in-law had really meant, though Aslam was to discover a glimmer of the truth not long after.

☙

When Bahlol Lodhi had died the previous year, there had been many claimants to the throne. His most beloved wife, the self-assured and ambitious Bibi Ambha, had immediately pushed forward her son Nizam Khan as heir. She had faced scorn for this presumption: Isa Khan, an ambitious cousin of Bahlol Lodhi's, had remarked that a goldsmith's grandson could not be Sultan of Dilli.

That contemptuous remark had incensed Bibi Ambha and hardened her resolve to make sure her son indeed became Sultan of Dilli. Before the summer had ended, she had won over the nobility by a combination of charm, persuasion, and, it was rumoured, both bribes and promises of position. By the time the rains had arrived last year, Nizam Khan had ascended the throne as Sikandar Shah Lodhi.

The celebrations for the first anniversary of his coronation were in full swing, and Aslam had come to offer his congratulations, with Zubair and Raheem in tow. Raheem, in any case, came to the palace often enough, to deliver commissioned pieces. Zubair or Aslam visited the palace only if summoned by Bibi Ambha, now the Dowager Empress: it would be insulting for her to have to discuss a brocade with anyone less than the owners of the workshop.

The three men kneeled before the screen that shielded the lady. The gifts they had brought, both for the Sultan and for his mother, had been conveyed to her.

From beyond the screen came a murmur of pleasure, a soft sound of joy. 'This is beautiful,' said Bibi Ambha. 'I remember, in I think the eighth year she brought me a gift, your mother had made something a little like this. Little pearls sewn all around the edge, and I had suggested she try doing something more intricate with pearls and silver thread.' The old lady's voice softened, sliding into the distant past. 'What a very admirable woman she was, and how beautiful her work.'

She stopped, wrenching herself out of the past. 'Thank you. I shall make sure the Sultan receives these; I thank you on his behalf too.' She paused, then added, in a clear, ringing voice that echoed in the chamber: 'And I would like to take this opportunity to recognize the work you have been doing for the imperial family all these years. In acknowledgement of your merit, it is hereby ordered that your workshop will now be the sole purveyor of brocades to the imperial palace. All we need by way of brocade, you will provide.'

Aslam bowed lower and declared his gratitude. Informally, he had occupied this position for several years; this, however, was an official appointment, and highly coveted. It brought favoured status when it came to being awarded contracts for peripheral areas of the Sultan's regime: henceforth, Aslam would be approached first if brocaded cloths had to be ordered for the royal elephants' caparisons, or for the Sultan's tents when he went on hunting trips and into the battlefield. For rich robes to be bestowed on meritorious courtiers, and gifts for emissaries from foreign lands. For chaadars to be placed at shrines.

It would all be his brocade.

When they emerged from the palace, besides the usual crowd, there was a small group of men, clad in pristine white, kneeling on the ground in neat rows. They were chanting something—it was impossible to distinguish the words; the noise of the crowd around drowned out everything—but every now and then they would lift their heads in unison and shout, 'For shame, Sikandar Lodhi, for shame!'

Aslam stopped in his tracks at the sight. 'What on earth is happening here?'

It was Raheem, standing beside him, who supplied the answer. 'I've seen them before,' he said. 'They're the Hussaini Brahmins.'

Aslam turned to the younger man, his brow furrowed in puzzlement. 'What's that?'

'They believe that one of their ancestors, by the name of Rahib Dutt, fought alongside Imam Hussain. They say Rahib Dutt was a merchant who lived in Kufa. When he heard about Imam Hussain's battle against Yazid, Rahib went there along with his seven sons, and fought valiantly. All his sons were martyred, but Rahib Dutt survived.'

'Rubbish,' Aslam said, his tone brusque. 'There were no kafirs at Karbala, martyred or not.' He was turning away, gesturing to Raheem to lead the way through the crowd, when he realized that Zubair was not beside him any longer. Aslam turned to look over his shoulder, to see Zubair standing stock-still, his eyes wide, staring.

Aslam followed his son's gaze, to the Hussaini Brahmins.

In the centre of the front row, standing a head taller than the others, was a man who caught the eye. Perhaps in his mid or late twenties, he was broad-shouldered and slim-hipped, his moustache neatly trimmed, his features clean-cut. His tunic and dhoti were of well-starched muslin, and his turban had an edging of crimson and gold. There was about him an air of self-assurance, of knowing what he was about.

Zubair was staring at him as if he had seen the face of God.

'What is the matter with you?' Aslam huffed, grabbing his son by the elbow. 'Come on, we have to be getting back.' Zubair let himself be pulled away, but he turned once, at the edge of the crowd, to look back at the group of Hussaini Brahmins. All of them were now on their feet, and the tall man was looking at Zubair, a faint smile lingering in his eyes as he did so. The moment his gaze met Zubair's, he lowered his head a fraction, as if acknowledging an acquaintance.

The crowd closed in behind him.

Just fifty paces ahead, and Zubair made a hurried excuse—he had forgotten something back at the palace; he would catch up with them—and retraced his steps. He was back outside the palace gates within a minute.

The Hussaini Brahmins were dispersing, sent their way by a small contingent of palace guards. The protest seemed to have been a non-violent one, and Zubair, looking on, wondered what it had been all about.

'Don't push.'

The tall man had reached out a hand and clasped the shaft of the lance held by the nearest soldier. 'I am not fighting back. And I am not even fighting; you know that.' The soldier wrenched the lance out of the man's grasp, and with a roar of anger, hit out at him with the flat side of the weapon. The man dodged neatly, and side-stepped to avoid the soldier's rush the next moment.

'We're going,' he called out, even as he whirled about. 'We're going, but we'll be back!'

And with that, he raced to catch up with the rest of the group. Zubair hesitated; then, on a whim, he followed.

Zubair caught up with the man soon enough, and was gratified when he smiled in immediate recognition at Zubair's touch on his arm.

'Salaam, young master,' said the man, his eyes gleaming with what might have been deemed mischief in a boy. In a man, they enhanced his attractiveness, the sense of playfulness.

'Salaam,' returned Zubair. 'But "young master", I am not. I am a commoner, no nobleman at all.'

'But a wealthy and influential commoner,' said the Brahmin. 'I saw you, coming out of the palace. Obviously after an audience. And your clothes'—a slim, long finger indicated Zubair's fine muslin jama and pajamas, the muted brocade that edged his turban and cummerbund—'your clothes are not those of the average commoner.'

There was a twinkle in his eye, but there was something more. Flirtatiousness? Zubair felt a light-headedness come over him. He did not know what lay ahead, but from the look on the man's face, it seemed clear his interest in the other had not gone unnoticed. Emboldened by the laughter in the man's eyes and the smile on his face, Zubair moved forward, closing the distance between them.

'A commoner, still,' he replied, looking up into the man's face—he was a head taller than Zubair, and this close, Zubair saw that his eyes were brown rather than black. 'My father owns a brocade workshop; the Dowager Empress has long been a patron, and we have just been appointed purveyors.' Perhaps it was boastful, but he wanted to make a good impression.

The man's eyes widened. 'I am impressed,' he said, 'that such an important personage should stop to talk to me.' He grinned. 'I am Brahmdev Dutt.'

'I am Zubair, and as I said, no important personage at all. You are the one who is important, I think, that you should stand so boldly before the palace and shout at the Sultan.'

The light-hearted gleam in Brahmdev's eyes sobered into speculation. 'Ah.' He pursed his mouth, eyeing Zubair with interest. 'That caught your attention?'

Zubair nodded.

'And you have no idea what it was all about, I take it?'

Zubair shook his head. 'No. From all I have heard, Sikandar Lodhi has been an exemplary ruler this one year he has sat on the throne. He has put in place a good administrative system. He wants the welfare of his people. They even say he goes out, in disguise, to see how his subjects live, what problems they have. What more could one want of a ruler?'

Brahmdev sighed. 'See. This is the sad reality; that people will blindly believe all that the Sultan and his sycophants will put about as the truth. Nobody even bothers to stop and think.' His gaze bored into Zubair's face. 'Do you want to know the truth? Do you want to know what is really happening?'

Zubair nodded, too tongue-tied to speak.

'Come, then; let us sit somewhere nearby, and we shall have a chat. Yes? Come.'

They made their way through the bazaar, and, a little way beyond, to a domed pavilion that stood by itself on a little mound. An old tomb, perhaps; but it was removed from the bustle and crowd of the bazaar. A good place for a private conversation.

Brahmdev Dutt settled himself down and looked narrowly at Zubair. 'So you think Sikandar Lodhi is a good ruler?' he asked, without preamble.

And before Zubair could reiterate all that he thought of as the virtues of the Sultan, Brahmdev began describing the many ways in which Sikandar Lodhi was persecuting the Hindus of his realm. They were to no longer shave their beards or the hair on their heads. They were also to once again pay the jaziya, the dreaded tax imposed on all who were not followers of the true faith.

'But his mother, Bibi Ambha, was born a Hindu,' pointed out Zubair. 'How can he so go against the faith of his own mother?'

'He has grown up being referred to as "that son of the Hindu goldsmith"; he probably feels he must prove himself a good Muslim.' Brahmdev's lip curled in contempt. 'So he takes it out on us.'

'Was that why you were protesting outside the palace?'

But no; that was because Sikandar Lodhi had banned the practice of taking out tazias during Muhurram, an old tradition that might have been expected to only affect the Shia Muslims of his realm, but which had the Hussaini Brahmins up in arms too.

Every year, when Muharram came around, it was observed with a procession through the streets of Dilli. Tazias, representations of the tomb of Hussain, led the procession. Bright, carefully crafted bamboo structures covered with cloth, decorated with tinsel and flowers, they were so colourful an affirmation of life that they seemed incongruous in a procession of mourning.

Behind the tazias came the mourners, howling and weeping as they moved forward. Some would be thrashing themselves with flails and beating their breasts. Others would carry metal strips with which they beat their own backs, stripping off the skin, letting the blood flow where tears were insufficient.

'We are Brahmins otherwise, but at Muharram, we mourn as fervently as any other,' said Brahmdev. 'To take out tazias at Muharram, to recite elegiac poems, to weep for the martyrs: this is an important part of the observance of this day for us. Who is this upstart Lodhi to deny us our rights like this?'

He straightened up, smiling as he did so. His expression had lightened; his eyes were twinkling merrily now. 'But less of this bleak talk. Tell me more about yourself.'

10

Spring stayed late that year, the cool of winter leaving the city with reluctance. The mahua and the neem blossomed late, and though the days grew longer, the sunlight was bleak. The cold lingered on, and Aslam caught a chill. His wife and daughter-in-law spun nervously about the sufferer's bedside, offering unguents for his chest, hot broths, bitter potions and poultices prescribed by a dozen different physicians and charlatans, including a tantric whom Firoza's maid had fetched from his haunt at a nearby shrine.

'It will run its course,' said the most experienced of the hakims. 'But I don't think there is any need to worry; it will settle, give it time.'

The old hakim was proven right as the days went by. Aslam grew slowly, almost imperceptibly, better. Firoza, her anxiety for her husband now somewhat lessened, began to worry that Shahana had not yet conceived. So many months had gone by, she said to her daughter-in-law: surely there should be a babe in her womb by now? But Shahana could only flush and shake her head, and finally Firoza was obliged to send a discreet note to Shahana's sister-in-law, Waqar's wife, Mariam.

Mariam had been more a mother to Shahana than Shahana's own rather frail mother had been. It was she who had helped ease the passage from girl to woman, she who had taught Shahana all that was expected of a gently brought-up lady: the graces, the duties, the responsibilities.

In response to Firoza's letter came a reassuring one: Mariam would come next week, and would talk to Shahana. All would be well.

ʚ

Mariam came as per her promise, and Firoza was discreet enough to leave her alone with Shahana after exchanging greetings and enquiring briefly about the welfare of the family. Mariam smiled, said all that was expected, and gave Firoza a mysterious, confiding smile as Firoza took her leave to return to her own room. Half an hour later, having had a quiet conversation with Shahana, Mariam emerged from the zenana with her young sister-in-law. Firoza, hovering impatiently in the courtyard outside, was told that Mariam wished to take Shahana to an old woman she knew who might be of help. They would go in the bullock cart that waited outside; it would not take more than three-quarters of an hour.

Their destination was a place close to the riverbank, where the old woman lived in a single room in the middle of a grove of babool trees. The acacia was in flower and studded with tiny golden blooms, each a perfect sphere. The woman was, in some ways, reminiscent of those flowers: there was a sunny exuberance about her, a cheerfulness that was reflected in the crows' feet about her eyes, and in the gap-toothed grin she gave when Mariam told her all about how her young sister-in-law was yet to bear a child.

The old woman smiled at Shahana. 'It is all in the hands of Allah,' she said. 'But perhaps I can help.'

She bustled around, disappearing into her hut—through the open door, Shahana saw that it was spotlessly clean on the inside, its walls plastered and painted white—and remained ensconced for the next few minutes. When she came out, she held a tiny bundle in her hands: a light handful of assorted bark, twigs, dried leaves and other indistinguishable things. She placed it, tied up in a square of muslin, in Shahana's palms, while she went to the nearest babool tree and plucked a handful of fluffy golden flowers. These she pressed into the bundle, and tied the ends of the muslin together. A couple of sentences, and her instructions to Shahana were complete.

'Go, child,' she said, smiling benignly at Shahana. 'May you find what you seek.'

As they walked to where the bullock cart stood, outside the babool grove, Shahana murmured, half to herself, 'I wonder if he lost his heart to another woman, even before he married me. If there was no other in his heart, would he not at least be curious about me? Would he not have come, even once, to me?'

Mariam stopped in her tracks. 'Not even once—?' she whispered, aghast. 'I did not realize.' She cupped Shahana's face in her hands and saw tears well up in Shahana's eyes. 'Do not cry, my dear. Do not cry. It will all be well. There is Allah up above, and he will look after his children.'

Shahana said nothing, but that evening, when she was alone in her room, she opened the little bundle the old woman had given her. From it, she picked out all the babool flowers and set them aside in a little bowl. The rest of the contents of the bundle she rewrapped and placed in the chest where her clothes were stored. The old woman had instructed her to brew an infusion and get Zubair to drink it. 'To beget sons,' she had said.

Shahana had thought long and hard about it, and had decided that that could wait. At least for a while, until she figured out who her husband really was, and what he felt.

For now, she would be content with attracting his attention.

She took a single babool flower, its yellow fluff now limp and wilted, and went to Zubair's room in the men's quarters of the haveli. There, in the middle of his bed, she placed the bloom. It looked diminutive, perhaps even accidental: as if it had blown in on a breeze through a window left open. But there were no babool trees around here, not even one in the yard outside.

She whispered a prayer that Zubair would understand. She would keep placing one flower on his bed every evening until he came to her, to ask her what she was up to.

Then they would talk.

When she brought Shahana back home from the old woman's abode in the babool grove, Mariam took a few minutes to quietly tell Firoza the truth. Firoza was stricken: her first reaction was to go hurrying to Shahana to confirm the disgraceful truth. When she knew for a fact that it was, indeed, as Mariam had interpreted it, Firoza fell to the floor and wept, cursing the womb that had borne a son so lost to any sense of responsibility. She railed, she exclaimed, she apologized on Zubair's behalf to a mortified Shahana. She wished he had never been born.

But she did not realize, till the next day, how matters truly stood.

Aslam, by now, was much improved. The cough was better, the fever gone, but he was still weak, and this in-between state was getting on his nerves. He was a man used to activity, and this enforced rest was galling. It made him bitter and irascible.

'I know just the thing,' said Gulrez, when he came visiting. 'I will take you to the Baoli of Hazrat Nizamuddin Auliya. It will be a nice change of scene for you, and the waters of the baoli will take away the last vestiges of this illness.'

Firoza leapt at the opportunity to go to the baoli, for next door to it was the dargah of the much-venerated Hazrat Sahib. She told neither Gulrez nor Aslam what was on her mind, but merely insisted that she would accompany them to the baoli.

Gulrez was the one who helped Aslam down the steps of the baoli so that he could take a dip in the healing waters of the step-well. That done, and both men chatting quietly as they sat in the sun and dried off, Firoza went to the dargah. The place was crowded with devotees, young and old, Muslim and Hindu, men and women—though the women, of course, were not allowed inside the mausoleum of Nizamuddin Auliya. Instead, they could sit outside, in the corridor surrounding the tomb, to perhaps peer in through the pierced stone screen. More often, though, to just draw comfort from the proximity to one of Dilli's most beloved saints.

Firoza seated herself against a pillar, drawing her voluminous cotton dupatta around her, closing her eyes as she began to murmur her prayers. *Hazrat Sahib, intercede for me. Intercede for this poor soul, so lost and so beleaguered. Pray for my husband, Hazrat Sahib, that he may recover completely and wholly. Pray for my son, that he may awaken to a sense of his duty. Pray that we may be blessed—*

'You should be getting back, my beautiful Zubair,' said a deep voice. 'They must be wondering where you are.'

Firoza, jolted out of her prayers by that familiar name, shook her head the next moment. There were probably hundreds of Zubairs in Dilli.

'Oh, Raheem is competent enough. I do wish, though, that I didn't have to go.' The man's voice dipped to an inaudible murmur, but those few words had been enough for Firoza to recognize him. She stumbled to her feet, and, the next moment, was standing in front of her son.

A stray ray of sunlight, peeking between clouds, was shining down on him as he stood next to another man. The rest of the crowd of worshippers, seekers of blessings, destitute and oppressed, blurred into a uniform, unseen mass: these two stood out, sharply defined in the sunlight, as if the Almighty had chosen that moment to show them off together. Zubair, slim-figured, his features delicate; the older man's beauty more emphatically masculine. So different, and yet seeming to fit so well together.

They were standing, ironically enough, in the paved space between the tombs of Hazrat Nizamuddin Auliya and his dear friend and follower, Amir Khusro. Perhaps there was, too, the same relationship here? Friends, close friends who drew succor by being together? Firoza let that idea go almost as soon as it had occurred to her; there was something in Zubair's face that gave away his feelings. She did not know the other man, and she did not care. Her son she knew very well, and he could hide nothing from her.

'Zubair,' she said, the effort of keeping her voice level making her tremble. 'Zubair, come home with me. We need to talk to you.'

☙

'He only regards me as a friend,' Zubair said quietly. 'This has never been mutual.'

'But he knows that you—you love—him,' Firoza said. Her voice quavered; she was sitting beside Aslam, and it was Aslam who was supposed to be having this conversation with Zubair, but Firoza could not possibly have sat silent. This was her son, and he had shocked her in a way she could never have imagined, not in the wildest of dreams.

'Yes. I do love him, and he knows it. I told him.' Zubair's expression was now one of unabashed defiance.

'How can you? To love a man—if you had left your wife for another woman, I might have lived with it. But this? How—'

'Brahmdev,' said Aslam, sunk in thought all this while, suddenly spoke up. 'Isn't he the Hussaini Brahmin we saw outside the palace? Is he the reason you have been coming home so late? Do you leave the workshop every day to go and meet him?'

Yes, he did. Sometimes they met in the bazaar, to sit under a tree and talk; or to just walk along, strolling, talking. Or they went to the beautiful Bagh-e-Jud, where both Mohammad Shah Sayyid and his successor, Bahlol Lodhi, were buried: their tombs were impressive, but it was the surrounding garden, verdant and tree-shaded even in summer, that was the attraction. Sometimes they went to the riverside, and took a boat to cross the Yamuna and go to Brahmdev's house on the other side.

'He has a house on the east bank of the Yamuna?' Aslam's left eyebrow quirked up.

Zubair was proud to be able to boast that the one he loved was by no means a penniless wretch, an adventurer looking to feather his nest. 'Yes. And land, many bighas; I have been there, he took me around. His ancestors were originally from the Punjab, and one of them had been in the service of a Sultan, who rewarded him with land—'

Aslam held up a hand. 'I do not wish to know.' He added, in a gentler voice, 'I know the heart cannot be governed. While I cannot understand how a man may fall in love with another man, I know it happens. But.' He cleared his throat. 'But you have to remember: on you is the responsibility of bringing forth the next generation.'

He paused. 'Much as I dislike your friendship with this man, I fear that if I try to break the bond, it will only cause you to cling even tighter to him. So let us reach a compromise, shall we? You do your duty by us, by your wife, by your family. And in return, I will not stop you being friends with this man.'

Zubair had found, for the fourth day in a row, a small, wilted babool flower on his bed. The first two days it had merely been a wilted flower; now it was a dry one, its fluff disintegrating into yellow powder when he picked it up. On the first day, he had simply brushed it away as an oversight on the part of the maid. On the second day, he had been taken aback by its presence, and had—at breakfast the next morning—asked his mother if she knew who had put the flower on his bed. Firoza had shaken her head, but Shahana, sitting beside her, seemingly engrossed in spooning out yoghurt into individual bowls from the large earthen container in which it had been set, glanced up at him. A quick glance, which told him what he needed to know. She was responsible.

There was no help for it. He did not know how she felt, but like him, she too must be under pressure: from her own folk, and from his. If they could find common ground somehow, they might get this business out of the way. Then they could lead their own lives, even if tied to one another.

That evening, he went, cringing inwardly, to her chamber. 'I should have come here much before,' he said awkwardly, once she had seated herself opposite him. 'I beg your pardon.'

He was still unsure, uncertain about how to approach the topic, when to his surprise, Shahana spoke up. 'You love another, don't you?' she said softly. 'That is why you do not need me.'

The hurt inherent in that second sentence hit him hard, and sent a wave of guilt washing over him. He was tempted to deny it, but decided that the truth, even if harsh, was necessary.

'There is another in my heart,' he admitted. 'But'—he forged ahead, wanting to get this awkward conversation out of the way—'I know I am at fault, but can we at least be friends, even if there is no love? Otherwise, it will be unbearable.' He flushed at the implication, and glanced involuntarily towards Shahana.

She said nothing for a while, and then what she said surprised him. 'You cannot give her up?'

'No.'

'But why not marry her then? Or'—her eyes widened in shock—'or is she a married woman? Another man's wife?'

Zubair shook his head. 'No. Please don't ask me more about it. It is—painful.' Yes, indeed it was. Those whose love was requited were the happiest people in the world, and those who loved but were not loved in return, the most wretched.

Shahana caught the meaning of his words, perhaps the tone, too. 'She does not love you back, is that it? It is a one-sided affair?' There was sudden hope in her voice, a gleam in her eyes.

Zubair gazed at her and felt sympathy for this lonely

young woman, his wife. 'I am sorry,' he repeated. 'Nothing will come of it, Shahana. Do not hope for me.'

☙

To Zubair, it was a conundrum: Shahana was his wife, with whom he was dutybound to have children; but Brahmdev was his love; and how could he possibly withhold this latest development from the one he adored most? In any case, it could not remain a secret forever; sooner or later, if Allah willed it, he would become a father. And how hurt Brahmdev would be if he came to know of Zubair's infidelity only when it was over and done with.

'Infidelity?!' Brahmdev could not suppress a loud guffaw at that. 'My poor, dear Zubair! Do you mean you would much rather impregnate me? Me, the father of three sons? What would my wife say, eh?' He went off into peals of laughter, and Zubair, watching him, felt the hurt of one whose love is not just spurned but mocked. Worse, mocked by the object of his affections.

When Brahmdev had finally stopped laughing, he touched the tips of his fingers to his ear lobes, as if begging Zubair's pardon. 'But if you could only see yourself.' He grinned. 'My dear, beautiful boy, how naïve!'

It was hurtful, but Zubair swallowed down his resentment. Brahmdev had told him, just a few minutes back, that they would perhaps not meet for several months now: Brahmdev was going travelling. 'I have been stuck in Dilli all too long,' he had said, 'and my work has come to a standstill; there are men I must meet, work I must undertake. Who knows how long I will be gone?'

Zubair's heart sank at the thought of being bereft of Brahmdev's company. These last few minutes, this one last afternoon by the gently rippling waters of the Yamuna, were to be savoured, all the more because they may not return for a long while. He pushed aside his hurt and smiled sunnily, listening as Brahmdev told him of a man, living in faraway

Badayun, who was convinced he was the heir to the throne in Dilli. They laughed over the lunacy of the man, they joked about the ambitions of fools. Zubair blinked away tears and hoped Brahmdev would not see them.

11

Four years later
900 Hijri (1495 CE)

'I heard something interesting the other day,' said Raheem as he placed a naqsha—an unusual border of tiny leaves, enclosing a space patterned in roses—in front of Zubair. 'Have you heard of Sheikh Hassan? His grandfather, Sheikh Abu Lala, was much esteemed in the town of Rapri,'—he saw the impatience in Zubair's face, and hurried to finish what he was saying. 'It is said that Sheikh Hassan is wildly in love with the Sultan, but the Sultan loathes him.'

Zubair's eyes narrowed as they rested on the naqsha. A bystander might have thought he was scrutinizing the pattern, gauging its suitability to be woven into a brocade.

'And what made you say that?' Zubair asked, in as conversational a tone as he could manage, a tone that hid his fear that Raheem might have discovered Zubair's love for Brahmdev, and was obliquely taunting him for it.

'Why, that naqsha, of course.' Raheem pointed to the roses scattered across it. 'Don't tell me you've forgotten the Sultan's nom de plume. Gulrukhi, he calls himself: rose-cheeked. Someone in the marketplace had been reciting one of the Sultan's verses, and that stayed with me when I made this naqsha.'

Zubair nodded. Of course; it was well-known that Sikandar Lodhi was a fairly accomplished poet, writing in Persian. They said he was fond of music, and a great patron of the arts—an old gentleman known to Aslam, a scholar of some repute, had even said that the Sultan was planning to have several outstanding works of literature translated from Sanskrit to Persian. And yet: he was, too, a shrewd general and a canny administrator, not merely a dreamy-eyed poet.

Brahmdev and his clique held that he was a vicious tyrant,

the eradication of all Hindus the sole guiding principle of his life.

Zubair was undecided. He did not know, yet; but he had a feeling there was more to the truth than he, or any other commoner, could tell.

In the meantime, his life had been changing. Shahana, to his utter relief, had conceived soon enough. It came as a surprise to him that he enjoyed being a father; baby Nadeem, all pink toes and toothless smiles, had wriggled his way into Zubair's heart in a way Shahana had never even hoped for. In a way even Brahmdev had not achieved.

Nadeem was now a toddler, three years old and hard to restrain. Aslam and Firoza doted on him. Shahana spoilt him, knowing full well that he was destined to be the only child Zubair would deign to give her. Shahana's brother Waqar and his wife Mariam treated him as they would treat one of their own grandchildren: adored, indulged. Gulrez, who had died the previous year after a sudden and disastrous attack of malaria, had been so fond of the child that he would often come by, just to play with Nadeem or bring him a small gift.

And there was the workshop. They were flooded with work, most of it for the palace. It was busy, exciting, intoxicatingly so. Zubair was now handling the workshop on his own, assisted by Raheem; Aslam, getting on in years, was happy to sit back. 'I do not need to earn any more money,' he said. 'I can rest now.'

Life was good.

If only Brahmdev were there too, and not in some unknown, distant corner of the world. Zubair missed him, more deeply with every passing day.

That day in the workshop, Zubair had no idea that his yearning to see Brahmdev would be satisfied so soon after, or that it would leave him more distressed than joyous.

Two days later, a note arrived from Brahmdev. As always,

it was far too short. *I am well*, wrote Brahmdev, *and will be in Dilli shortly. Many thanks for conveying that letter I had entrusted to you. It was work well done, and your contribution to the cause is appreciated by all.*

It sounded stilted, wooden, depressingly businesslike. But then, thought Zubair, that was an important part of Brahmdev's personality, too. Over the years, though the Hussaini Brahmin had never quite explained everything to Zubair, the younger man had begun to realize that Brahmdev was involved in some plot to dethrone Sikandar Lodhi. That first time Zubair had seen Brahmdev, standing in front of Sikandar Lodhi's palace, shouting defiance, was no flash in the pan; there was more. But what exactly that more was, Zubair had no idea. From stray remarks that Brahmdev made, he gathered that Brahmdev and many of his fellow Hussaini Brahmins were working together to convince others of the Lodhi's inherent evil; to mobilize funds to aid those left homeless or ruined by his tyranny; to whip up public sentiment against the Sultan.

Where Brahmdev fitted into it all, Zubair had no way of knowing. But every now and then, from whichever part of the land he might be in, Brahmdev would write to Zubair, requesting a favour. An enclosed note had to be delivered to so-and-so, to be left there where it would be picked up by another. Or Zubair would have to go to a certain money-lender, and collect from him a sum of money that he would then have to pass on to another. It was all very clandestine, and Zubair sometimes wondered where it would all lead.

It was not that he minded running these errands for Brahmdev; he just wished his beloved would find it in himself to thank Zubair for his contributions with a little more feeling, a little less of the formal, predictable congratulations.

❧

The old woman with her hut in the babool grove was known to everybody around as Bibi Bayabaani. Shahana was too shy to ask who had given her that epithet; but perhaps it was a harking back to the Sufi saint Shah Turkman Bayabaani, whose dargah lay far to the north, near the tomb of Razia Sultan. Like the mystic, Bibi Bayabaani too chose to live away from settlements, in the wilderness—the bayabaan—by herself. Like him, she cherished solitude.

But, as Shahana had discovered thanks to Mariam, Bibi Bayabaani was wise in the ways of nature. She was a talented healer, and kind. A good listener, and, what Shahana sought most of all: a friend, someone who could listen to her woes without passing judgement and without offering advice that was unsought.

Shahana had begun to frequent her abode among the babool trees, seeking healing of various kinds. Sometimes she brought little Nadeem along, letting him play while the two women sat and chatted in front of Bibi Bayabaani's hut. Squirrels and birds would chirrup and tweet in the trees and bushes around; once an inquisitive mongoose poked its head out from the undergrowth and gazed at them. Nadeem would break off a twig, as he had done today, and use it to draw lines in the sandy dust under the babool trees.

'Look,' said Bibi Bayabaani in a whisper, 'he is drawing letters. Letters! At his age?'

Shahana smiled, ever the proud mother. 'My brother has taught him. Waqar is a calligrapher, and he and Nadeem are devoted to each other.' She reached out a hand to affectionately tousle her son's hair. He ignored her, too engrossed in drawing the curving bowl of a bey, the second letter of the alphabet. Shahana looked back up into the placid face of Bibi Bayabaani.

'Waqar's own sons have no talent at all for calligraphy, so he is even more eager to teach Nadeem. Waqar says he is far more accomplished than most boys this age.'

Bibi Bayabaani said nothing to that, and went on with her work—sorting through a heap of twigs, newly harvested, and stripping them of leaves and flowers. After a while, Shahana revealed what she had come for.

'I have done all I could to find out who he is in love with,' she said softly. 'But I cannot tell, and it is driving me mad.' She pursed her lips. 'I have searched his room, but there is nothing there, no trinkets, no letters, not even the scent of a woman. Yes, I have sniffed.' She closed her eyes briefly, as if doing so would shut out her humiliation. 'I do not know who it is.'

'And how will knowing who it is make a difference?' Bibi Bayabaani had finished stripping the twigs of leaves, flowers and buds; using a sharp knife, she now began peeling the bark off the twigs in long, spiraling curls. 'Will you go to her and beg that she jilt your husband?'

She paused. 'You had said your husband does not ill-treat you. Is that true, still?'

Shahana nodded. 'He is kind, and friendly. He comes a few times a week to my chamber, to sit with me, to talk, to play with Nadeem.'

'And?'

'And nothing. That is all. I am a friend, that is all. Help me, Bibi; can you not?' The question took the form of a plaintive cry.

Bibi Bayabaani set aside her work and took Shahana's hands into her own, her palm dry and calloused, her knuckles knotted but her fingers strong. 'I am no miracle-worker,' she said. 'Just a healer. There is nothing I can give you to change a man's heart. But if you will accept it, I will offer some advice. Yes?'

When Shahana nodded yes, Bibi Bayabaani added, 'Be like the babool.' She glanced up and around at the trees that surrounded her home. They were no longer in bloom, but the flowers had given way to seed pods, shaped like strings of large round beads on a thread. 'Do you know how vital the babool is supposed to be? It's called the "healing tree" because every part of it can help cure something or the other. The Jains believe that it represents the cycle of life and death.'

Shahana was staring at her, puzzled and a little annoyed at what she perhaps regarded as mindless rambling. Bibi Bayabaani gave her a small, swift smile of reassurance. 'Heal. Give of yourself. Both to others and to yourself. Be generous, be kind, to him: trying to hold on to him at all costs will only push him away, just as the babool's thorns injure anyone who tries to grasp it too firmly. If you will give willingly of your warmth, if you are truly a friend to him, he may realize it.' She still held Shahana's hands, though her grip had relaxed. She caressed Shahana's soft palm with her fingers. 'And be kind to yourself, do not push yourself so far that you punish yourself in the process.'

'How much more can I give to him than I have given already?' Shahana murmured to herself later as she walked back with an exhausted Nadeem fast asleep in her arms, his head lolling on her shoulder. 'I have nothing left to give.'

Zubair was startled awake by someone shaking him. 'Zubair!' A male voice hissed. 'Zubair, wake up!'

He was already wide awake, the once-familiar voice recognized even in the darkness. Zubair threw off the covers and sat up, blinking in the moonlight which filtered through the muslin curtains at the window.

'Brahmdev! What are you doing here?'

'Shh! I don't have time; I must leave at once. Listen, can you keep this man hidden in your house? Till sundown tomorrow?'

Zubair had not even realized there was another in the room. Brahmdev's gesture made him look towards the doorway, where a bulky figure stood just inside, dark against the curtains. The man stepped forward into the moonlight: a tall man wrapped in a dark shawl, his turban and dhoti startlingly white against the shadows. He moved a little jerkily; there was something wrong, perhaps, with one leg.

'But who'—Zubair was hushed by Brahmdev's hand on his arm, pressing urgently.

'I cannot tell you now,' Brahmdev whispered. 'Please hide him; anywhere here, but your household must not know. Nobody must know. Yes?'

Zubair's mind was racing, considering options for hiding places that might be safe from curious eyes. While the family itself was small, they had a number of servants, and there was much coming and going through the day. He thought of various rooms, even of the tehkhaana, the basement to which they retreated in summer—and then he hit on the solution: one of the storerooms that lined the back wall. There were several of them, used for everything from grain to spare mattresses, large cauldrons to broken furniture that might have its wood one day repurposed. In one of these the man might stay, safely out of sight.

He smiled, happy to be of service to Brahmdev. 'Yes,' he said. 'Of course.'

He had been careful to be quiet while leading the fugitive to the storeroom, but even then, Zubair could not sleep the rest of the night. He tossed and turned, went a couple of times to the storeroom to ensure that all was well, and then returned to his room to pace about, unable to even lie down.

His sleepless night helped, in a way, for Zubair to act out the plan he had decided upon: to insist that he felt too sleepy and heavy-headed to do anything today. He could not summon the energy to go to the workshop, and wanted fresh air. He would lie under the kadamba tree—which happened to be opposite the storerooms—and doze there.

His behaviour caused commiseration and concern, but his suggestion of sleeping under the kadamba tree was greeted with astonishment. 'You must be out of your mind,' snapped Aslam. 'Why there, of all places?'

But Zubair shrugged it away and insisted that he knew best what he wanted. Breakfast over—and he was careful to eat little, picking at his food to give the impression of lethargy—and he went out to the kadamba tree. Under this he set up a charpai, but before he lay down on it, he looked carefully about to make sure there was no one within sight or earshot. Then, surreptitiously, he made his way to the storeroom in which he had locked his unbidden guest the previous night. A quick exchange of whispered words through a gap in the door's panels, and he was assured that all was well; the man had not been found out.

Zubair returned to the charpai, steeling himself to maintain a vigil that would stretch over the rest of the day.

He had not the slightest inkling that, from a distant window looking out onto the row of storerooms, he had been watched from the moment he had stepped out. Shahana, smelling a rat, had quietly followed her husband and seen it all. She could not tell, of course, who might be in the storeroom; to whom Zubair had spoken through the chinks in its door, but she suspected. Her husband had smuggled his clandestine lover into their home.

A newlywed Shahana, shy and unsure of herself, would have worried herself into a fever of jealousy; an older, more mature Shahana did not waste any time in needless fretting. She marched out to the storerooms and headed for the kadamba tree. Zubair, alarmed to see her approach, scrambled up from the charpai as soon as he saw her.

'Who is in there?' she asked, coming to a stop in front of him. 'Please don't tell me there's no one; I know you have someone hidden in that storeroom.'

For a moment it looked as if Zubair would indeed try to deny the allegation; but he heaved a sigh of resignation and confessed. 'I don't know who the man is,' he admitted. 'I am keeping him here as a favour to a friend. My friend will take this man away by sundown today.' He saw the scepticism in her expression, and hurried to explain. 'He's the dearest friend I have, Shahana. I cannot deny him anything.'

Shahana believed him, but she was curious, too: curious about this friend, and about the man he had asked Zubair to harbour for these few hours. So she made sure that at dusk, when Zubair might expect to be relieved of his charge, she was back in the room from which she could keep an eye on the goings-on outside the storeroom. She was there, watching despite the gathering shadows, when Brahmdev arrived—on horseback, presumably, since she heard the clip-clop of hooves stopping at the main gate. She watched as Zubair escorted him to the storerooms, and the fugitive was released from the little room in which he had spent the day. She saw him come out, and hurry away with the man who had come to fetch him. Heard the galloping of horses fading into the dusk, and saw Zubair slump on the charpai, drained suddenly of energy.

Shahana wondered what it had all been about.

Zubair was back at the workshop the next morning, catching up with all that had happened the previous day, while he had been at home. Raheem had been scheduled to visit the palace to deliver a consignment of brocades, and had had a successful visit.

'We have more work coming our way,' he said. 'A good bit, too. Do you remember that piece, with the pattern of lotuses on a purple ground? I was told Bibi Ambha liked it so much, she wants it replicated in deep blue. She sent a special note'—his brow creased, and he uttered a soft curse. 'I am an idiot. I left it behind in the palace, in all that confusion. Never mind; I remember what it was.'

'Confusion? What happened?'

The evening before last, an armed intruder had been found in the palace, trying to creep into Sikandar Lodhi's private chambers. He had been caught, but had proved very adept with his dagger: he killed two of the guards and wounded another three before making his escape.

'Despite a limp,' Raheem said. 'They say he dragged his left leg a bit.'

A wordless dread took hold of Zubair with those words. 'A limp?' he repeated. 'Then he could not have got too far, they must have overtaken him.'

But he had not; the fugitive had made good his escape. And in doing so, he had left the palace guards tense and worried. The previous day, when Raheem had gone there to deliver the brocades, a false alarm had sent the entire brigade of the guard into a frenzy, rushing about, pulling out weapons, securing gates, and arresting a couple of men they deemed suspicious.

'All to no avail, of course,' said Raheem. 'They were perfectly innocent. I suppose the palace guards are nervous after what happened.'

Ordinarily, unless it was raining or blisteringly hot, Zubair would have walked to the riverside to hire a boat and take him across. It was a walk of no more than a quarter of an hour, and he enjoyed the ambience of the Yamuna's shores: the birds, the breeze, the fishermen, their boats bobbing gently in the waters. The reeds that lined the bank, and the feathery pink flowers of the faraash bushes. It soothed him.

Not today, for he was here on urgent, stressful business: he was crossing the Yamuna to confront Brahmdev. To assuage his own fears, to find out what the truth was. For surely there must be more to it. Brahmdev could not have meant to put Zubair at risk.

But Brahmdev was a different Brahmdev, not the man he had known. The silk in his voice was gone, the warmth in his eyes had turned to ice. 'You always said you wanted to help the cause,' he said. 'Have you changed your mind? Do you think Sikandar Lodhi should be allowed to stay on the throne, then? Are you scared?'

Zubair, indignant and hurt, pointed out that it was not just him, it was also a question of his family. By harbouring a fugitive who was accused of attempted assassination,

Zubair had got himself into a position fraught with danger. And that danger extended to his parents, his wife, his son. All would be branded traitors along with him.

Brahmdev heard him out with a small, calculating smile playing on his lips. When Zubair was done, he said, 'All that is done; there's no use crying over spilt milk. I won't involve you in the future, but I need one last favour. I will bring a man to you tomorrow. Employ him, make sure he is introduced to the palace. I want him to be the one frequenting the palace.'

Zubair stared, wide-eyed and aghast. 'No! No,' he sputtered. 'You can't!'

'But I can, my Zubair,' Brahmdev said, his smile now vicious. 'If you will not agree, Sikandar Lodhi's men will receive information that you sheltered a would-be assassin. After all, the cart-driver who took him away from your house with me saw him. As did others; I made sure there were passersby who could see him well, limp and clothing and all.' He reached out for the small silver plate beside him and picked up a paan. 'It will be far easier for you to introduce my man to the palace than to face arrest.' Delicately, carefully, he placed the paan in his mouth and began chewing.

12

Zubair spent a sleepless night. Brahmdev's perfidy—nay, outright blackmail, that was what this was—had shaken him to the core, wiping out every shred of affection for the man. Zubair felt revulsion for Brahmdev, and mixed with that loathing was a good measure of self-contempt. He had been gullible: too eager to please, too besotted to realize that he was being played for a fool.

One thing was clear as daylight: Brahmdev would carry out his threat if Zubair tried to resist him. And when that happened, Zubair would not be the only one to suffer. He must take steps to ensure the safety of those most precious to him.

'Abbu,' he said to Aslam at breakfast. 'And Ammi,' he turned to Firoza. 'Someone I know has just returned from the haj, and it made me think, do you not wish to go, too?'

His parents were taken aback, as he had thought they might be. Both Aslam and Firoza had long harboured a dream of travelling to the blessed city of Mecca to pray at the holiest of Islam's sacred sites. The faith decreed that this pilgrimage was obligatory, to be accomplished at least once in a lifetime by those who could afford it. And affording it was a crucial factor: sea voyages to and from Arabia cost a goodly sum. Added to that was the money needed for such a long journey. The provisions that must be carried, the gifts, the money for accommodation and travel on land. The bodyguards that had to be hired to protect travellers from brigands and cutthroats.

They demurred, putting forward reasons of economy, of tiring and long travel in old age, of being away from home—but Zubair had come prepared; he was not going to retreat without a victory here. He countered every excuse, he cajoled and coaxed and held out the promise of blessings for the whole family. He reminded them, in a subtle way, that they were getting on in years.

By the time they rose from breakfast that morning, Aslam and Firoza had agreed in principle. Firoza had even begun worrying over how they would manage: what to pack, which servant to take, how many gifts and what to prepare. Zubair watched, his heart a little lighter.

That evening, when he had returned from the workshop, he came to Shahana's chamber. In a face as expressionless as he could make it, he told her that he wished for a divorce. Once his parents had gone on haj, he would like Shahana to move out with Nadeem. To her brother Waqar's home, if that was what suited them all; to another home, if she preferred. He would make arrangements.

He had supposed she would be shocked, and might want to know the reason for his decision. He had it all sorted out in his head. He would say that he could not love her, he still loved another. It pained him to pretend fidelity to her, when there was no such thing between them. He wished to be freed of her.

But Shahana surprised him. She blinked when he broke the news, but instead of crying or pleading for reasons, she simply shook her head. 'No,' she said. 'No, I will not go.' She paused, regarding him with an intensity that unnerved him: it was almost as if she was trying to read his mind. 'This morning,' she finally said, 'out of the blue, you convinced your parents to go on haj, and that too as soon as possible. And now you want me to leave, and Nadeem too. You are getting rid of us. Why? What danger looms, that you must be the lone man standing when it hits?'

He was beginning to realize she was too canny for her own good.

'We will talk of this once they've gone,' he said, without answering her question. 'Please don't talk to Abbu and Ammi of this. Please.'

ઙ

Frantic preparations began for the journey almost at once. Shahana supervised the pickling of limes and raw mangoes, to be taken in jars for the journey, while Firoza got the cook to make quantities of crisp, flaky savoury breads to last them through the months ahead. Dried fruits were cleaned and packed in bags, along with smaller bundles of spices: 'Who knows how much something as common as a stick of cinnamon will cost in foreign lands?' Firoza said. Quilts were aired, sheets mended. No new clothing was needed, of course—this was, after all, a solemn pilgrimage, not a happy jaunt—but new lengths of cloth were bought, to be given as charity. Raheem was made to design a suitable naqsha that the workshop's best weaver wove into a brocade, to be offered at the Great Mosque of Mecca, the Masjid-al-Haram.

Finally, it was all done. Everything was packed, every last item on Aslam and Firoza's long list checked and rechecked. They had spent much of the last week going to various friends and relatives, taking their leave of those dear to them.

Firoza was weeping when she was helped into the bullock cart by Zubair, who was going to escort his parents to the starting point of the caravan in which they would be travelling. He was murmuring to her, gentling her fears, soothing her with reassurances. Aslam, who had initially meant to ride alongside with Zubair, changed his mind and climbed into the cart too: it would be good for Firoza to have him beside her.

Shahana and Nadeem saw off the little cavalcade—a second cart carried all their provisions, as well as the two servants in attendance—before going back in.

That evening, Zubair talked to her again. He had given up the pretence that all was well; with his parents gone, there was no longer any need to maintain a façade of calm normality. He told her, outright, what had happened. Not, of course, that Brahmdev had been the object of his affections, but just that he, Zubair, had considered him a very good friend. A friend who had proved disloyal.

'Disloyal?' Shahana stared, horror-stricken. 'He isn't disloyal, he's criminal. How could you—' she shook her head, marvelling at the mess her husband had gotten into. 'What will happen, though? What *can* happen?'

Zubair shrugged. 'He brought that man he wanted introduced to the palace. His name's Damodar. I've taken Damodar to the palace, shown him around, had him meet the officer, Mirza Yasin Mohammad Khan. Damodar seems to have made a very good impression.' He shook his head. 'I don't know what Damodar means to do. Perhaps nothing that will be found out.'

'In which case there might be nothing to trace back to you?' Shahana's voice was hopeful.

But Zubair doubted that very much, and Shahana, looking at his woebegone expression, knew that she was being unduly optimistic. This Damodar could not have been inveigled into the palace for no rhyme or reason; and given the underhand way in which Zubair had been blackmailed into the job, it was clear to the blindest eye that some evil was afoot.

Mirza Yasin Mohammad Khan was part of the imperial household, entrusted with the job of choosing, purchasing, and handling all drapes, upholstery and other cloth used by the palace. He was an important man, and well aware of it. Damodar, from his very first meeting with Yasin Mohammad Khan, had set about flattering the man. He listened attentively, even when the Mirza was talking of something completely inconsequential; he was lavish in his praise for the courtier's taste and sensibilities. He was the perfect sycophant, and it sickened Zubair to see how readily Yasin Khan allowed himself to be led by the newcomer.

Before the month was out, Yasin Khan had ordered that

from then onwards, Damodar be the only one from the workshop to come to the palace. The message was couched in somewhat diplomatic terms. Zubair and Raheem were senior men, whose presence at the workshop was needed; it would be better to depute a younger man for the stressful and hectic visits to the palace. Damodar, since he had learnt the ways of the palace so well in such a short time, was perfectly suited for the job.

Zubair set Yasin Khan's letter aside with a sense of foreboding. This was what Damodar—surprisingly capable and much more knowledgeable about brocade work than an apprentice might have been expected to be—had been aiming for. But what did he have in mind as a final goal? Another try at Sikandar Lodhi's head? Or something else?

With Firoza and Aslam gone, and Zubair away at the workshop all through the day, Shahana was left alone with Nadeem at home. He, used to being pampered by his grandparents, had become irritable in their absence: he missed them, and could not see why his mother did not have the time or the inclination to indulge him the way his grandparents did. Shahana, worried for Zubair, could do only so much to keep her increasingly unruly toddler occupied. He whined, he threw tantrums, he cried for his grandparents.

Eventually, Shahana took to visiting Waqar's home frequently. Nadeem enjoyed it, for here was an entire household full of people who adored him and would do anything to keep him amused. Mariam was as a doting grandmother to him, and Waqar, already impressed by the child's talent for calligraphy, began teaching him the nuances of the art. Shahana, surrounded by nieces and nephews and other relatives, could, for a few hours, forget that danger lurked somewhere ahead for Zubair.

She was at Waqar's home one day when a note arrived

from the workshop. It had been written by Raheem and sent to their home in Ghiyaspur; from there, the steward had sent one of the servants to Waqar's home in Khizrabad, bearing the note.

Zubair had been arrested and dragged off to prison, accused of conspiring to assassinate Sikandar Lodhi. Raheem had gone to the palace to see what could be done. Perhaps Waqar Sahib would come there? It might be useful.

Waqar, summoned by his panicking sister, calmed her down and told Mariam to keep Shahana with her while he hurried to the palace. He was gone most of the day. When he returned, he was grim-faced and tired. He had little to tell: there had been another attempt on Sikandar Lodhi's life, but again, Allah be thanked, the would-be assassin had been killed before he could do any harm. The man was Damodar, from Zubair's workshop, and introduced into the palace just a few months back.

'I was not allowed to see your husband,' Waqar said. 'But I have been assured he is well. They know, I suppose, that the workshop is purveyor to the palace; perhaps that has some bearing on how they're treating Zubair.'

But would that be sufficient, wondered Shahana. Would Zubair's position as a purveyor make a difference to what punishment was meted out to him? Could there be any chance that he might escape execution?

Zubair was not the only one who had been arrested and imprisoned on a charge of conspiring against the Sultan. The captain of the palace guards had immediately swung into action, sending a group of his men to the workshop to arrest Zubair. Damodar, it had been realized quickly enough, was a Hussaini Brahmin; and so, in conjunction with the kotwal of Dilli, the captain had come to the conclusion that the Hussaini Brahmins had had a hand in this latest attempt on the Sultan's life. After all, they had been vociferous in their criticism of the Sultan all these years; that they should conspire to murder him was nothing extraordinary. The kotwal himself went out with a contingent of his sturdiest men to round up the Hussaini Brahmins they knew of.

One of these, a grizzled and tubby man named Maheshwar Dutt, wound up in the same cell as Zubair. He was a talkative man, seemingly resigned to his fate.

'It's all because of this,' he said, tracing a forefinger along the front of his throat, indicating a faint line. 'This marks us; each Hussaini Brahmin carries this mark as a reminder of our connection with Karbala.'

Zubair nodded; he knew about the mark, since Brahmdev too bore it and had explained its significance to him.

'Damodar had it too,' said Maheshwar Dutt. 'But he was killed before he could do anything, and now they've begun questioning us.' He rubbed his thigh under the thin dhoti that he wore. 'Though what they will be able to find out, I don't know. I know nothing, and I doubt if any of the others do, either.'

Zubair did not know what to say. The fetid, close air of the tiny cell choked him, and the screams that pierced even the thick stone walls of the prison made his skin crawl. He could only imagine what methods Sikandar Lodhi's men were employing to get at the truth. How long before it would be his turn? His stomach lurched at the thought.

Maheshwar Dutt had been in prison before, briefly, on several occasions. 'The Lodhi knows I don't like him,' he said, with a wry grin. 'The bastard.' His hand drifted down to his knee, which he massaged with increasing vigor. 'His men know it, but what can they do? They try to scare me. They beat me up.' He let out a laugh, a harsh cackle that set Zubair's teeth on edge. It began to dawn on him that Maheshwar Dutt was by no means as blasé as he pretended to be. He may have had previous experience of being interrogated, but instead of leaving him inured to the experience, it had only served—as was natural—to make him dread it.

He had not died, though. They had not hurt to cripple, and they had not executed him. Perhaps there was yet hope. Zubair asked Maheshwar Dutt why.

The man shrugged, his good-natured expression clouded. 'I suppose their captain is a perceptive man. Perhaps he can tell all I am is bluster. I have no heart for these grand plans to murder the Lodhi, to be honest. I have a wife and family; I cannot afford to be so reckless.'

It did little to calm Zubair or to help assure him that he would be spared the worst abuse of the torturers. What it did, instead, was to remind him that he too had family. Thank goodness he had been able to get his parents away in time. He hoped Shahana would keep her head down, and not draw attention to herself.

☙

Waqar and Mariam continually reminded Shahana to stay calm, to remain optimistic and to trust in Allah to have mercy. She tried, for a while, to follow their strictures. Then, unable any more to restrain herself, she demanded that Waqar send Raheem to the palace, to seek an audience for her with Bibi Ambha. Waqar was thunderstruck: Shahana had taken leave of her senses, she would get them all thrown into prison, if not executed.

But Shahana stood her ground, and Waqar had to finally relent. 'It's audacious,' he murmured, shaking his head after he had sent a note to Raheem. 'You will have us all killed.'

Perhaps Bibi Ambha thought the request audacious too, but she had had prior experience of the audacity of this family's women. Perhaps she was curious. Perhaps, too, she really did feel that Zubair merited something more than torture and summary execution.

At any rate, Shahana was granted an audience for the next day. She was to present herself at the palace an hour before noon. Raheem, by virtue of being one known to the Dowager Empress, was allowed to accompany her. Shahana would of course take a maid with her. Mariam insisted on going along as well.

'I am not so very intimidating that you need bring such a retinue,' the Dowager Empress said. The words were admonitory but the tone was not, and Shahana took heart from what was said. Bibi Ambha's beauty had mellowed over the years: she was still a remarkably handsome woman, her face striking and her hair streaked with silver. What she had gained over the years was a dignity and grace far beyond the mere physical beauty of a younger woman. She commanded the space in which she was, just by being herself.

There was, too, something about her that invited confidence. It could have been her early memories of Zubair's grandmother, Aabida, who had come to Bibi Ambha with a request on behalf of her husband many years ago. Perhaps it was the memory, too, of Aslam's many years of service, of the countless brocades crafted so painstakingly for her. She was patient, she was dignified and gracious.

When seeking an audience for Shahana, Raheem had already conveyed to the Dowager Empress most of what Shahana wanted to plead for. All that was left for Shahana to do was beg, and this she did with all her heart, reminding the Sultan's mother of their family's loyalty, of Zubair's own years in the service of the palace.

Bibi Ambha heard her out, and when Shahana fell silent, she said in her grave, even voice, 'It is eventually up to His Majesty. All I can do is put in a plea for mercy. But you realize, of course, that it will be dependent, too, on the evidence? If there is clear proof that he is indeed guilty, I can do nothing. I will not do anything, then.'

There was one wish, though, that she could easily grant: that Zubair be allowed one visitor. Raheem, trusted by the palace, could see him. Once every three days, no more. And with the express understanding that he would not conspire to help the prisoner escape.

Shahana bowed her head in gratitude. That, in itself, was consolation.

Interlude

'Uff,' Mohsin says. 'What adventures our family has had. And what women, too. Regular firebrands, like Razia Sultan.'

He has been away from home these past few days, on a trip east with his father. My son had heard a rumour that there had been rain somewhere near Mathura, and that had been enough to make him decide that an expedition to Mathura was in order. To forage. Imagine, all the way to Mathura to forage. The man has lost his wits.

So have we all, I suppose.

I said nothing; I let them go. But while they were away, it struck me that I was sitting around all day moaning and complaining about my weakness and my aches and pains; what if I should die, and my story died with me? So I got out my papers, my pens and my ink, and I sat down to write.

That is what Mohsin has been reading, now that he is back. They did not, after all, go all the way to Mathura. Mathura is too far, and when the horses and donkeys are all dead, and there is little water and even less food for men, Mathura is even further away. A couple of kos outside Dilli, and they turned back. Empty-handed, it is true; but at least they are back, and we are together again. I ask for no more.

'Shahana reminds me of Aabida,' Mohsin adds. 'Though initially I thought she was a cringing and weak sort of woman.'

'Just shy,' I say. She was that, a woman inherently quiet. Not given to talking a lot, happy with her own company. It took a great deal of effort for her to speak to a stranger, for instance, and even more to approach a stranger in the first place. But beneath that shyness was also a steely resolve.

Mohsin puts down the last of the pages he has been reading. The expression on his face is thoughtful; he wants to say something, I can sense it. But he does not, not until I ask him. Not even until I push him.

'You may take offence,' he says, shaking his head, trying to fend me off.

'Take offence? Why?'

It takes some prodding from me for him to finally speak up. 'About your father,' he says. 'Zubair. Though I don't see why you go on referring to him like that: it's so distant. As if he didn't mean anything to you, he was just a stranger.'

Briefly, I wonder if that is part of the truth. Because my father was not there for a substantial chunk of my early life; my memories of him from when I was a toddler, and a little beyond, are sketchy. I remember snatches. Sitting in his lap, staring with fascination as he sprinkled salt on earthworms that had crawled into our home during the monsoon. Running through a field of green chickpeas and gathering up fistfuls of the tender green beans. Watching while he placed them on a perforated disc of iron and roasted them over a small fire. Looking up into a starry sky and seeing the Milky Way stretching overhead. 'The road to the stars,' I can hear him say.

Those are his only words I remember from back then. That handful of scenes are the only memories from those few years.

Later, of course, when I was a grown man, I became reacquainted with him—but that is a story for later.

'No,' I say. 'No, it is not that I think of him as a stranger. Far from it. But you must remember that this account of our family is written not just for you and me but perhaps for many generations to come. It is better we be identified by our names, as individuals. Not by our relationships.'

'I don't agree,' Mohsin says.

Just a few months back, he would have simply said it was silly. Our boy is growing up.

'Of course we are identified by our relationships,' he says. 'I am your grandson. Father's son. Not Nadeem's grandson, not Shaadaab's son. I know your names, but to me the relationship is all that matters.'

'To you, yes. But to people who might read this years from now? What if your grandchildren read this? When they read "grandfather" will they know enough not to think of you, but to think of me? If I write "Nadeem" though, that will be less confusing.'

'What if there are two Nadeems in the story? What if there are two Shaadaabs, two Mohsins?' I marvel at his tenacity, his stubbornness in holding on to an idea. But I have no time for fruitless bickering over this matter.

'There are no duplicates so far,' I say, dismissing the matter. 'When it is time for you to write your part of the story, you can do as you please. For now, this is my story and I will tell it as I wish.'

Mohsin has just returned from a morning's foraging, and he is pleased with himself. Even before he comes into my room, I can hear the relieved laughter, his own and his father's.

'Thanks to Gokul,' says Mohsin, in response to his father's praise. 'You should see how he ferrets out these roots and things. The birds and that squirrel I got, but the rest of it Gokul found.'

There is a murmur of appreciation from my son. He and I have not seen this Gokul yet, but we have heard about him from Mohsin. Gokul—such an apt name, that—is the son of a cowherd who lives in our neighbourhood. To be more accurate, the son of a man who used to be a cowherd. No doubt his cows have long since died. Starved to death, if not slaughtered by those with no longer any compunction about eating cattle.

Mohsin had told us, many months back, that Gokul and a couple of his brothers, along with their father, had taken to foraging in the area. They seem to be singularly good at it: they have succeeded in keeping a family of seven alive through this famine, no mean feat.

But I was talking of Mohsin. The success of his latest foraging expedition has made him smug for the time being. Enough to sit on judgement on his ancestors.

'Such a bunch of naïve and gullible fellows in our family,' he says, seating himself beside me. 'First Daanish, taken in by Mushtaq. Then Qasim, also taken in by Mushtaq—Ya Allah, how Mushtaq must have laughed his head off, to have so completely fooled two generations of the same family! And then Zubair, to get himself into such deep trouble over a man who didn't even reciprocate his love.'

'Perhaps we tend to see the best in people,' I say gently. 'Or at least to take people at face value. We aren't suspicious by nature.'

'Gullible,' Mohsin says, a hard finality in his voice. 'And it always hurts other people too, doesn't it? Not just the ones who are fool enough to fall into the trap, but their families as well. Their wives, their children.'

In all truthfulness, I cannot deny that. I have borne the brunt of it, and Ammi did too. She, worse than I, because I at least had the love and attention of several other relatives as well.

It occurs to me that while the men in our family may not have boasted of the most iron wills or the best judgement, the women have been, many of them, just the opposite. Strong-willed, determined, clear-sighted. They had to be, I suppose, in order to compensate for the poor decisions of their menfolk. Ammi, I know, forced herself to set aside her reticence and to take it upon herself to rescue my father from the mess he had got himself into.

13

The day after Zubair had been arrested, early in the morning, Maheshwar Dutt was dragged off to be questioned. He resisted, screaming his innocence. He kicked, clawed, tried to grab onto anything that might keep him inside the cell—and since the cell was empty as a beggar's bowl, the only purchase he could get was on Zubair. Zubair found himself pulled along by Maheshwar Dutt, clouted for no fault of his, and flung back so hard that he fell.

When Maheshwar Dutt was brought back to the cell a little after noon, he was much the worse for wear. His face was a mass of bruises, his left eye swollen shut. Deep welts criss-crossed his back and the backs of his thighs, and his dhoti was soaked in blood. Zubair tore off a broad strip of cloth from the bottom of his tunic and used it to wipe away some of the blood. There was no water; no herbs that might be applied to staunch the bleeding. No brazier, even, on which a pad of cloth might be warmed and placed on an aching muscle to soothe it. Zubair looked on, helpless. He was still wondering what to do when the door of the cell clanged open, and there, pushed into the cell by the soldier on guard, was Raheem.

It was a tight squeeze: the cell was small for its two inmates, let alone a visitor, but Zubair was so relieved to see Raheem, he did not mind sitting scrunched up, with Maheshwar Dutt's torso in his lap. Raheem talked quickly, aware that he might be ushered out at any moment. He told Zubair what had happened, how Shahana had pleaded his cause with the Dowager Empress; how investigations were still ongoing. How it might all boil down to the evidence of Mirza Yasin Mohammad Khan: if he were willing to admit that he was the one who had asked for Damodar to be the liaison for the palace, the focus might shift from Zubair. But

Yasin Khan was away right now, visiting Rewari; he would return, perhaps, by the end of the week.

Zubair shook his head despondently. 'He will not admit that he asked for Damodar,' he said. 'That would be tantamount to admitting his own guilt. Why would he?'

They sat, sunk deep in gloom, for a minute or so, the only sound in the tiny cell the ragged breathing of the injured man.

'If only I hadn't given in to Brahmdev!' Zubair burst out. 'How could I have been such an idiot?'

As he was leaving, a few minutes later, Raheem asked, 'Is there anything I can get you? I may be able to come again, perhaps in two days' time. Do you need something?'

Zubair shook his head, before glancing at Maheshwar Dutt, who seemed to have fallen into an exhausted sleep. 'Go to our hakim and see if there is anything he can suggest.' He nodded slightly, indicating the battered man. 'That's all.'

It was not until the next morning that Maheshwar Dutt was finally able to sit up, groaning and wincing, and eat a little of the dry roti that had been shoved inside their cell by the guard the night before. His jaw was painful, his gums sore and two of his teeth missing, so he had to hold the roti in his mouth to soften it. It was appallingly slow, but he finally finished, and sat back against the wall with a shuddering sigh.

'Why did you blame Brahmdev for your worries?' he asked, without any preamble.

It took a few moments for Zubair to understand what he was saying, and in what context. 'You heard our conversation yesterday?' he finally said. 'It is the truth. Brahmdev Dutt is the reason I am here today. I suppose I was gullible, too. Ruled by my emotions. And he took advantage of that.'

Because they had become friends of a sort, Zubair told him about Brahmdev. He felt embarrassed about admitting that he had been in love with the man, so he omitted that detail. After all, one might commit crimes and be guilty of lunacy for a dear friend, might one not?

'Ah,' Maheshwar Dutt said when Zubair had fallen silent. 'So that is what happened. I have been wondering about that. He isn't one of us, you know,' he added.

Zubair looked up, surprised. 'Not a Hussaini Brahmin? But I've seen the scar on his neck—'

The other man shook his head, a small movement that made him suddenly wince and immediately freeze. 'No, that's not what I meant,' he said, when he was somewhat comfortable again. 'He's a Hussaini Brahmin, all right. I mean Brahmdev Dutt isn't really one of those who oppose Sikandar Lodhi for his bigotry.'

'But—but the first time I met him, he was at the head of a group protesting outside the palace.' He told the man all that had happened, from that very first meeting, to the many occasions when Brahmdev, travelling to distant lands, had directed him to do this, do that: all for the cause of bringing down Sikandar Lodhi. Zubair admitted that he did not like the idea of killing the Sultan in cold blood; deposing him, or defeating him in battle, would have been honourable, not assassination.

Maheshwar Dutt chuckled at that. 'Brahmdev, and honour?' He snorted. 'That man would not know honour if it was labelled as such. He has no honour to speak of.'

And he proceeded to tell Zubair the truth about the man Zubair had worshipped these many years, before his idol had proved to have feet of clay.

Brahmdev was a soldier of fortune. 'If you can call one who does not actually bear arms a soldier,' added Maheshwar Dutt. For Brahmdev's weapons were guile and deceit: he used them, combined with his irresistible charm and good looks, to feather his nest. He changed employers and loyalties the way other men changed their clothes, and it was always the potential employer who offered the greatest incentive who won his loyalties—for the time being.

For the past several years, almost since Sikandar Lodhi had ascended the throne of Dilli, Brahmdev had been in the pay of a prominent nobleman from Badayun. This man claimed to be a near relative of Alam Shah, the Sultan whom Bahlol Lodhi had replaced, and who had retired to Badayun years before Bahlol had finally entered Dilli.

'Who knows who the man really is, but he has got it into his head that he has some sort of claim to the throne,' Maheshwar Dutt said. Zubair remembered, then, a long-ago conversation he had had with Brahmdev: Brahmdev had mentioned this man, and had laughed about the man's lunatic idea of being heir to the throne.

Alam Shah's relative—if, indeed, he was that—may have lofty ambitions, but he was also eccentric. Or overly cautious, miserly. He had a small troop: so minuscule that it would certainly be laughed at if it ever tried to attack Dilli. He did not intend to expand this troop, either, until he was as certain as he could be that Dilli might be his.

For this task, he had employed Brahmdev Dutt. Brahmdev's job was to, by hook or by crook, get Sikandar Lodhi off the throne of Dilli.

'As if that would leave Dilli free for anyone to come and stake a claim to it?' Zubair shook his head, marvelling at the naïveté of the man. 'There is the Sultan's son, Ibrahim, for one: there can be no contender for the throne more obvious than him. And there are bound to be others, generals and nobility in Dilli who could make a bid for an empty throne.' He could not resist a chuckle of dry mirth. 'It baffles me that Brahmdev was so easily fooled.'

Maheshwar Dutt did not shake his head this time; it was, he knew, too painful. All he did was to purse up his lips in obvious disagreement. 'He isn't the fool here,' he said. 'Brahmdev is paid well; and he makes sure he does not get into trouble. There is no real danger in standing in front of the palace and yelling abuses. What he does do, and he does it well, is to use others.'

As he had used Zubair. Brahmdev had suspected, from the moment he had seen Zubair, richly clad and obviously in favour with the palace, that Zubair was of some importance. Then, when Zubair had approached him—Maheshwar did not comment on Zubair's motive behind that approach—it had occurred to Brahmdev that the young man might be used to help Brahmdev plant his own man in court. An assassin. Zubair realized, with sudden and hurtful clarity, that the interest he had seen in Brahmdev's eyes that first day, the flirtatiousness, the attraction, were all carefully cultivated. Brahmdev had seen a prey, and had tailored his behaviour to set a trap.

'It was calculated,' Maheshwar Dutt said, his voice now weary, fading. 'All carefully planned to use you to the fullest.'

Shahana had known, deep in her heart, that nothing would come of all their efforts. Bibi Ambha could do only so much. And why not? After all, Sikandar Lodhi was her son; how could she be benevolent to one accused of conspiring to murder him? Yasin Mohammad Khan, Shahana had no hopes of. He would never admit to his part in the affair.

She had, therefore, spent her days thinking, trying to come up with a plan. A scheme had begun to form in her mind soon enough: an audacious, mad scheme, but perhaps its very audacity meant it might work. She could only hope that some miracle might happen, and she would not need to implement her plan.

At the end of the week, Raheem came to announce that Yasin Mohammad Khan was back. Far from speaking up in defence of Zubair, he had added to the accusations: he had always felt Damodar was cagey; he had opposed the man's coming to the palace, and had been suspicious. Zubair was wholly to blame. Complicit, in fact.

Shahana did not wait to hear the all of it. Leaving Nadeem with a maid, she hurried out and away.

A quarter of an hour later, she was at the babool grove in which Bibi Bayabaani lived.

It took her a while to explain it all to the old woman, and to put forward her request. She stumbled at the last, her throat choking as she bent her head to Bibi Bayabaani's hands, where they rested in the old woman's lap. Shahana pressed her face to them, taking in the scent of grass and woodsmoke, fruit and soil. The essence of Bibi Bayabaani, her intrinsic connectedness to nature.

Bibi Bayabaani placed a gentle hand on Shahana's head. She did not caress, she did not soothe; it was more like a blessing than anything else. 'You ask for much, Begum Sahiba,' she said. 'Something like this is so fraught with danger. Nature can be very whimsical, very unpredictable.' She saw the determination in Shahana's expression, and added. 'I do not know how tall your husband is, or what his build is. How can I know what will be the correct dosage? And if I do not know the correct amount to use, it can prove fatal.'

But Shahana had thought it all over very carefully, and she had the answer to that as well. She would come, not later than the following day, bringing with her a set of Zubair's clothing. That would give Bibi Bayabaani a good indication of Zubair's height and build.

Bibi Bayabaani had little option but to agree. 'You are playing with fire, Begum Sahiba,' she cautioned, as her visitor took her leave. 'I am not happy doing this.'

Shahana, already veiling herself for the walk back to the cart outside the grove, stopped. 'Neither am I, Bibi,' she admitted. 'But what else can I do? I cannot sit back and let him be executed.'

Instead of going back home, Shahana got the bullock cart to take her to her brother Waqar's home in Khizrabad. She would need his help, and that of Raheem—the only person so far allowed to visit Zubair in prison—in order to carry out her plan.

'Are you mad?!' Waqar had set aside his pen as soon as his sister had asked to speak to him; but he had not been expecting this. 'Are you out of your mind, Shahana, to traipse about like a—a wanton?'

Shahana looked him in the eye, unafraid. 'I have come to my brother's home,' she said. 'And that because I want to get my husband out of prison. There is nothing wanton in what I am doing.' Waqar opened his mouth to protest, but Shahana did not let him. 'Come with me to the workshop,' she said. 'I need you to accompany me there so that I can talk to Raheem. It is essential that we enlist his help; without him, it will be impossible.'

Before Waqar could stop her, Shahana had swept out of the room and had gone, hurrying down the corridor outside. Waqar scrambled up from his place on the mattress and ran after her, calling frantically. He was able to stop her just as she was about to step over the threshold, and his hand on her shoulder made her turn around.

He was furious now, but Shahana was too determined to let that cow her. 'Do not stop me,' she said quietly. 'Do you know what my husband did? When he feared that this might happen—that he would be arrested—he sent his parents off on haj, and he was ready to divorce me, so that my son and I could be safe. He did that for us, and you say I should just leave him to his fate?'

'Of course not,' Waqar retorted, testily. 'When did I ever say that? All I'm saying is, there must be some other way.'

Shahana stared up into his face. 'What?'

Waqar had to give in and get into the bullock cart with Shahana. The journey from Khizrabad to Ghiyaspur took less than an hour, but all the way there Shahana was subjected to a series of admonitions by her brother. Waqar said, over and over again, all the things he had already told her. How in her demureness and propriety lay the honour of her family. How a simple act of thoughtlessness could ruin everything. How a woman's greatest jewel was her chastity.

Finally, Shahana could not pretend to ignore him anymore; she reached out and rested her hand on Waqar's in a gesture that echoed the fondness that had existed between them in their childhood. Waqar was many years older than her, but in those long-ago days, he had been his little sister's most ardent protector. He was the one at hand to scare away the geckos she was so frightened of; the one to take her to a colourful fair and buy her pretty glass bangles. The one to hold her when she twisted an ankle and had to be coaxed to allow it to be massaged. He had been confidant and friend, elder brother and father figure.

'We are going to rescue my husband,' she said. 'And I am with you, my brother. There can be no impropriety.'

Waqar looked taken aback at that, but mollified too. He patted her head in a somewhat awkward way.

'But what do you have in mind, Shahana?' he whispered. 'What do you mean to do?'

Shahana, perhaps from a superstitious fear that her plan would be jinxed if more people knew of it, shook her head. 'I will tell you when it is time,' she said. 'It will be better for you, and for Raheem, if you don't know exactly what is happening. It is just that I need Raheem to go tomorrow to the prison, taking something for my husband. A letter, and a small package. I need to tell him this.'

And that was all she would say. No matter how Waqar cajoled and wheedled, Shahana stayed silent.

Outside the workshop, where the cart drew to a halt, Waqar made Shahana remain in the cart while he went indoors to fetch Raheem. A scant couple of minutes later, the naqshband was outside. He stood decorously beside the cart, his gaze lowered even though Shahana, shielded by the cotton fabric that hung as a curtain over the back of the cart, was in all effect veiled.

Shahana told him all that she had told Waqar—and withheld all that she had withheld from her brother.

'Do you think you could go there tomorrow, to visit him?' she asked. 'You are allowed a visit only once in three days, is it not? When did you last go?'

Raheem had gone the previous day, but he did not think he would be stopped if he went again the following day. 'The guards do not seem especially alert or interested. A bored, lackadaisical lot, Begum Sahiba,' he volunteered. Then, as if he thought that might send Shahana's hopes up, he added, 'not that they would sit back if they found anything suspicious.'

'You have already taken some food and some medicine,' Shahana said. 'And that was allowed. There were no questions asked?' Reassured, she heaved a sigh. 'Very well. I will get for you, tomorrow before noon, some more medicine which you must take to him. A letter too, which I will give. He must read the letter as soon as you hand it over, and he must tell you whether he agrees to it or not.'

Waqar, looking a little embarrassed at Shahana's imperious behaviour, interrupted. 'Raheem may not be free tomorrow,' he said. 'With Zubair not at the workshop,' he said, addressing Raheem, 'all the work must have come onto you. Can you spare the time?'

Shahana was beginning to say that it was a matter of urgency, but before she could finish, Raheem had shaken his head. No, he told Waqar; it was not a bother. He understood the urgency. And, in any case, he had meant to go, because Zubair had asked him for something important. A leather folder that was kept at the workshop, in which there were some documents Zubair wished to see.

He was carrying it, in fact: he had been going through the papers when Waqar had arrived. He held it out, a weather-worn folder of scruffy brown leather, overstuffed with yellowing pages. 'It is mostly correspondence with the palace.' He bit his lip. 'Perhaps he feels that it could be used to prove his loyalty? I don't know.'

'May I have a look at that, please?' Shahana asked.

So Raheem handed the folder over to Waqar, and Waqar passed it to Shahana. She opened the folder and had a cursory look at the papers inside. They were as Raheem had said: documents that affirmed the confidence the palace felt for the workshop. Each document in it, from the farmaan decreed in the name of Her Imperial Highness the Dowager Empress Bibi Ambha, to the many orders, the letters of commendation and gratitude, spoke of that trust. Shahana flipped through them, wondering what it might be that her husband meant to use to secure his release, if that indeed was his objective in asking for the folder.

She turned over the last page, and frowned. This was not the end of it. On the back flap of the leather folder was a pocket, closed with the help of a couple of wooden buttons. A pocket that may not be immediately discernible if one were not paying close attention, but definitely there.

Shahana opened the pocket and peered inside. There were more papers there, folded neatly and tied together with a thin string.

She pulled them out, undid the string, and unfolded the topmost page.

It was a letter, and the way it was addressed made her eyes open wide in shock.

My beloved, my beautiful Zubair.

She closed the folder and placed it beside her in the cart. 'I will return this tomorrow when I bring you the package to take to my husband,' she said softly. 'Thank you, Raheem Sahib.'

14

Bibi Bayabaani had been expecting Shahana, and when her visitor arrived, it took the old woman no more than a couple of minutes to carefully spread out Zubair's pyjamas and jama on the ground and examine them. She asked Shahana a few questions, murmured to herself a while, and then withdrew into her hut.

When she emerged a few moments later, she carried in her hand a small packet made of palash leaves, folded over and tied with thread. 'I have already told you how it must be used, and when it should take effect,' she said, placing the package in Shahana's outstretched hand. 'Do you remember it all?'

'I remember.'

'Then go, Begum Sahiba, and may Allah be with you.'

From the babool grove, Shahana went to the workshop. This time, since the distance was not great, she had taken her palanquin, with a maid in attendance. The maid and the palanquin had waited outside the babool grove for her; now as the kahaars lifted the palanquin and set off towards the workshop, the maid fell into step beside them. Within a few minutes, they were at the workshop, and Raheem was already outside, waiting for her.

It took a few moments, no more, for Shahana to hand over the packet she had received from Bibi Bayabaani, along with the leather folder she had taken the previous day, and a letter she had written earlier that morning. 'He is not to open the package until he has read the letter,' she said. 'Remember, he must read the letter in your presence, and give you a definite answer.' She paused. 'Once you have returned from the prison, will you please send word to me? I need to know what my husband said, what is his answer.'

A few hours later—it was just after lunch, though Shahana had been too sick with worry to eat anything—Raheem returned from his visit to Zubair. He did not merely send word; he came to the house. Shahana bustled out into the men's quarters and talked to him from behind a curtain of vetiver grass.

'I have done as Begum Sahiba had instructed,' Raheem said. 'The master has said that he will do as you wish. He read the letter, and then he took the package you had sent.'

Shahana drew in a deep, shuddering breath. Till this moment, she had not been sure: it all depended upon Zubair, after all, and he might have refused to have anything to do with this mad scheme of hers. But now the way was clear, and it was time to set the plan in motion.

She thanked Raheem, and then quickly gave him the rest of his instructions. 'Thank you,' she said, when he had confirmed that he understood, and that he would do as she said. 'You had better go now. I will leave soon, too, for my brother's home. We cannot afford to be late.'

☙

Shahana could not tell when she would return home. It might not be till the wee hours of the morning; it might not be till later. She had no wish to leave Nadeem in the care of a maid for that long, so she took him along with her, with clothes and a favourite toy wrapped in a bundle, to Waqar's home. Mariam, who had been given to understand that Waqar would be accompanying Shahana to the prison in an effort to allow Shahana to meet Zubair, was happy to have Nadeem stay with her. This was his home too: he had spent many days here, he enjoyed being with his cousins. He would be happy.

'But do you think it is proper?' she said, walking Shahana to the front door. 'The prison is no place for a gently bred lady to go. Let my husband meet him; that will be better.'

Shahana had heard the same words from Waqar too, and

had countered them, as she countered Mariam now. 'There is no hope that he will emerge alive from the prison,' she said, shocking a horrified gasp out of Mariam with those words. 'It would be cruel to deprive me of that one meeting, just for a reason so flimsy.' She patted Mariam's hand. 'Do not worry. You know me; you brought me up. Would I do anything that would shame you?'

Then, with a gentle request that Nadeem be kept in hand and not allowed to run amok across the house, Shahana walked out to where Waqar stood, waiting beside the cart that was to take them to the prison.

It took more than an hour to get from Waqar's home in Khizrabad to the palace and its ancillary administrative buildings in Jahanpanah. By the time they reached the prison, the last blush of the setting sun had gone, turning the sky a palette of greys. The sconces along the outer walls of the prison held flaming torches, and the guards at the gate, fresh on the night watch, were alert-eyed and suspicious. The bullock cart was made to stop well away from the gate, and Waqar—who had alighted from it even before it had come to a standstill—was told to go back the way he had come.

Shahana, sitting inside the cart, straining to overhear the conversation, could catch only snatches of it. Waqar's pleas, the guard's refusal to let anyone in at this time. Shahana waited until she realized that Waqar was not making any headway. Then she gathered her veil closer about her head and shoulders and got out of the cart.

Waqar shouted to her to get back into the cart, but she ignored him and came up to the guards.

'I cannot,' Shahana said, speaking not just to Waqar but to the guard as well. 'My husband—I have a terrible feeling there is something wrong.' She allowed a whimper into her voice. 'Please, if you will not let us in to meet him, will you have a guard go and see if he is well? Once I know he is safe and well, I will go.'

And from this position she would not budge. The guard

got angry with Waqar, berating him for letting her disrupt their work. Waqar, his nerves frayed by Shahana's obstinacy and her obvious distress, turned on her, only to have her burst into tears. He could not see those tears, but the way she clung to his arm, wailing and becoming increasingly hysterical, shook Waqar. 'Do you have no heart?' he snapped at the guard. 'Will it be so very difficult to do what she asks?' He paused before flinging at the man his trump card. 'You do know, don't you, that the Dowager Empress has put in a word for the prisoner? The condition my sister is in, what will happen if she goes to Her Highness and complains that you lack even basic humanity?'

Of course they knew that the Dowager Empress had sent word that Zubair be treated with gentleness; that was why he had not yet been subjected to the gruelling questioning and torture that were a routine part of investigations. Maheshwar Dutt and the others had been beaten and whipped, scalded and branded with hot irons. Zubair had only been questioned through the night, and made to go without sleep, food and drink for most of the day before that. He had been left exhausted and worn, not subjected to bodily harm.

It was because Bibi Ambha had put in a word for him. Until there was concrete proof against Zubair, he must not be harmed.

The guard sighed, exasperated. He knew when he was beaten. 'I will find out.'

This man was on guard at the gate, and here he was to remain. To find out about Zubair, a message was passed on to one of the guards just inside the gate, and from there, presumably, someone was sent to check on Zubair. Waqar and Shahana stood outside, she still clinging to his arm.

It seemed an eternity before news came, and then it came in a rush, a flurry of flying feet. A man came hurrying out of the gate, eyes wide as he came to the guards at the gate.

'He's dead,' he announced. 'His heart has stopped.'

Shahana let out a strangled scream before collapsing in Waqar's arms.

ᘓ

When she came to, she wept and pleaded to be taken to Zubair's cell, but Waqar put his foot down. 'No,' he said. 'Get into the cart; I will deal with this.' He looked surprised when Shahana assented, but perhaps he guessed she was too distressed to resist. He helped her into the cart and was about to move off, back towards the gate, when Shahana reached out, putting a hand on his arm.

'Please,' she whispered. 'Please, whatever happens, get him out as soon as you can. Tell them I shall kill myself if they keep him there any longer. I will go to Her Highness and kill myself in front of her.'

It was melodramatic, ludicrously so, and Waqar tut-tutted. 'You are overwrought, Shahana,' he said, and winced the next instant, when he remembered that she, newly widowed, had cause enough to be overwrought. He patted her hand, trying to make amends for his faux pas. 'I mean—it will not help for you to get so emotional. I will talk to these fellows; leave it to me.'

'But you will make sure he is brought out of there as soon as possible?' Shahana asked, grabbing his hand. 'As it is, they did not let me see him. Had they allowed me in, I might have been there, beside him…' Her voice broke off on a sob.

Waqar was required to wait for nearly half an hour before the chief prison-keeper emerged, a portly man with a bristling beard and stark white moustache. With him came the guard who had carried the information to him; they had both been to the cell where Zubair had been found dead.

The discussion between the men was low-voiced enough for Shahana to not be able to hear any of it. From the way the prison-keeper was shaking his head in response to Waqar's pleading—her brother had his hands folded, his shoulders stooping into a servile bow—it seemed the man was refusing to let Waqar have the body. The conversation went on for what seemed an eternity, with Waqar pleading, cajoling, pointing in the direction of the palace—invoking Bibi Ambha? Finally, when it appeared that neither side would budge, the prison-keeper relented. Perhaps the thought that Shahana might complain to the Dowager Empress unnerved him; perhaps he realized that there was no point hanging on to the dead body of a prisoner whose crime had never been proven.

An impatient gesture, a sharp bark, and the prison-keeper had given his consent. Waqar hurried to the cart to tell Shahana that he was being allowed into the prison to bring out the body. She must stay in the cart. Shahana nodded. 'Where would I go?'

And thus it was that Zubair was carried out, wrapped in a rough, moth-eaten sheet that had seen better days. Two guards and Waqar bore him out of the gate while the prison-keeper looked on.

Behind Shahana, the cart-driver suddenly seemed to realize that the drama of this evening was about to culminate in a corpse being laid in his vehicle. 'I will not have that, Begum Sahiba,' he said, standing beside the cart, his eyes lowered deferentially. 'My cart will be defiled. I will have to burn it.'

The little knot of men had stopped at the gate. The prison-keeper had a paper in his hand, which he was showing to Waqar. They set their burden down on the ground, and one of the guards reached up for a torch. It was pulled down out of the sconce and held so that Waqar might read what was written.

Shahana said, 'I have travelled in your cart often enough. Surely—'

The man cut her off. 'Yes, Begum Sahiba; but please, this time, no. It is a question of not just my faith, but of my livelihood. If my cart has to be destroyed because it is polluted, what will I do? How will I earn a living?'

'I will buy you a new cart if it comes to that,' Shahana said. At the gate, Waqar had scribbled something on the sheet of paper and handed it back to the prison-keeper. 'Besides,' she said, her voice a whisper, 'there is no corpse.'

ᘓ

Zubair groaned.

His eyes were impossibly heavy and his head hurt, as if someone had cleaved it in two. That might have made him want to keep lying still, eyes closed, if only he was not so thirsty. Parched beyond belief. When was the last time he had had more than the tiniest of sips of water? And even now there would be little, what with him and Maheshwar Dutt having to share the minuscule daily ration they were given.

Maheshwar Dutt. The cell. The dankness, the stench.

All of which were missing now.

The memories came flooding back abruptly, so suddenly that Zubair's eyes flew open.

It would have been completely dark had it not been for the dim light from a single diya that burned somewhere near: Zubair could not tell. He could not even tell where he was, or how he had got there. It was not the prison at any rate; Shahana, looking down into his face with a look of worry on her face, would not have been allowed in. Waqar, beside her, might have got permission for himself. And Raheem, the third person present, had been with him. When? Just a short while ago? In another lifetime? Zubair closed his eyes, his head swimming. Images came and went in his mind. Brahmdev, laughing uproariously, slapping his thighs and holding his sides, unable to contain his mirth. Damodar, leering in a triumphant way. Brahmdev, arm in arm with Damodar, advancing, his eyes gleaming red. 'My beautiful Zubair,' he was saying, but his mouth dripped red blood and when he lifted a hand to Zubair's cheek, it held a dagger, the light glinting on its blade.

'I don't care anymore,' Zubair said. His words were slurred. 'I will bring you down. I won't forgive you.'

'He's hallucinating,' said Shahana. 'Bibi Bayabaani had told me he might. I'll get the antidote she gave.'

Even with the antidote, it took several hours for Zubair's symptoms to die down. Not completely; Bibi Bayabaani had warned that some of the side effects of what she had prepared might last for months, even years. Perhaps the numbness in his fingers would never go. Perhaps his head would hurt for a long time. Perhaps the spectre of Brahmdev, lurking in his mind and grinning manically at him, would remain.

'But at least,' Zubair said when he woke from a restless sleep long after midnight, 'that will remind me I have to destroy him.'

Shahana was now the only one sitting beside him. She had sent Waqar and Raheem off on other errands: Waqar to fetch a bundle of clothes and other belongings of Zubair's that Shahana had left at her home nearby, and Raheem to the riverbank. There were still at least three or four hours to sunrise, but if Raheem were able to rouse a boatman who could take Zubair across the Yamuna and out of Dilli before dawn, it might mean the difference between life and death.

Zubair, now sitting up with two bolsters behind his back, looked about him. Now that his head was clearer, he could finally see where he was. 'The workshop? You brought me here?'

'If we are pretending you are dead, this is the best place,' she said. 'Either at our home or Waqar's, there would be servants around; we could not escape being seen.'

Zubair nodded. He reached, with a trembling hand, for the suraahi Shahana had placed beside him. She anticipated him, and having poured out a tumbler of water, handed it to him.

'It will be difficult for you,' he said quietly. 'To deal with the questions, and the censure.'

'Perhaps the censure will be reduced somewhat if people regard me as a widow,' Shahana said in a flat voice. 'That is the way of the world, is it not? A man's death goes a long way in erasing all the wrongs he has done.'

She shrugged. 'It will all be well. As long as I know that you are safe. You will write, will you not? Write, and let me know how you are. Wherever you are.'

'I feel stupid and guilty for having put you through so much distress,' Zubair said after a while. 'It will be so hard for you, to bring up a child on your own.'

'On my own, no. My brother and his wife are very fond of Nadeem. And your parents will be back within a few months.'

Zubair's expression grew even more worried at that thought. 'You will tell them the truth, won't you? They deserve to know, that I am not dead.'

'Of course.' She smiled. 'I will tell them, and you will make sure you write often, long letters. They will like that.'

They sat in somewhat uncomfortable silence for a while. Then, because it seemed preposterous that she should have done so much for him, and he had still not told her everything, Zubair confessed to Shahana. He told her about Brahmdev, about his one-sided affection for the man. And about the vicious betrayal.

'He used me,' Zubair finished. 'All those things Maheshwar Dutt described, I could recognize. I could tell where and how he had taken advantage of me. What a fool I was!' He closed his eyes, mortified at his gullibility.

A few deep breaths, and he regained control. 'I had got Raheem to bring me a folder in which there are many of his letters,' he said. 'Letters which show, clearly enough, that he is conspiring to bring down Sikandar Lodhi. After I read your letter and discovered your plan, I gave the folder back to Raheem, so that he could safeguard it until I could take it away with me.' There was a sound at the front door of the workshop, and he stopped.

It was Waqar, bringing with him the bundle Shahana had packed. She opened it, right there on the floor to show Zubair: clothing, dagger, dried fruit, a pouch stuffed with silver coins. Some pieces of brocade, too, 'which you might sell if you are in dire need,' Shahana said, repacking the bundle.

'You have provided well for me.'

Before Shahana could say anything, Waqar interrupted. 'You are still your family's son, and Shahana's husband. You must be provided for.'

Zubair shook his head. 'I am also an able-bodied man, well capable of providing for myself. Let me get out of Dilli and away, then I will begin work. I can correspond with Raheem and start selling brocades in other cities. I doubt if we will get much work from the palace now.'

Far away to the east, beyond the belt of trees that fringed the eastern bank of the Yamuna, the sun was just below the horizon: a peach-gold hue suffused the edge, blending into a band of surreal mauve above. Even further up, where the sky was still an intensely deep blue, a scattering of stars glittered like spilled coins.

'It'll be light soon,' Waqar said, as Zubair placed his bundle of belongings in the boat that Raheem had hired. The boatman was already seated, oars at the ready. Raheem had stayed behind at the workshop to clean up and make sure there remained no signs of Zubair's office having been used during the night. Waqar had insisted on going along with Zubair to the riverbank—he could not possibly go on his own, not in the still dizzy, weak condition he was in—and had even offered to cross over with his brother-in-law. Zubair needed to rest, to recuperate: in a big town, perhaps, like Mathura, where he might find a convenient sarai where he could stay for a few weeks in comfort.

Zubair had turned down the suggestion to go to Mathura.

A largeish village, while it may not have the facilities of a town, might be more conducive to his health. Quieter, gentler, with fewer chances of him suddenly running into someone who might know him.

In the few short minutes since they had arrived at the bank of the Yamuna, the stars had almost all vanished from the sky, and the sky itself was not quite as deeply blue as it had been. It was getting lighter by the moment; the sun would be up before Zubair had crossed the river. Waqar embraced Zubair and murmured a wish that he would be protected by the Almighty, before he moved away, back to the cart. Shahana came forward.

'I do not know when and if we will meet again,' she said. 'But may Allah preserve you and keep you safe and well.'

Zubair cleared his throat. 'I am sorry,' he said at last. 'For not having been a better husband.'

Shahana shook her head. 'I told you, some years ago, I think, that you and I were doomed to love people who would not love us back. How true that has turned out to be.' She drew in a deep breath. 'But if you are safe, if you are happy, I will be content with that.' She nodded, a resolute look in her eyes, her lips set in a straight line and her jaw firm. 'Go now,' she added. 'Goodbye.' She stepped back, as if putting a distance of a few feet between them would signify the breaking of that tenuous tie. Or at least a willingness to let go.

Zubair hesitated, wanting to say so much, to apologize once again. Then, with a quick nod, he turned and got into the boat on shaking legs. Even before he had sat down, the boatman had begun to ply his oars.

Shahana stood on the sand, watching as the boat drew away, silhouetted against the gold of the rising sun. Around her, the clamour of the waterbirds grew steadily calmer, until all she could hear was the occasional tweet or chirrup, the gentle swish of the waves of the Yamuna licking at the shore.

Interlude

'I find that impossible to believe,' Mohsin says. There is scorn in his eyes.

'Why on earth?' I say. 'People sacrifice a lot for those they love. It is nothing strange.'

He shakes his head vigorously. 'Not that. I mean that bit about Bibi Bayabaani providing some sort of drug that made him appear dead.' He utters a sceptical laugh. 'That doesn't happen outside of fairy tales.'

But this is something I remember hearing, not just from my mother, but—many years later, when my father had re-entered my life—from him too. Both of them, as also my uncle Waqar, described it the same way, though of course my father, given that he had been unconscious through a substantial portion of the adventure, could only remember part of it.

'It was some herb called angoorshefa,' I tell Mohsin. 'I believe it is mostly to be found in the distant mountains, far to the east. But Bibi Bayabaani was a healer of some repute, so she probably had it with her. She told my mother that it was so dangerous, she had to be very careful with the dosage. A certain amount, and my father would only sink into something like a stupor, his heartbeat slowing till it was barely discernible. Even a pinch more, and he would die. Or end up paralyzed for life.'

Mohsin obviously does not believe me; that look on his face is not merely one of doubt, it is of sheer disbelief.

I try to explain a bit more. 'She was a very skilled healer, but sometimes her treatments seemed to not be founded on anything that the trained hakims would have even considered treatment.' I remember, when I was a small boy, I had been plagued with a terrible stomach ache, and my mother had taken me to Bibi Bayabaani. I remember the old lady laying me down on her charpai, and gently lifting my tunic off my stomach.

'She massaged my stomach for a minute or so,' I recall. 'And then, while I was still lying down, she tied a black thread around my big toe. Then she told me to close my eyes and pray, asking to be healed.'

'And? Did it work?'

'The pain disappeared within a few minutes,' I affirm.

This time Mohsin cannot contain himself. He lets out a snort, which he tries hurriedly to change into a cough when he sees I am looking offended.

'Perhaps the old lady was in league with the djinn,' he says. 'Do you remember that friend of mine, Osman? Osman had a distant uncle who used to claim he had a genie servant. Osman said that whenever he went to visit his uncle, the uncle would say, "Tell me what you want. Halwa-e-gajar? Green almonds from Kabul? Pedas from Mathura?" And when you chose something, even something completely bizarre, he would never bat an eyelid. He had a closed basket, which he would place in a wall niche, and then he would say, "My servant, hear: my friend wants so-and-so thing. Get it for us now." And half an hour later, even if you had been sitting there all the time watching the basket, you would open it and find exactly what you had asked for.'

I cannot tell if Mohsin is making fun, or if he truly believes in this. I too have heard of people—not Bibi Bayabaani, I must add—who claim to have djinn as servants. I am one of those who do not believe in such things. Allah made us human, and it behooves us to use only what paltry powers we have as humans to make our way through life.

'Let us go to bed now,' I say, putting an end to the conversation. 'It has been a long day, and I am tired.'

☙

I woke this morning to the sound of life. In the golden light of the dawn, I opened my eyes to a world for once not silent, not dead and decaying. As I went about my ablutions—which, thanks to this hellish drought, now consists of simply rubbing exposed parts with an old rag—I let my ears grow accustomed to the birdsong that floated in from the tree outside our home.

It is a semal, a silk cotton tree, a venerable giant that towers above all the other trees. From it comes a chorus of sounds: the twittering of birds and the excited squeaks of the squirrels that chase each other across its branches. The tree is in bloom, its fleshy red flowers littering our neglected courtyard. Mohsin had heard somewhere that the buds of the tree could be cooked and eaten; he collected some and tried cooking them with whatever spices he could find in our depleted stores, but the end result was hardly palatable. We ate the dish stoically, though, comforting ourselves with the thought that it was, at least, nutrition.

Nutrition, too, for the birds and the squirrels, who are better off than us, with smaller bellies to fill. And fewer worries. They are contented, happy in the abundance the semal offers.

Spring is here, and dare we hope that this means there will be a change for the better? Surely this huge tree, its roots drawing enough water from deep in the earth to feed its flowers, is a sign that the land is recovering? My heart fills with hope.

Around noon, Mohsin comes racing into the house, the front door slamming behind him, his breath coming in great gasps as he shares his news.

Gokul's father and one of Gokul's brothers, returning from a foraging trip along the riverside, were set upon by a group of starving beggars. They beat Gokul's father and brother to death, and took away every single object on them, from the few roots they had dug up to the threadbare clothing they had been wearing.

'Gokul told me,' Mohsin says, 'that the only thing left behind was the dried mud that had got rubbed off the roots, and remained in his father's palms. That was all.' His eyes are wide, staring and glazed over with the shock of it.

The death of two relatively able-bodied members of the family has meant that the task of foraging, of somehow getting hold of some sustenance, must now be divided among the littler ones. 'His youngest brothers are two and three years old,' Mohsin adds. 'How will they find anything?'

The five people who are left—Gokul, the two little brothers, a baby sister and their mother—are in a bad way. There has been so little to eat, the mother has no milk now for her baby. 'The rest of them are managing, but it is the baby who worries them. Gokul's Amma is trying to feed her thin gruel, but the baby just cries.'

We fidget and look away. We are men; what do we know of such things? My son and I are both fathers, but of course we have left all the bringing up of children to our womenfolk. We can offer nothing but sympathy now.

It has been two months today since the Baadshah Humayun died, and there is news in the bazaars that Hemu, the ambitious general who has an eye on the throne, is moving westward towards Dilli. He is still a long way off, so I am not worried. The new Baadshah is still far away in the west, but there is time for him to make his way to Agra, to stop Hemu before he gets much further.

We have been so busy keeping alive that neither I nor Mohsin have had the inclination to continue with my chronicling of our collective past. I have the time, yes; I will admit that. But the heart, the soul? They are too full of worry, too crowded to do anything but fret.

I am alone at home today, for Mohsin and his father went out yesterday with Gokul on a foraging expedition. They intend to range far, and have been gone all of yesterday. The sun is now setting, and all I have eaten today is a handful of withered fruit from a peepal tree. Even as I ate them, I remembered a long-ago vaid prescribing these to my grandfather when he had lost his appetite in the wake of an illness. How ironic, that when there is nothing else to eat, there is this. If it whets my appetite, I can do nothing.

I wonder where they can be, this son of mine and his son. Have they found something to eat? Are they headed home?

That night, two months back, after I had told Mohsin the thrilling events of how my mother Shahana had contrived to get my father Zubair out of prison and away to safety, I had dreamt of them both. Not together. Not as, I suppose, other people dream of parents: not a unit, not mother and father side by side. I dreamt, oddly, not even of a scene I had witnessed. In my dream, I saw Shahana standing on the bank of the Yamuna, and Zubair standing in a boat that tossed about on the waves of the Yamuna. He was not looking at her; his gaze was somewhere far off, across the river. But she was watching him, all her attention focused on him: as if, if she were to look away, she might die.

The next morning, of course, Mohsin had resumed his questions, the how and the why and the what. Questions, thankfully, which are pertinent to this story, so I will provide a brief gist of the answers I gave.

Shahana and Waqar had, of course, been aware that they would face many questions over the next few days. Their acquaintances and neighbours knew of Zubair's arrest and incarceration, and had been badgering them ever since in an attempt to find out more. Waqar went to the local mosque and talked in private with the imam there. Perhaps some money was given, a donation for the upkeep of the mosque. The sombre news of Zubair's sudden death in prison was announced, and special prayers were offered for the soul of the bereaved.

There will always be some who are too inquisitive to be satisfied easily, and they wanted to know why Zubair had been buried so secretly, in such a clandestine way. To these, Waqar and Shahana gave the impression that Zubair had been so badly tortured, so mutilated that Shahana herself could not bear to look upon his face. 'But tell no one,' they cautioned. 'If word were to get to the palace, we might be in trouble.'

The palace had already severed its connections with the workshop. Raheem had received a messenger from Mirza Yasin Mohammad Khan, bringing with him a sum of money to cover outstanding payments due to the workshop. There was a letter, too, in which Raheem was told in no uncertain terms that neither he nor any other representative of the workshop need come to the palace again.

While all this was happening in Dilli, Zubair was rebuilding his life. After recuperating in a village near Dilli, he travelled to Banaras, the eternal city of Kashi. The city of the Ganga, its waters lapping at the steps of its countless ghats. A city of temples, yes; and the faithful flocking to wash their sins in the river—but also a city of commerce. Kashi had been, for many centuries now, an important centre for trade: the Ganga, of course, brought and took away many boatloads of goods, but meeting at the city were also some of the major highways in the land. The road from Bengal to Lahore, and the one from the mountains to the far north, deep down into the peninsula, met at Kashi. It was a melting pot, a cosmopolitan city where merchants from near and far rubbed shoulders with mendicants and mercenaries, pilgrims and priests.

Kashi was not just a city getting rich on its location: it also produced some of the finest textiles in the land. Silk and cotton, yes: but also brocade, and that was what drew Zubair to Kashi. He knew brocade workers in the city, men who owned workshops like his own, and he went to one of these, Faisal.

He told the man, behind closed doors and in complete secrecy, all that had happened. He explained his predicament, asserted his innocence, and begged to be allowed some work. Zubair had chosen carefully, for Faisal was a man with a reputation not just for excellent brocades, but also for kindness. He welcomed Zubair with open arms.

Zubair began work, and soon discovered that Faisal had only one naqshband, an old man now short-sighted, his hands no longer steady enough to do the fine work of the naqshas. A new naqshband was needed, and Zubair knew just whom to approach. He wrote to Raheem.

In Dilli, though the workshop had lost the business of the palace, it had acquired new buyers. Some were simply people with a taste for the macabre, excited about buying brocades from the workshop whose owner had died in such dramatic circumstances. But there were others who valued the brocades for what they were.

Zubair set about forging ties between the Dilli workshop and Faisal's. Copies of Raheem's best naqshas would be sent to Kashi, and Faisal's brocades, carefully chosen by Zubair keeping in mind the tastes of the Dilli clientele, would be sent to the capital. Within a year of his supposed death, Zubair had begun on the work of taking the workshop to new heights, and of building his fortune, a fortune which he intended to put to just one use: to destroy Brahmdev.

☙

I have spent these hours fretting over my son and grandson, wondering where they are, and how they are.

Night falls, and now too anxious to be able to just sit around more, I ease up the bar on the front door and step into the lane outside. All is still, silent as the grave. I sit down on the threshold, too worried to go inside, too tired to stand.

I am sitting on the threshold, my chin sunk on my chest, when I am jolted out of my stupor by the sound of approaching footsteps. I scramble up despite my frailty, stumbling as I try to scurry back into the safety of my home.

'Abba! Abba, wait!'

It is my son. My knees buckle with the relief of it, and to my horror, tears trickle down my cheeks. Tears? Where has my body been able to spare the moisture for tears?

But it is them, Mohsin and his father, and even, hovering

in the background, an emaciated boy of indeterminate years. Gokul, I assume.

'We've got some things to eat,' Mohsin says as he helps me inside. 'And Gokul will be living with us from now on. You don't mind, do you? He has no one left.'

ଓ

Gokul's mother has remarried. Her new husband is a money-lender; I suppose she was driven by desperation to approach him for a loan. What transpired, the conversation they might have had, is not known to Gokul. My son and Mohsin have already spoken to him; it is from them that I hear what has happened.

'The money-lender refused to let her bring Gokul into the house,' my son tells me, while Mohsin takes Gokul inside. 'The younger children he accepted; Gokul, no.' He tells me that the money-lender, however, has agreed to send some millet for Gokul every month. When they went to Gokul's home yesterday, they found the boy alone and distressed, and he told them all that had happened. They took him off to forage in an attempt to distract him, and got back late this evening. They have brought Gokul with them, as also a small sack of millet that his new stepfather had sent for him.

'The poor child,' he says. 'He must feel so rejected, abandoned in this callous fashion. What a heartless mother.'

I cannot help but wonder. Was she heartless, though? Or did she simply see that her younger children could be saved from starvation if she gave herself to the money-lender? And was she responsible for the money-lender's agreeing to send millet for Gokul? I doubt if he would have offered to support this boy out of sheer magnanimity.

Poor Gokul, I think, as I stretch out on my bed and pull up the sheet. Poor child, to have his father dead, his mother and siblings gone. How alone he must feel, how lonely.

Between us, we can try, at least, to help him feel that he is not alone. Perhaps I will involve him in documenting the story of our family. I will dictate it to Mohsin, and Gokul can listen as I talk. We will have more time, now that the millets are there to supplement what they have foraged. In some odd, roundabout way that makes me feel guilty: I realize that by marrying the money-lender, Gokul's mother has sacrificed herself not just for her son, but for us too. The thought unsettles me.

☙

I have said my prayers, I have had my meagre breakfast of a swallow of water and a few ber. Since the wee hours of the morning, a constant murmur has filled my ears: the sound of Mohsin's voice as he tells Gokul everything. All about our family, our failings, our idiosyncrasies, our many flaws. At first, I felt uncomfortable at the airing of our dirty linen; then I told myself that it does not matter. Half the people—no, more; most—in this long story are long gone; how will one small and insignificant boy knowing about them change anything?

When Gokul enters my room, following Mohsin, his eyes are full of awe. Wonderment, perhaps even a certain amount of disbelief. He has been told about ancestors who have been friends with Sultans, and who have nurtured enemies of the realm. He has heard of sages and fools, of those who neglected their own families to pursue an illusion.

'What will we talk about today?' Mohsin asks, settling himself on the thin reed mat beside my bed, reaching for the sheets of paper he has taken out in preparation for our session today. Gokul, seeing me nod, sits down on the mat. He looks awkward: we will take time to adapt to each other, to grow comfortable.

'Shall I complete the bit about Zubair?' I ask. 'And how he had his revenge on Brahmdev?'

Aslam and Firoza returned from the haj the year after Zubair had been arrested. To meet them at the port of Surat, where their ship docked, Raheem sent a nephew of his, a youth named Mudassar. Mudassar gave them a letter from Zubair, informing them of all that had happened. Of course they were shaken, and Firoza cried and fretted most of the way from Surat to Dilli; but by the time they were home, they had reconciled themselves. Shahana, who had lived these past months in Waqar's home, returned to her in-laws' home in Ghiyaspur, Nadeem in tow.

Raheem and Mudassar, between them, became Zubair's eyes and ears in Dilli. His vengeance against Brahmdev was plotted out through them.

The first thing that was done was for Raheem to hire a man to shadow Brahmdev: to keep an eye on whom he met, where he went, what he did.

The second thing was to have Raheem take Brahmdev's old letters to the palace, to lay them before the officers of the law, for them to see who was at the heart of the conspiracy against the Lodhi. The day Raheem submitted the letters, he went to visit Brahmdev at his home across the Yamuna. 'My master had kept your letters,' Raheem informed Brahmdev. 'And I have taken them to the palace today.'

To Brahmdev's suspicious query—why would Raheem tell him that?—all Raheem said was, 'Because it would be too simple if you were merely arrested and executed. There should be a chase, shouldn't there, otherwise where is the thrill?' Then, without waiting for more, he left.

That very evening, word was brought from the spy Raheem had employed: Brahmdev had left his home shortly after Raheem had visited him. He was headed downriver from Dilli, and the spy would follow.

'Good,' Zubair said, when the news was brought to him later that month by Raheem, who came to Kashi. 'He dare not show his face in Dilli now. And I will not let him rest anywhere else.'

And thus began Zubair's vendetta. Wherever Brahmdev went, the man who shadowed him did too. Whenever Brahmdev homed in on a possible client—a wealthy and ambitious nobleman, perhaps, with an axe to grind or a clandestine battle to fight—the spy looking on would report. Within days, just as it looked that Brahmdev had got a commission—a letter would arrive. It was always anonymous, and filled with unsavoury details. How Brahmdev had failed in the task assigned to him by the nobleman in Badayun; how his mishandling of it had brought shame and disgrace to the man who had hired him; how Brahmdev's precipitate flight from Dilli had meant that he had neither completed the job, nor paid back the vast sum he had taken for it.

He was unreliable, dishonest. He was already in trouble with the imperial authorities in Dilli, and for him to be seen in any part of the empire would spell death for him. And also, of course, for anybody else who gave him shelter, or supported him in any way. Brahmdev was poison.

It took many months, several years, but it whittled away Brahmdev's business, and with it his confidence, his wealth, his everything. He could not return to Dilli anymore; his sons were briefly imprisoned, but released when they proved to know nothing of their father's doings. The next day, Brahmdev's wife left for her natal home, deep in Mewar, taking her sons with her. No one ever saw them again in Dilli, and as for Brahmdev, he was last seen trying to persuade a shopkeeper in Jaunpur to let him have a sack of millet on credit.

'That is it?' Mohsin says. 'So lame?'

'He got his just deserts,' I say. 'He had used Zubair, and Zubair had his revenge.'

'But Brahmdev never even knew why he was ruined, and by whom,' Mohsin insists. 'Where's the fun in vengeance like that?'

'Fun was not Zubair's motive. He was furious. I suppose the hurt of that betrayal was too deep to be easily assuaged.' I can only surmise. For all I know, had my father been less attached to Brahmdev, he might have not suffered such hurt, and he might not have been so ruthless in his vengeance.

'But let us set that aside,' I say, turning back to Mohsin. 'That story is done. There is the next story waiting to be told.'

'Yes.' He nods. 'Yours.' He turns to Gokul. 'My grandfather's name is Nadeem, by the way. If you hear him talking of Nadeem, it means him. He has some odd notions about why it must be so, but we humour him.' He winks at me.

The impudence of the boy.

15

Dilli

Twenty years later

921 Hijri (1515 CE)

One of Nadeem's cousins had come to Dilli, on his way to the imperial capital at Agra. Shamsher was the son of one of Zubair's sisters, and had lived all his life in Dariyabad, in Awadh. Now he had inherited property in Agra thanks to the death of his father-in-law, and Shamsher was eager to launch a new life as a moneyed man about town. A first step in that direction was to acquire a little town polish in Dilli, even if it was only for a few days.

Aslam and Firoza had died within a year of each other. Aslam, returning from a journey to Agra with Raheem, had breathed his last six years back at a busy sarai along the highway. Firoza had collapsed on hearing the news, and had taken to her bed, never to rise from it. They were both gone, and Zubair of course believed dead by all but his immediate family—but Shahana still occupied the house near the workshop in Ghiyaspur, and there was Nadeem, now twenty-three years old. There was too his wife Ismat, Waqar's daughter, a slim and fragile woman whose delicate beauty had dazzled her husband until it had dawned on him that there was little to Ismat beyond her beauty. He had soon begun to find her overly needy and childish, looking to him to entertain her, indulge her and cater to her every whim. It had put him off completely and utterly. They had a daughter, followed by a son—now five years old—and Nadeem considered his duty done.

Shamsher and his family, his wife and four children, were of course staying with Nadeem in Ghiyaspur. The womenfolk, Shahana, Ismat and her daughter, Shamsher's wife and his two daughters, had quickly made friends with each other. The zenana rang with the laughter of the girls. Frequent outings were being organized, to the riverside for a picnic; to the dargah and baoli of Hazrat Nizamuddin Auliya; to the shops. Sellers of fine cloth, of jewellery and cosmetics, were ushered in all through the day so that the visiting ladies (even though neither of Shamsher's daughters were yet ten years old) may buy what they wished.

'It is getting suffocating in that house,' Shamsher said, with a laugh that did little to hide his exasperation. He must have realized the implication of what he had so carelessly said, and hurried to make amends. 'I do not mean that we are in any way uncomfortable—'

Nadeem grinned at him. 'It is all right. Think of this as a holiday, for your family and for yourself.'

'We are imposing on you.'

Nadeem tut-tutted that self-deprecatory remark away with all the grace of a man who can afford to be hospitable. He had never known want; he was amply provided for. Zubair, whom he did not remember at all and had not seen since his early childhood, ran the workshop in Kashi; Mudassar here in Ghiyaspur. Raheem had retired some years back, but his attachment to the workshop was so deep that he came by every now and then, just to be quietly happy in familiar surroundings, among people and work he knew and loved.

Today, too, Raheem was there, and just as well. Shamsher's two young sons, eight and ten years old, had been taken under his wing and were being shown around the workshop by Raheem. The boys' excited chatter could be heard every now and then over the rhythmic click-clack of the weavers' looms. Every now and then, too, there would be the sound of running feet, and there had been a brief shriek of amused fright as a startled gecko scurried across one child's foot and up a wall.

Shamsher, sitting with Nadeem, apologized for the poor

manners of his children, but Nadeem brushed it away. 'I remember what it was to first come to the workshop, and have Raheem show me around too. I can understand.'

It was said to put Shamsher at his ease, but the truth was less simple. Nadeem's first visit to the brocade workshop he would inherit had been no happy outing as it was for Shamsher's sons. For Nadeem, it had been a visit under duress: a reluctant child compelled by an anxious family to at least attempt an interest in something he was indifferent to.

ଓ

Nadeem looked out of the window beside which he sat, in what had been once Aslam's office and later, for some years, Zubair's. The sun shone bright outside, on a beautiful spring day. The faintly citrus scent of orange jasmine blossoms, their white stars studding the bushes in the garden, drifted in on a breeze. A pair of sparrows hopped about along the paved path, and from somewhere in the trees came the unmistakable kot-roo, kot-roo of a barbet.

'Do you know what it feels like, to see magic before your eyes? Magic you have created?' Nadeem asked. A rhetorical question, and one Shamsher recognized as such. 'That was how it was for me. I don't remember the first time I held a pen, but my uncle told me later that my eyes lit up when I drew that first wobbly line on the page.'

His eyes lit up even now, at the long-ago memory of that day, even if all his memories of it were second-hand. Waqar, proud of his sister's son, relieved that here was one, unlike his own son, who had the talent. Waqar, eager to share his love for his art with another who understood it.

'I fell in love with calligraphy very early,' Nadeem said quietly. 'Do you know how it is taught? Or rather, how my uncle taught me, which may not be the same thing.' He reached out for the pen and the inkstand that was never far from him. 'This, see.'

Having dipped the nib of the reed pen in the ink, Nadeem pressed it firmly to the paper before him. A neat black square, tilted so that it formed a diamond, now sat on the white of the page. 'This,' said Nadeem, 'is called a nuqta. A dot.' Swiftly, his pen barely lifting, he drew seven more nuqtas under that first one, the corner of each touching a corner of the ones above and below. A small tower of eight nuqtas, perfectly aligned and each a replica of the others.

'And this,' Nadeem finished, 'is the first letter. Alif.' With a single stroke of his pen, he painted a vertical stroke beside the tower of nuqtas. The exact height of the tower, the same width, but a single stroke. 'This is how my uncle began, by teaching me the importance of proportion, of beauty. That's what calligraphy is all about, you know. Beauty, balance.'

He stared down at the sheet of paper, at the neat column of nuqtas and the alif beside them. 'This is art, Shamsher,' he said, his voice low, brimming with reverence. 'And I am fortunate enough to have been given the gift of this art.'

Waqar, of course, had been pleased that his favourite nephew showed such an aptitude for the calligraphy that Waqar had taught him. Even at six years of age, Nadeem was far more skilled than Waqar's own elder son, who at twelve, still struggled to shape his letters. Waqar had more or less given up on the boy; he would have to, and quickly, find some other occupation for the boy, since it was impossible to hope that he might suddenly show a talent for being a qaatib, a calligrapher.

Waqar's pride in Nadeem's calligraphy was countered by Aslam's equally strong unease at seeing the boy drift away towards a field in which he might have harboured a mere interest, but could afford no more than that. 'He is destined for brocade,' Aslam said, first grumbling only to his wife Firoza in the privacy of their chambers, and then outright, to Shahana, and finally to Waqar. 'It is all very well that he shows a talent for letters, but that must remain a hobby. He will inherit the workshop; there is no one else to take it over.'

Waqar was a canny man, and Aslam's words had shown him something he had not considered earlier. He had a young daughter, several years younger than Nadeem; ten years from now, if the boy was the owner of one of the biggest brocade manufacturers in the realm, there could be no more eligible match for little Ismat. It would be to Ismat's benefit if Nadeem were to be turned away from calligraphy and towards brocade.

Nadeem, too young to understand any of this, was left out of the deliberations that were to decide a good chunk of his life: the decisions about whom he would marry and what work he would do.

A few days later, Shahana woke him up early, and once he had eaten his breakfast, took him away to be carefully dressed. Nadeem had been getting ready to go outside and play before sitting down to practice his calligraphy; he had wondered aloud, and baulked at his routine being changed so summarily. Shahana had explained gently that he would be accompanying his grandfather to the brocade workshop. As she combed his hair, she told him what he could look forward to: the beautiful patterns, the lovely richness of the brocades, the colours. 'It will all someday be yours,' she had said.

Nadeem had been puzzled; what would he do with so much brocade? Even if, grown up, he needed a lot of it to have his clothes made?

But Shahana had simply laughed at that, before she kissed him, called him a good boy, and took him to Aslam.

The hanging mat of woven reeds at the doorway to Nadeem's office was pushed aside and a little head poked in. Shamsher's younger son, his eyes gleaming with excitement. 'Abbu,' he said, 'Come and see!'

Behind him, Raheem appeared, smiling as he ushered both boys in. 'I think we should let your father talk to Nadeem Sahib,' he said.

'But Abbu would never have seen a shikargah naqsha before! Do you know what that is, Abbu? Like a forest, so fine—'

Raheem intervened. 'Perhaps it will be more convenient if I were to bring it in. Your father is comfortable here, the noise of the workshop may displease him.'

The shikargah, 'the hunting lodge', were patterns that depicted a profusion of living creatures, all woven into the brocade as if it were not a piece of cloth but a section of the jungle. Cheetahs or lions would leap through this space, following in the wake of a prancing gazelle. An elephant, though caparisoned, might be glimpsed between two trees, while a peacock, its tail forming a cascade of tiny but perfect teardrops, might perch on a branch. All of them, birds and animals, would have been crafted from fine gold or silver thread, or in muted silk threads woven on a bright ground.

The naqsha that Raheem brought and spread out carefully on the mattress in Nadeem's room depicted a forest. It was a mosaic of large leaves and stylized flowers, their curving stems enclosing a panoply of wild creatures. Here, a blackbuck lifted beautifully spiraling horns to the skies; there a tiger, each stripe defined, reared up, ready to spring on the unsuspecting antelope. There, beyond, was an elephant, its trunk curving up. At the bottom, a row of parakeets, all jauntily curved beaks and long sweeping tails, marched along the edge of the forest.

'Isn't it beautiful, Abbu?' Shamsher's younger son breathed. 'But I wish the tiger wouldn't kill the deer. Instead of that elephant—it is beautiful, I don't mean I don't like it,' he added, glancing up apologetically at Raheem, 'but instead of that, it would have been so much more fun to have a hunter with a bow and arrow. That would be a story! A hunter killing the tiger before it kills the deer.'

Shamsher burst out laughing; Raheem and Nadeem smiled too, but a look was exchanged between them, a look that did not go unnoticed by Shamsher.

He did not, however, get a chance to speak the question in his mind, because his elder son had questions.

'Why would a naqsha have to be made?' the boy asked Raheem. 'I thought the weavers made cloth in the workshop, not drawings like this naqsha.'

Raheem's voice was patient when he answered. 'The naqsha is the plan, the map, of what will be woven. A weaver cannot just sit at the loom and begin working with the threads as he likes, you know. The weaver is no artist; and you need an artist to think up something like this.'

'But can the weaver not be also an artist?' the younger boy asked.

'He may. Even then, he will need to have a naqsha to refer to. If he works without a naqsha, it will be a mess. Every thread of every colour must be planned: where it will be inserted, where it will leave the pattern.

'The naqshband is not just an artist, he is more,' Raheem continued. 'He must know what motifs will be woven into the brocade, and how. How many threads, how many warp and how many weft—' Raheem stopped, suddenly aware that this was too much for a child. 'An entire story may be told in a naqsha,' he finished, with a smile.

It was only when Raheem had taken the children away, this time to give them a snack, that Shamsher turned back to his cousin, an enquiring look on his face. 'Why were you so amused?' he asked. 'Something made you laugh, when my son made that silly remark about the naqsha.'

Nadeem smiled. 'My reaction, many years ago, was similar. Raheem had shown me a shikargah naqsha too, and I had pointed out things I didn't care for. In my case, it was a mahout on an elephant. I thought he had no business being in the forest; a monkey might have looked better on the elephant's back.' He laughed, but there was a ruefulness in his laugh that did not escape Shamsher.

ঙ

Shamsher accompanied Nadeem home for lunch. The boys, still bubbling over with the excitement of their visit to the workshop, had raced off into the zenana to recount their experiences. Shamsher and Nadeem had sat down in one of the rooms of the mardana, the men's quarters, that overlooked the garden outside. A fine meal had been laid out for them: kebabs and pulao, fluffy naan-e-tanuri, and an array of relishes, cooked vegetables, and sweetmeats. Shamsher was a hearty eater and did justice to the repast; Nadeem merely picked at his food in an abstracted manner.

'Brocade, no matter how exquisite, I could not summon up any love for,' Nadeem said, when the meal had been cleared away. 'You know, it's when you love a woman: once you have fallen in love with one, do you have eyes for any other?'

Shamsher looked a little abashed at that; it was an open secret that he was devoted to his wife. Not like Nadeem: Ismat inspired in him no love, not even a passing feeling of anything approaching pleasure. At best, he was indifferent to her; at worst, he wished he could be rid of her.

He put the thought aside.

'The pen captured my heart long before,' he said. 'There was no room in it for anything else.'

'But you seem to have settled in well. You looked completely at home in the workshop today.'

Nadeem shrugged. 'Our grandfather could not possibly have gone on much longer. Both he and Raheem were getting on in years. It would have been cruel to leave them to their own devices.'

Shamsher nodded sympathetically. 'But you still do your calligraphy. You have your pens and ink in your office at the workshop.'

'How can you abandon your love completely? If someone were to forcibly separate you—Allah forbid—from your begum, would you stop loving her? Can distance dim that fire? Does it not have the opposite effect?

'I make sure I keep my hand in,' he added. 'And lately, I have even begun showing off my skill as a calligrapher. My uncle Waqar does not like it; he thinks I should focus on the workshop, not get distracted.'

'Or maybe he is jealous.'

'From your mouth to God's ears.' Nadeem could not resist a smile. 'If my uncle is jealous, it can only mean that he thinks I am good enough. And if he thinks I am good, I must be better than good.'

Bahlol Lodhi had held on to the throne of Dilli for nearly forty years, a period during which he had worked hard to not just cement his position as Sultan, but to expand the territories of his realm. Sikandar Lodhi, succeeding his father after Bahlol's death, had continued the work, expanding the empire to spread from Gujarat to Jaunpur, to Bengal in the east.

One strategic stronghold, however, eluded Sikandar: Gwalior. The Sultan's many attempts to subjugate this prized territory were frustrated, and he came to the conclusion that a focused campaign required a base close to his target. Dilli, in this sense, was too far to be a good headquarters; in order to keep an eye on Gwalior and to swiftly move troops, he needed to be closer to his objective.

In the year 910 of the Hijri calendar—the year Europe knew as 1505 Anno Domini—Sikandar Lodhi began work on this resolution, by building a palace at Agra. By the following year, he and his court had moved to the city. Dilli was no more the capital of the empire; Agra was.

Ten years it had been now since the court had shifted. Some people had been anxious that Dilli's loss of status would send the city into a decline, but Aslam had been optimistic. He had firmly believed that even if the Sultan and his court moved to Agra, Dilli's position as a city of culture, of aesthetics and wealth, would remain. He had also decided that it was a good time to approach the palace once again. 'The Sultan will be busy in military campaigns; that is his objective in shifting to Agra—and his ladies, I feel, might find themselves at least a little at a loose end,' he had told Raheem and Zubair. 'Perhaps this is the time to try and win them back.'

So, a couple of months after the last group of palace officials and servitors had moved to Agra, Mudassar and Raheem had gone with a very exclusive package of brocades to be gifted to the harem at Agra. Aslam had personally chosen the brocades that made up the package: the most exquisite, the most unique in colour, in combinations of silk and metallic threads, in patterns. It was a gamble, similar to Aabida's initial forays into the palace: the offering of tantalizing gifts in the hope that they would win admiration, and subsequent employment.

For the first few years, there had been nothing. The gifts were sent back, regardless of how fine they were. But there was also no rap on the knuckles, no curt command to desist.

'There is hope,' Aslam had said firmly, and had continued to try. On the Sultan's birthday, and on the anniversary of his accession to the throne, Aslam or Raheem, accompanied by Mudassar, would go to Agra to present the cream of the crop from the brocades woven over the past year.

Finally, five years earlier, the gift was accepted. True, it was just a petty official who took the gift, looked sharply at Aslam, and handed over a gold coin, minted to mark the Sultan's birthday. But Aslam chose to interpret it as a sign of acquiescence. Had the palace finally decided to let bygones be bygones? After all, for them, Zubair had been dead these many years; and his fault had been somewhat lessened by the revelation of the true culprit. Perhaps it was felt that by depriving the workshop of their custom, the palace was cutting off its nose to spite its face. In the years since Zubair's so-called death, the workshop had rebuilt its reputation, its brocades now finer than ever before, the collaboration with Faisal's workshop in Kashi reaping rich dividends. They were indubitably the finest brocade workers in Dilli or Agra, and to distance oneself from them was to deny oneself the best.

Perhaps, too, there was the fact that Bibi Ambha had been replaced by her daughter-in-law, Dilawar Begum, as the chief lady in the Sultan's harem. Bibi Ambha, devoted to the son she had helped put on the throne, had been no shrinking violet as a young woman; older now and even less bothered about public opinion, she refused to vegetate in the palace at Agra.

As part of his plan to conquer Gwalior, Sikandar Lodhi had invaded Dholpur, a town which appealed to him otherwise too. Enough, at least, for him to visit it frequently and stay for extended lengths of time. He built palaces and fortresses along the route between Agra and Dholpur, and his mother, who accompanied him, stayed in them. Dholpur was a jewel, its palaces of stone bright as burnished gold, its surrounding forests green and rich, the Chambal River broad, life-giving. Bibi Ambha must have liked it more, perhaps, than Agra, because she spent a good bit of time here. When she died, it was at Dholpur that she was buried.

Dilawar Begum now presided over the harem in Agra. Perhaps she was more forgiving than her mother-in-law had been; perhaps, simply, she valued good things more than she valued such vague ideas as honour.

Slowly but surely, the workshop was allowed back into the palace.

☙

'Well, what do you think?' Mudassar said.

Nadeem looked across the naqshas that had been spread

on the low slope-topped desk before him, then to the many brocades, carefully spread out to reveal their patterns, that covered the mattress in his room at the workshop. 'They're beautiful,' he said, a little cautiously.

Mudassar looked faintly piqued, but he did not express any irritation he might have felt in words. 'That's all? You don't think we might be better off showing the green brocade with the parakeets, rather than this one with the peacocks? And this naqsha? I had a disagreement with my uncle Raheem over this. He thinks it is too prosaic, not something we need bother showing at the palace.'

'If that's what Raheem thinks—best follow his advice. He knows the palace like none other.' Nadeem hesitated. He knew Mudassar would not like what he was about to say, but it was necessary. 'You will have to make the trip to Agra on your own this time,' he said. 'It is the anniversary of Grandfather's death, and I have to accompany Ammi to the grave. I cannot possibly come.'

Mudassar was not happy, but there was no help for it. He packed away the brocades and left Nadeem's room, carrying the naqshas with him and calling for one of the apprentices to bring the brocades.

16

Shahana knelt beside the gravestone and washed it gently. She had already washed Firoza's gravestone, which was beside Aslam's, and Nadeem had offered to perform the task for Aslam's grave. But Shahana had refused; these people, she said, had been good to her, in-laws as loving as parents. This was the least she could do for them. In fact, all of it, she would do. Washing the graves, placing flowers on them. Burning incense and reading from the Quran. Offering prayers at the wall mosque in the graveyard, a diminutive structure marked by three small arches. It was her prerogative as their daughter-in-law.

Ismat stood nearby, holding the Quran and the small basket of fragrant jasmine and roses that they had brought. The look on her face was unreadable; it was impossible to tell whether she was indifferent or bored, or merely waiting in a dispassionate way for when she might be needed.

Nadeem rose to his feet, the empty terracotta water pot in his hand. Shahana needed him to fetch more water from the nearby tank, a small shallow one that was meant for the ablutions of those who might wish to pray at the mosque. It was a little way off, half-hidden by an amla tree and the wall of the mosque. The graveyard was deserted at the moment, the only sound the swish of the grass as Nadeem made his way between the graves towards the mosque.

He was bending, dipping the pot into the water, when Nadeem caught a movement off towards his right, in the shade of the amla tree. A stray animal, thought Nadeem; but no, it was no feral cat or pariah dog sniffing about in the undergrowth. It was a man, standing just at the point where the edge of the wall mosque hid most of him. Had Nadeem not been standing where he was, he would not have noticed him.

A strange man, thought Nadeem as he straightened up with the water pot now brimming. Obviously no vagrant, seeking shelter in the graveyard. No; this man was neatly dressed in well-stitched, even expensive clothes. His salt and pepper beard and moustache were trimmed, and his turban carefully tied. A man of means. A man, too, who seemed vaguely familiar, though Nadeem could not place him.

The man looked Nadeem full in the face, his eyes friendly and a smile on his lips. 'Nadeem?' he whispered. His gaze travelled past Nadeem, towards the graves where Shahana used a clean rag to wipe one end of the slab. 'Is that your wife with your mother?'

Nadeem's eyes widened. 'Abbu?' he whispered. 'Is it you?'

ଔ

'How could you be so foolhardy?' Shahana exclaimed, though she was careful to keep her voice low. 'To show your face here in Dilli—oh, so foolish!'

Zubair gave her a small, reassuring smile. 'It has been nearly ten years since Sikandar Lodhi moved away to Agra. Also, barring a handful of people, nobody will even suspect me of returning to Dilli. Unless as a ghost.' The smile broadened into a grin. 'And I have changed, haven't I? It's been a long time.'

Shahana shook her head, obstinate in her refusal to let go of her anguish.

'If it's any consolation, I don't show my face anywhere I'm likely to run into people who might know me. In Ghiyaspur, for instance: I haven't been near the workshop or home.'

Nadeem had gone off to stand beside Ismat while Shahana had come hurrying to the husband she had not seen all these years. Ismat, her head and shoulders decorously veiled, stood silent and still; Nadeem could not resist glancing towards his parents every now and then. Zubair and Shahana stood under the amla tree beside the mosque, its feathery leaves throwing a dappled shade over them. Crickets sang in the grass around, butterflies fluttered amidst the tiny wildflowers, and a couple of parakeets feasted on the tart fruit of the tree. Shahana seemed to notice none of it; all her attention was focused on Zubair.

'You should have written to tell me you were coming,' she said.

'Why? So that you could forbid me?' He shook his head. 'It had been so long: I was missing Dilli. I ached to see Nadeem—' he broke off, perhaps realizing that he could not say the same for this woman. His wife, but unloved, even though for a brief while there had been between them an intense companionship. A conspiracy, too, that persisted. She was an accomplice in his endeavour to be alive and dead at the same time.

'How are you?' he asked. 'Are you well?'

'As well as can be expected. At this age, what more can one hope for?'

They spoke briefly, in muted tones, so low that their voices did not carry even to Nadeem and Ismat. There was little they did not already know about each other's lives: their letters, though infrequent, contained all that was of worth. Zubair knew of Shahana's love for her grandchildren, the fulfillment she had found in her affection for them. She knew of the way he had poured his life into the workshop at Kashi; how he, though never appearing in public as a representative of the workshop, had tied his life to it. Faisal had retired some years previously; his son had taken over, but Zubair worked closely with him, and with the workshop here.

And he knew of Nadeem's love for calligraphy, his desire to make the art his life. He had gauged, over the years, the dilemma his son faced, pulled two ways, and still unable to decide whether to follow his heart or his head, his duty towards his family or his passion.

Shahana and Ismat left soon after, and Nadeem could not stay much longer. He was expected back home, because food had been cooked for charity. Nadeem, along with the men servants, would take the cauldrons full of khichdi and roasted meats to the lane outside the local mosque and distribute the food to the poor who thronged the area. He would not be back home till late in the afternoon.

Zubair said he would wait. Meeting Nadeem was his main purpose in coming to Dilli; he would not return without spending some time, at least, in talking to the son he had not seen for so many years.

They agreed to meet at the riverside, away from the settlements. Along the sandy banks of the Yamuna, where fields gave way to scrub and wild grassland and finally to forest, there was little chance of running into anybody who might recognize Zubair.

'Here,' said Nadeem, holding out a bundle wrapped in muslin, when he met Nadeem later that day. 'Malpuas,' he added, as Zubair pulled away the muslin to reveal an inner package crafted from dried dhak leaves. 'We have a cook now who makes the most delicious malpuas. Ammi got him to make some as soon as she got home, because you like malpuas.'

Zubair settled himself against the base of a venerable old gular tree, its branches festooned in clusters of fruit ranging in colour from bright green to yellow, through orange and blush-red. 'I thought she would have forgotten,' he remarked, opening the leaf package to look at the small stack of syrup-soaked fried pancakes, fluffy in the centre, pleasantly chewy along their browned edges. 'Mmm.'

Nadeem watched him eat. 'Ammi remembers a lot about you,' he said, after a while. 'She keeps telling the children about you. What you like to eat, what colours you like in your clothing. There are plenty of stories that Grandmother had told her about you as a child, all your antics and mischief, and Ammi passes them on to her grandchildren.'

Zubair laughed at that, but it was rueful laugh. 'She has already made sure that my grandchildren have no respect for me.' He wagged his head.

'That's not true. Ammi has a lot of respect for you. You can hear it in her words. If she talks about you, it is with affection.'

Zubair looked up, surprised. 'I did not mean that as anything other than a joke,' he said. 'I know how your mother feels.'

'Then? Why do you not write more frequently to her? All your letters come to the workshop, and all you write about is work. Brocades, weaves, naqshas, orders here and deliveries there. There is nothing in your letters for your family. You have forgotten us.'

A stunned silence followed that emotional outburst. Zubair set aside the half-eaten sweets and placed a hand on Nadeem's shoulder. 'I am truly, deeply sorry,' he said, 'if you have felt this way. Nothing interesting happens in my life anyway, you know. It is your mother's letters, full of the news of you and your children, that are enjoyable. I am always hungry for more.'

Nadeem stared into his father's face. One face young, unlined and smooth, the eyes clear and innocent. The other, a mirror of that face as it may be twenty years from now: weathered, older, the eyes calmer and wiser. More knowing. Perhaps not knowing all—not even about oneself, for even that may take a lifetime—but at least not as naïve.

'Yes,' Zubair murmured to himself, even though Nadeem had not said anything, only given him a long look of silent reproach. 'Yes. I suppose she, and you, may be hungry too. Even if the news I share is of no consequence to anyone. I have been remiss. I promise to write more frequently.'

Nadeem could say nothing for the next few minutes. Zubair went back to eating the malpuas, savouring them as one who had not eaten a favourite food for years. But of course, thought Nadeem as he watched his father, it was not as if there were no malpuas to be had in Kashi; there would be, why not. It was not the malpuas. It was the thought behind them, that Shahana had hurried home and ordered that malpuas be made, because the husband who had suddenly appeared in town and who would disappear just as suddenly, liked them.

'I have been told all about your love for calligraphy,' Zubair said when he had finished eating. 'And the corresponding indifference for the workshop.'

Nadeem was beginning to protest, but Zubair cut him short. 'I understand your feelings,' he said, and proceeded to tell Nadeem some of what he had already told Shahana. He was matter-of-fact, agreeing that it was unfair of the family to expect Nadeem to devote himself to one thing when his heart was in another. He commiserated, he listened; and he offered a solution. Mudassar should choose the most promising of the apprentices and train him. Mudassar had none of the talent of his uncle Raheem, but he knew the workshop fairly well. It was essential that he find someone who might eventually succeed him as clerk and manager, advisor and spokesman.

'Mudassar is no naqshband, though,' Nadeem pointed out.

'No, he isn't. A good naqshband is hard to find. What you need is somebody who understands the overall work well, someone who can talk to a client—at the palace, in particular, where they are so finicky. Someone who knows everything, back to front, inside-out. Gulrez was like that, and Raheem. If only there could be another like that…' His eyebrows snapped together suddenly. 'I wonder.' It was said in a whisper, so low that Nadeem barely caught it.

'Wonder what, Abbu?'

Zubair shook his head. 'Nothing. Perhaps it will not come to that. I wish,' he said, smiling at Nadeem, 'to see what your calligraphy looks like. I have heard such praise of it, but your letters are all written in the most prosaic of hands. Will you oblige, my son?'

Nadeem rose to his feet and rummaged around in the undergrowth nearby, finally emerging from it with a long, straight twig in his hand. This became his pen, the soil under the tree his paper. In flamboyant, sharp strokes, he inscribed his name, and then, after a pause to think, he added, *Ghiyaspur, Dilli. By the bank of the river Yamuna as it bends south towards Mathura.*

'Thank you for not adding my name to it,' Zubair said solemnly. 'Best not leave any evidence of my being still alive.' He grinned, but his expression turned solemn again: this time not in jest. 'You are very skilled indeed. I am no expert, but even I can tell. It would be a crime to wrench you from this.'

'Abbu,' Nadeem said later that day, when they were getting ready to part ways, Zubair to return to the obscure sarai he was staying in, 'I—thank you. Thank you for coming. And thank you for talking to me. You—' he ducked his head, embarrassment getting the better of him. 'You are the only one of the family who has not tried to compel me to leave my calligraphy.' He chanced a quick look at Zubair, and the gentleness in his father's face encouraged him to continue speaking. 'Everybody says my calligraphy can be nothing more than a pastime. You are the only one who understands.'

His voice had risen to a strident cry of petulance. Zubair looked on, his gaze sympathetic, until his son had fallen silent.

'Nobody will be benefited by needless harrying and badgering,' he said finally. 'It is not as if you will develop an affinity towards the workshop if you are pushed into it.' He shook his head. 'And for everybody to fret and worry is no use. Worry serves only to destroy.' He smiled suddenly. 'Chinta aisi daakini, kaat kaleja khaaye; Vaid bechaara kya kare, kahaan tak dawa lagaaye.'

Nadeem, caught off-guard, blinked. 'What? What was

that? A verse about worry? Say it again; you were too quick.'

Zubair recited the couplet again, this time slowly, stopping briefly after every phrase.

'Anxiety is that thief, that cuts away your liver and chews at it. What will a mere vaid do, his medicine will be all futile.' Nadeem was so delighted, he clapped. 'I am impressed, Abbu. I had no idea you were a poet too. That's excellent.'

'It's not mine.' Zubair grinned. 'And the man, though he speaks in these couplets, is venerated not for his poetry but his wisdom.'

'And who might this be? A mystic? One of the great Sufis, like Hazrat Nizamuddin Auliya or Qutb Sahib? Chiragh-e-Dehli?'

'No. A julaaha, a weaver, originally from Kashi, but now living in the north, near Gorakhpur. A simple old man, but very wise. His name is Kabirdas.'

'A weaver? A friend of yours, Abbu?'

Zubair shook his head. 'No, no friend. In fact, Kabir says he has no friends and no enemies. All he wishes is the good of everybody.'

Nadeem raised an eyebrow. 'A weaver, and a philosopher? I would not have thought the two would go hand in hand.'

Zubair responded with a shrug. 'Who is to say what path a man's thoughts will take him down? And Kabir has quite a following. Such a following, indeed, that it brought down on him enemies who got Sikandar Lodhi to sentence him to death. Not once, but thrice.'

It was an interesting tale, and one that Zubair knew well, even though he had not been witness to the dramatic, even fantastic, events that had taken place nearly twenty years earlier. 'That was just after I had reached Kashi, in the wake of my supposed death,' Zubair explained. 'I was terrified of being seen by Sikandar Lodhi's men; it was all too fresh back then.'

Even twenty years ago, Kabir had acquired quite a

following, and those of people from both the major faiths: Hindus and Muslims alike flocked to him, drawn by his simple philosophies. Do no evil, do not hanker after worldly goods. Be humble, put your heart and soul into all that you do, and never put off what must be done. Be patient, be soft-spoken, look for God within yourself.

Simple words, easily understood, and expressed in metaphors and idioms that the common people could relate to. This was a man like them, neither wealthy nor well-born, who knew hardship and want as they did. He did not speak high-blown, mystifying philosophy, he did not surround himself with an aura of superiority.

Kabir became popular—much to the horror of the guardians of both the religions he so heretically warned against. The Muslim clerics and the Hindu priests, for once, were united: they loathed Kabir equally, and so it was that when Sikandar Lodhi came to Jaunpur in the wake of his conquest of that city, a delegation of pandits and maulvis journeyed from Kashi to Jaunpur, a distance of some thirty kos. They pleaded for mercy, they begged Sikandar Lodhi to come to Kashi and do justice. Punish the heretic, O Sultan, they said, for he blasphemes and derides our religions.

'Sikandar Lodhi came to Kashi: I suppose he was curious,' Zubair said. 'The pandits, I think, could probably not have influenced him much, but the maulvis were enough. They complained so vociferously of Kabir's heresies, an orthodox Muslim like the Lodhi was incensed enough to condemn Kabir. He sentenced the weaver to be drowned in the Ganga.'

But the river did not comply: Kabirdas floated up, wet but very much alive. Then Sikandar Lodhi sentenced Kabir to be burnt alive. This too failed: the fire left him unscathed. An elephant was then brought along, to crush the prisoner underfoot. Again, Kabir was left unhurt: the animal backed away, and would not harm the man.

'There are some,' said Zubair, 'who fervently believe that

Sikandar Lodhi did not try just three times to kill Kabir, but again and again. Dozens of times, dozens of innovative and gruesome ways. But Kabir was indestructible, and finally the Lodhi had to bow his head. Kabir was banished from Kashi, and left the city soon after. He has wandered all across the Doab, the plains between the Ganga and the Yamuna, these past years, and now he lives in the village of Maghar, near Gorakhpur.'

'That must be a full life, don't you think?' Zubair said. 'To have influenced so many. To have converted a king, to have defeated death.' He smiled to himself. 'But not for me, I think. I am content with leading a life less full.'

Nadeem laughed. 'You, not a full life? The adventures you have had!'

Nadeem sat cross-legged on his mattress, a clean sheet of paper before him. On his right, within easy reach, sat the qalamdaan, a rectangular pen case of carved wood. Inside were the two qalams, the reed pens he worked with; beside them, in the form of a little box with a hinged lid, fitting into the pen case, was the dawaat, the ink well.

Nadeem had spent the past few minutes working the mixture of kohl, gum and water into ink. He poured it carefully into the dawaat, and then, having selected a sheet of paper and positioned it atop the rough pad of paper he used as a support, he settled down to work. His right leg bent, the paper resting on his knee, he carefully drew up ink into the qalam and drew a line, tapering as it went, curving and broadening into the swirling belly of a letter.

This piece of calligraphy was a panel that would be transferred to stone, which would be then carved for a nobleman's tomb. It was painstaking work, and he had to keep in mind how it would look translated to stone, going from two dimensions to three. Hard work, taxing work. Work he adored.

His attention was focused so entirely on his work that he failed to notice the movement at the door. Ismat saw him bent over his work, and waited until he had straightened after completing the downward flourish of the letter he had been crafting. Then, in what she recognized as a tiny break between one letter and the next, one word and the next, one refilling of ink and the next, she cleared her throat.

'Abba was not pleased that you hurried away like that yesterday,' she said.

Nadeem had expected something like this; Ismat did not approach him for anything other than complaints or requests. Requests, he knew by now, were invariably channeled through the children. He may not be the most doting of fathers but he was susceptible to their smiles and cajoling. One of them would be sent to Nadeem, bearing a gift—a sweet, perhaps, or a flower plucked for him from the garden—and once there was a likelihood of him being in a good mood, Ismat would put in an appearance and make her request known.

Today, the children had not been in evidence. Their mother was in a peevish mood, and had come prepared for an argument. Nadeem heaved a sigh of exasperation and set his work aside.

'I waited until everything was over, the last cauldron was empty. It wasn't as if I left in the middle of it all.' He looked up at her. 'If you've come here to pick a fight,' he added, 'please accept my capitulation. Whatever you think I've done, I apologize, even if I am not really to blame. I simply do not have the time or the inclination for a conversation with you.'

Ismat looked, for the briefest of moments, as if she would either slap him or fly into hysterics. He saw her struggle visibly to contain herself. Finally, with a cry of fury that rang within the four walls of the room, she swept out of it.

Circumstances tie us to each other, Nadeem wrote to Zubair. *I am beholden to my uncle Waqar for teaching me the art of calligraphy: he is my ustad, and you know what the Hindus say about gurus? They are owed a guru dakshina. Nothing they can ask of one whom they taught is too much. Also, there is the fact that without my uncle's help, you might never have been able to escape, all those years ago. My uncle is deserving of my gratitude, and my marrying Ismat was part of my guru dakshina. As for her, she lives for the wealth that the workshop generates. Which, I suppose, is why she frets so much if she sees any signs of my ignoring the workshop.*

Help me, Abbu. Tell me what your Kabirdas would say, what words of wisdom, to live with this? How does one live without love?

It was several months before a reply came. Zubair, despite his promises to write, was not the best of correspondents: his letters were stilted, and he did not have the easy way of recounting incidents, of being entertaining and warm, that characterized the letters of Shahana. But in this letter, after the hurried assurance that he was well, he went on to answer what Nadeem had meant as a rhetorical question.

I do not know if Kabir has said anything specific about relations between husband and wife. But he does say, often enough, that one must look on all with love and goodwill. It is difficult, especially when two people in a relationship are tied to each other by bonds that are not of love. But love can take other forms, can it not, than mere romantic love? I know I am undeserving of your mother, though her love for me I can never doubt. However, the esteem I feel for her far outweighs any love I could have felt: she has been, for many years, my greatest friend and companion. To me, that has become my love for her. Not romantic love, but something else. It is enough. Find a love, perhaps in your children, perhaps in your calligraphy, that will support you and be the love your wife may not offer.

Nadeem shook his head. Abbu was being obtuse. How could children take the place a woman should have in his heart? But Zubair was right about the calligraphy: his love for his art *did* warm his heart. If only he did not feel the need for something beyond.

The first of two blows fell just a few days after that letter had arrived from Kashi. Nadeem was getting ready in the morning to go to the workshop when a servant arrived from Raheem's home, panting and distressed. Raheem had passed away during the night, slipping gently and peacefully from life to death.

They had been expecting it; he was an old and very frail man, and had been ailing these past few weeks—but it still came as a shock. Shahana remembered how he had helped when Zubair had been imprisoned. Waqar came to the funeral, and praised the old naqshband's loyalty, courage, and sheer competence.

'But what will you do now that Raheem is gone?' Waqar said when he and Nadeem were returning from the graveyard later that day, after the funeral.

'There is Mudassar. He knows the trade like the back of his hand. And he has already identified one of the apprentices as a successor. Junaid is very good at his work, and Mudassar is training him well.'

'That is good. But Mudassar is no naqshband. And a brocade workshop, I gather, is not likely to succeed if it does not have a good naqshband. Your grandfather always said that more than half the secret of the workshop's success lay in the skill of Raheem and his father.'

Nadeem nodded in a non-committal way, but later that week, once Mudassar was back at the workshop after the obsequies for Raheem had been completed, Nadeem brought up the topic with him.

'You are here, and if Allah wills it, you will be here for many years still,' he said. 'Enough time for you to bring Junaid up to scratch. What we need is a naqshband like Raheem was.'

'Time yet,' Mudassar said. 'When I travel next to Kashi, I will ask your father if there is anyone he recommends. After all, whether the naqshband is here or in Kashi, it hardly matters, does it?'

'Didn't Raheem have any sons?' Nadeem burst out. 'That would have solved all our problems, a man with the ability and the talent inherited from a master!'

Mudassar shook his head wordlessly, but there was a guarded look in his eyes that Nadeem did not notice.

ଓ

The second blow fell exactly a week from that conversation, and this one obliterated even the shock and anguish Raheem's death had caused Nadeem. Mudassar got drenched in the rain while returning home from the workshop, and got a bad cold and fever as a result.

It might still have not been a disaster if Mudassar had not tried to make light of his illness. When the fever had abated after two days, he insisted on getting up. Not just getting up; getting out, and going to offer namaaz, to thank the Almighty for healing him. He refused his wife's pleas to rest, and helped by a boy from the neighbourhood, he went to the local mosque.

The boy was a gentle soul, earnest and conscientious. He was not, however, especially sturdy. And the offering of namaaz, involving frequent kneeling and rising, took its toll on an already severely weakened Mudassar. Getting to his feet after a prostration, Mudassar swayed suddenly, dizzy: the boy beside him reached out a hand to steady him, but it was futile. Mudassar was big-built, at least double the boy's weight. He crashed to the paved floor of the mosque, the back of his skull hitting the ground with a sickening whump.

He was brought home, deeply unconscious and bleeding from the skull. The family's physician, having examined Mudassar, suggested some decoctions that may help reduce the bleeding and act as a tonic. 'Keep him comfortable,' he said. There was an air of fatalism about the way he said it. A less tactful man might have said it was fortunate that Mudassar had fallen in the midst of saying his prayers: what more auspicious way to quit this world?

'He will be all right,' Nadeem reassured Mudassar's distraught wife. 'We will spare no expense. Allah will be merciful, Bibi. Trust in his mercy.'

But that evening, once he was back home, Nadeem wrote to Zubair. *Help me, Abbu*, was the gist of it. *Help me, because I am all alone now in a workshop I know too little about.*

17

The days went by, and Mudassar showed no sign of improvement. Nadeem wished, many times a day, that Mudassar would wake soon, and be strong and healthy. Then his conscience would needle him, reminding him that his wishes and his prayers were rooted in selfishness. Between the guilt, the fear, and the worry, Nadeem abandoned both workshop and calligraphy. He would sit at the workshop through the day—it was impossible to stay at home, with Ismat keeping an eagle eye on him—but he could not bring himself to lift his pen and do any work. As for the workshop's activities, they went on, somehow. Junaid, though talented and conscientious, was still a raw recruit.

Zubair, fortunately, seemed to appreciate the urgency. His letter arrived, brought by a special courier, within two weeks of Nadeem having written to him. *I wish I could come and handle the workshop myself,* Zubair wrote, *but you know that is impossible. But I have a suspicion that there is someone in Dilli who might be able to help. I have written to this person, and, to save time, have asked them to get in touch with you if they feel they can come to your rescue.*

Nadeem re-read the letter, and then read it all over again. Zubair's words were mystifying: why did he not say who this person was, who might help? Was it someone important? So important, that they might be doing Zubair a big favour by condescending to help his son? Or was there something else, something Zubair did not wish at this stage to reveal to Nadeem? Was this person a naqshband, or one who might, as Raheem or Mudassar had done, be able to supervise the workshop and be its face for the outside world?

It was all so confusingly ambiguous. Nadeem did not know what to make of it. Junaid, too, had not the slightest idea. Perhaps Zubair was calling in a favour from someone whose reaction he could not be sure of? All Nadeem could do was to wait and watch.

Five days after Zubair's letter, there came a large packet for Nadeem. The boy who brought it carried also a sealed letter addressed to Nadeem.

It was Junaid who brought the package into Nadeem's office and told him that the bearer had said he was to wait for an answer.

When Junaid had returned to his work, Nadeem glanced at the sealed letter, but did not open it: he was more curious about what the packet contained. He began to undo the strings that bound the long cylinder of unbleached cotton.

It was not one large sheet of paper rolled into a scroll, but several. Four sheets, each about a yard wide and a third high. Nadeem spread them out on the top of the slope-topped desk in his room and removed the thin layer of protective muslin that had been placed above the topmost sheet. Below it, revealed to his astonished gaze, was a shikargah naqsha.

And a shikargah naqsha like none he had ever seen before. As he peered at it, Nadeem marvelled at both the workmanship—the fine lines, the confident strokes, the perfect proportions—as well as the creativity of the piece. This was not the usual shikargah scene, with its tigers and deer pursued through a forest by hunters on horseback. Here was a deer, a fine stag, sporting a grand pair of antlers as it stepped delicately through a forest of banyans and peepals and mango trees: he could see, when he lifted the sheet of paper up and scrutinized it carefully, how each leaf, each branch, each tiny detail of every tree resembled the original tree enough to let there be no mistaking what it was meant to be.

A spray of rosettes showed, glimpsed between the aerial roots of the banyan: a leopard, its tail curved around one of the hanging roots, its eyes watching the deer. Higher up, perched on the branches of the peepal tree, sat a troop of monkeys: mothers with infants clinging to them, boisterous young ones playing among the leaves, a venerable old patriarch dozing against the bole of the tree.

There were more creatures: birds, both in the trees and in the air; a pack of wild dogs, racing through the undergrowth; a sloth bear, sharpening its claws on the trunk of a mango tree.

The drawings followed the stylized forms usual in the naqshas he had seen, but that form had been adopted and adapted by an obviously highly skilled and creative naqshband.

Nadeem let out his breath—he had not even realized he had been holding it all this while—and turned to the next sheet.

When he sat back a while later, his head was spinning. The three sheets below the forest scene were also shikargah patterns, each depicting scenes from nature, but like the first design, these too were unconventional. More so, even, than that magical little scene from the jungle; for these depicted animals and birds and other creatures in settings as he had never imagined before. A mountainscape, with a markhor, its spiral horns vividly etched, standing atop a knoll, with marmots and pheasants and partridge between tussocks of grass. A herd of elegant blackbuck crossing a desert, the sky above the undulating sand dunes etched with a flight of birds, while a pair of desert foxes played amidst driftwood.

And, lastly, a seascape. Palm trees swayed on a shoreline in the background, but the focus was on the waves in front: huge waves, frothing and towering, revealing a whale here, a shoal of fish there. Another shoal here, and sea birds poised just above, searching with eager eyes for a morsel. One gull held a tiny fish in its razor beak.

Whoever had made these was a master naqshband. Nadeem felt a sense of awe so intense, he could not resist the temptation to examine each pattern again. These had been made by someone with not just the skill and talent of an accomplished artist, but someone, too, who loved nature.

Nadeem set the naqshas aside and unearthed the letter from under them. Breaking the seal, he unfolded the paper.

Nadeem Sahib,

I received a letter from your esteemed father in Kashi, and he tells me that perhaps you may welcome these naqshas. Not just the naqshas, but some assistance as well.

For more than ten years now, I have assisted my father, Raheem Qizilbash, in his work. He did not allow me to accompany him to the workshop, but I feel he succeeded in bringing home to me much of the workshop. With the naqshas I have made over the years, and with the loom my father allowed me to set up at home, for me to get a sense of how the weaving is done, I believe I can—in all modesty—say that I know a good deal of what he knew.

I have chosen, from among the many naqshas I have made, four that I believe will appeal to you. I recall my father telling me you were fond of shikargah naqshas, but that you did not like the idea of animals being hunted. I trust these naqshas, then, will be to your liking.

Also, I trust that this will encourage you to give me an opportunity to prove myself. Your father informs me that you need someone by your side who might continue my father's work. I do not presume to think I could replace my father, for there was none as capable as him; but I assure you, should you allow me the opportunity, I will do all I can to show myself worthy of your trust.

If you would like to accept my services, I can come and meet you at the workshop today itself. The boy who brings you this letter and the naqshas has been instructed to wait for your answer.

May Allah uphold you and preserve you.

The letter ended there. There was no signature.

Nadeem re-read it, and then sat, staring into space, trying to make sense of it.

Raheem had always been reticent about his personal life, his family and his home, but Nadeem had been under the impression that he had no sons, only daughters. So who was this man who wrote, claiming to be Raheem's son? But surely a son would have been present at Raheem's funeral? Nadeem could not remember anybody being pointed out as such, though there had been other relatives, brothers and cousins and more distant relatives. When Nadeem had bemoaned the absence of sons among Raheem's offspring, Mudassar too had not denied it. He, after all, was Raheem's nephew; would he not know if Raheem had sons or not?

And why, even after Nadeem had pleaded with him so many times to recruit a replacement, had Raheem not thought of bringing his own son to the workshop? If the young man was so accomplished—and that would be apparent to anyone who saw the naqshas he had sent—why had Raheem not considered him? Or Mudassar?

But perhaps there had been other reasons. It hurt Nadeem to think it, but it might have been that Raheem had hoped for a better future than with this workshop for his talented son; perhaps he had wanted the younger man to go to another workshop, not spend his life attached to this one? The thought was galling. On the other hand, how old was this so far anonymous son? The naqshas were not the work of a child; an adolescent, at least, had made them. A youth past the age of being taken on as an apprentice at a workshop. Then why was he still sitting at home? Was he, perhaps, in some way, inadequate? Perhaps of poor moral fibre? A drunkard, an opium addict?

There was something fishy about all of this. But who was he to quibble, thought Nadeem, looking greedily through the naqshas again.

Whatever it was, this was a ray of hope.

He had no choice. A twig was being held out to a

drowning man; he would be mad to not reach for it. Taking a sheet of paper from his desk, Nadeem began writing a letter.

The boy who had delivered the packet took Nadeem's letter, and Nadeem settled down to wait. Raheem's home was not very far: it would take the boy perhaps a quarter of an hour, a few minutes more if he was prone to dawdle, to get there. It would take the sender of the packet some time to read the letter and to set out. Perhaps he might be at the workshop in an hour's time.

An hour came, and went. Another, and then another. The sun began its downward descent to the horizon. The looms began to go slower, work winding down for the day. Nadeem, unable to stay confined to his office, went out into the garden. He paced about under the trees, past the row of jasmine bushes, up to the gate that opened on to the lane outside.

The last of the weavers had gone long before the sun had set; they could not work, after all, once the light had begun to fade. Junaid came, hesitantly, to ask if he need stay back. Nadeem shook his head. 'No, why should you? Go; I will see you tomorrow.'

He sent the door keeper home to his hut tucked away behind the workshop: there was no need for him to wait around needlessly.

Another half-hour went past. Nadeem wondered what had happened. Had Raheem's son changed his mind? Had he developed cold feet and decided this was not, after all, for him?

It was just as he was beginning to think he had been duped, that he heard the unmistakable sound of a bullock cart: the squeak of its wheels, the tinkling of the bells round the bullocks' necks. Nadeem hurried forward, eyes bright with anticipation. It could only be him, Raheem's son. But why had he come in a cart? Had he brought more naqshas? So many that he had had to hire a bullock cart to transport them all? Or was there perhaps something wrong with him, some disability that did not allow him to walk much?

Nadeem burst through the gate and onto the lane outside just in time to see the curtain at the back of the bullock cart being lifted aside. A woman stepped out: a maid, obviously, from her clothing and demeanour.

A maid?

And behind her was another woman. Slim and petite, a young woman perhaps, though she was swathed so completely in veils that it was impossible to see her face. She jumped down from the cart with an insouciance and a disregard for dignity that might have drawn censure from most, and having drawn a couple of coins from inside her clothing, handed them over to the cart driver.

The cart went its way, and Nadeem stared wordlessly at the visitors. The maid stepped aside, making way for her mistress. The other woman walked briskly up to Nadeem and stopped in front of him. 'Thank you for your letter,' she said, in a firm, assured voice. 'I am Zarina. I am glad you liked my naqshas. Shall we go in, then? I did not think it would be decorous to call on you when the workshop was full.'

18

She was sixteen years old, and she had several older sisters. Zarina was the youngest of the lot, and her father had always liked her the most. 'Ammi says he pampered me silly, but the truth is, I was the only one of us siblings who had any sort of talent with naqshas. Naturally Abba was fond of me: he saw me as the last hope of the family.'

An exaggeration, Nadeem thought. Daughters were to be married off, to become wives and mothers, not to nurture a family talent or a profession. If this Zarina thought Raheem favoured her because he saw in her a way of keeping the art of the naqshas alive in his family, she was deluding herself. Raheem had been a fond father, no more.

Zarina laughed. 'I am joking, of course,' she said, even though he had not said he doubted her. 'Abba taught me the art, but not so that I could work.' The amusement was gone, evaporated as quickly as it had arisen. 'Ammi disapproves, but when your father's letter arrived, I thought: here is the perfect opportunity to do something with these naqshas. They have been lying around at home, all unused, these past couple of years, so why not put them to good use?'

Zarina was a voluble woman, open and frank, her vivacity a far cry from the taciturn and withdrawn demeanour of her father. Raheem had been a grave, quiet man, a man of few words. His daughter was the opposite.

But not in her love for the naqshas. Once she had settled into Nadeem's office—the maid sitting nearby, a stolid and silent symbol of propriety—Zarina had asked for the naqshas she had sent him earlier that day. With them spread out before her, she had spoken long and in great detail. The seascape pattern would work well in just two colours, a dull blue and a silver. But this one, the forest: this they could work in many more colours. She suggested some, and proceeded to explain how much effort each combination might involve. Also, accordingly, how much they might charge.

Even though her naqshas had convinced Nadeem of her talent, he was sceptical about her knowledge of the trade. It was too much to expect that someone so young—and a woman!—might know anything beyond what was logically connected to the naqshas. He conceded, privately, that having Raheem for a father, and being so inclined towards the art and skill, she might have made an effort to learn. But how much?

He set out to find out. Over the next hour, he asked her questions, he set problems before her. He trawled through years of memories, dredged up every single question he had heard put to his grandfather, to Raheem, and to Mudassar. How would it affect a pattern if this element had to be changed, or that? What effect would it have on the cost, on the time required to deliver it, on the final pattern? What patterns were most likely to appeal to whom?

In his perambulations through the garden while he had waited for this mysterious offspring of Raheem's, Nadeem had had ample time to think over these questions. He had realized, even then, that he would need to probe, to gauge the suitability of the man—as he supposed—for the post. Now, even though he questioned Zarina, he could not help but wonder why he bothered to do so. It was not as if he would employ her. As a naqshband, perhaps, it would be possible. She might work in the comfort and privacy of her own home, and send the readied naqshas to the workshop with a note explaining each pattern. But to have her replace someone like Mudassar, meeting clients, talking to them, answering their questions?

It was unthinkable.

And yet.

Yet, she was undeniably knowledgeable. Confident, articulate, intelligent beyond anything he could have imagined of a woman, and that too so young. He probed further, trying to discover more about her, why she wanted to do this work. It was not as if they were in financial difficulties; she was the only child now living with her widowed mother, and they were comfortably off. But she found it increasingly hard to just sit around at home and draw naqshas that no eyes but her own ever saw.

'I want more,' she said, baldly.

Nadeem had never met a woman like her. She was so refreshingly different, her candour so much more alluring than the artificial demureness of others. He wanted to get to know her better, and the best way for that, he decided, would be to get her to start working for them. Before the evening was through, he had formally employed her, and had promised that he would get the weaving started on at least one of her naqshas within the coming week. 'Please begin making more,' he added. 'It will be good to get some new naqshas into our business.'

Nadeem's announcement, that he had employed Raheem's daughter as a naqshband, was greeted with mixed emotions at his home. Shahana, though she rejoiced because her son was relieved, was inwardly sceptical: perhaps she doubted, as most would, that a woman could be as skilled a naqshband as a man. She feared, too, that Nadeem was being complacent. To her, it seemed he thought his worries were over now that he had hired Zarina; he set too much store by this wisp of a girl.

The mother worried for her son, fretted that he might fail.

With the wife, there was no such consideration. Years ago, soon after they had been married, Ismat had realized that Nadeem and she had nothing in common. No love, no companionship, no desire for any of those emotions that lovers, or spouses, sought in their partners. He wanted his calligraphy, and she contented herself with wanting a good life. Clothes, jewellery, the comforts of a large and prosperous household: all the things that could only be bought with a sizeable income.

For Ismat, the brocade workshop was and could be the only possible occupation for her husband. She hated that he preferred calligraphy to brocade; that he was good at it made her hate it even more. No matter how many works Nadeem might sell, no matter how wealthy the patrons who commissioned him to create inscriptions for them, Ismat could not imagine Nadeem's calligraphy ever being a replacement for the brocade workshop.

'But your Abba is a calligrapher, and he has been able to provide well for all of you,' Nadeem had pointed out on more than one occasion. Always, Ismat had retorted that it was different; Waqar was a genius in her eyes. There was no better qaatib in Dilli than her father.

The announcement that a highly skilled and very competent new employee had joined the workshop should come as a relief to Ismat, who seemed to dread the closure of the workshop with every passing day. But Nadeem knew his wife well, and had guessed that the subsequent revelation—that the new employee was a woman—would not be welcome at all.

'You tell me that your new naqshband is a woman because you seek to anger me, is it?' she said. 'Because you want me to be jealous? Well, I am not.'

Nadeem was taken aback. Before he could even think of a reply, Ismat continued. 'For there to be jealousy, there must be attachment.' She paused meaningfully, then, without adding more to that allusion, continued. 'Do not disgrace yourself, I pray. If you must have dealings with that woman, be discreet. Marry her.'

'Marry her!' Nadeem burst out laughing. 'Ismat, where will your imagination take you? The very thought!' Shaking his head in sheer bafflement, he left the house. Behind him, Ismat scowled, watching him as he crossed the courtyard and into the corridor, out of sight. When he was gone, she went inside to tell Shahana that she thought she might visit her parents today. It had been many days since the children had last been to Khizrabad, to their maternal grandparents' home; no doubt both generations were missing each other. Would Shahana like to come too?

☙

That afternoon, a visitor came to the workshop just as Nadeem was settling down to an after-lunch stint of work on the calligraphy he was doing. It was Waqar, standing unsmiling at the doorway to Nadeem's office. 'Can you spare an hour?' he asked. 'Come out with me, I want to talk to you.'

He had a bullock cart waiting outside, and gestured to Nadeem to climb in after him. 'Bagh-e-Jud,' Waqar told the cart-driver, and sat back. He glanced at Nadeem. 'We can talk in peace there,' he said. 'Without crowds of eager eavesdroppers listening to every word that is exchanged.'

Nadeem wondered what it was that Waqar might wish to be the topic of such a private conversation. It must have something to do with Ismat's visit to her parents today; she must have gone weeping to her father, complaining of ill-usage and injustice.

The Bagh-e-Jud was a vast parkland where Muhammad Shah, the third of the Sayyid rulers, had chosen to be buried, and after him, the first of the Lodhis, Bahlol. It was an expanse dotted with green, the spreading canopies of banyan and tamarind, neem and mango trees playing hide-and-seek with the domed tombs of the Sultans who lay buried here. Waqar got the cart-driver to let them down near the farthest of the tombs, the octagonal mausoleum of Muhammad Shah Sayyid. It was a beautiful tomb, well-proportioned and elegant. Nadeem had been inside before, to gaze in awe at the loveliness of the domed ceiling, its interior white painted with red and blue motifs. Today, they did not stop at the

Sayyid's tomb; Waqar simply went past it, instead turning to the right and taking the path towards the tomb of Bahlol Lodhi.

This was a building Nadeem had never been to before: he had only seen it from afar, a domed tomb of grey stone, its façade relieved by staid carving. More beautiful than the carving were the tiles in shades of bright blue, arranged in neat, geometric patterns around the top of the arched doorway.

'Oh,' said Nadeem, stopping suddenly. 'Can we, please, have a look at that?' He pointed to a building, domed and as large as Bahlol Lodhi's tomb, that sat just opposite it. 'I presume that is the gateway Sikandar Lodhi built?' He had heard that, some years earlier, Sikandar Lodhi had done his filial duty by commissioning the building of a grand gateway and mosque, to function as an adjunct to his father's tomb. Nadeem had seen it from a distance, its grey dome mirroring the dome of the Sultan's tomb beyond. It did not look very grand from a way off, but perhaps it might be better up close.

Waqar nodded in a non-committal way, as if it mattered little to him. He had not yet broached the topic on which he wanted to speak, and Nadeem felt a twinge of humiliation. Was his obvious excitement at wandering through this miniature necropolis too childish? Had it put Waqar off talking? His uncle's expression was impossible to read: perhaps pensive, perhaps a little tired.

Nadeem asked him, a little diffidently, what it was he wanted to say.

'We'll talk,' Waqar replied. 'Let's go on. We'll sit outside the mosque.'

From the garden outside, a flight of stone steps ascended to the gateway. The gateway itself was impressive in a forbidding sort of way, its solid stone façade sparsely decorated, and its sides battered, sloping in a style reminiscent of a fortress. Nadeem looked around him as he walked through: it was large and daunting, but that was all. It was, after all, just a gateway to the Sultan's tomb. The tomb was all, the gateway nothing.

The doorway opposite framed Bahlol Lodhi's tomb prettily. Nadeem stepped through it, paused to admire the view, and glanced briefly towards his right, where a row of inconsequential stone rooms stood, probably meant as a shelter for people visiting the Bagh-e-Jud. A passing glance to his left, where the row of rooms was mirrored—and he stopped, frozen.

Perpendicular to the back wall of the gateway stood the mosque, a small one topped with three domes, its façade pierced by five arches. The arches, the interior, the vaulted ceilings: all were covered in incised plaster, slathered on very thickly while still wet, and then cut painstakingly into patterns. Flowers, geometrical patterns, curling tendrils of vines. Calligraphy. Yards of verses from the Quran. Each letter perfectly placed, perfectly shaped, perfectly incised.

'Exquisite, is it not?'

Nadeem whirled about. He had forgotten all about Waqar, but there he was, a rare smile creasing the deeply tanned skin around his eyes, his teeth brown with the paan he was so fond of chewing.

'I have never seen anything so beautiful,' Nadeem admitted. 'It must have taken a long time to make, and many men.' He walked slowly along the front of the mosque, minutely examining the calligraphy that covered the arches. 'So beautifully done. Do you know who the qaatib was?'

'A man I know.' Suddenly, the smile was gone. Waqar's tone did not invite further questions; perhaps he did not wish to have a discussion on calligraphy and its practitioners. 'Come, Nadeem. Let us sit here. There's nobody around, we'll be on our own.'

They sat down, leaning their backs against the cold, hard

stone. Gazing with unseeing eyes at the mosque opposite them, the finely worked plaster of its façade thrown into stark relief by the bright sunlight washing over it.

'Ismat came home this morning,' Waqar said. 'Of course you have guessed that is why I came to see you.'

Of course.

'She thinks I intend to begin an affair with this woman, Raheem's daughter?' Nadeem shook his head. 'Surely you do not imagine that too?'

Waqar shook his head. 'Ya Allah, do you think me as dramatic and highly strung as my daughter? Ismat may be the apple of my eye, but I am aware of her ability to make a mountain out of a molehill.' He put a hand on Nadeem's shoulder. 'No, I am not weighed down by that fear. It was just that I was pondering this latest development, and I thought I should talk to you, man to man.'

Nadeem waited.

'Ismat told me that it was your father who contacted Raheem's daughter—what is her name?'

'Zarina.'

'Zarina. Zubair told her that you needed a new naqshband, and she came in response to his letter? She must hold him in great esteem.'

Nadeem had not thought of that; it had not even occurred to him. But one thing he had sensed: Zarina's passion for her work. He thought back to the previous evening, and to the sound of Zarina's voice, low and oddly deep for a woman, as she discussed the naqshas she had made. The enthusiasm that crept into her tone when she explained this part of her naqsha, or that; the excitement that was obvious in the way she gestured when talking of how this line may be worked in silver thread, and that in gold—'She loves her work with a passion,' he said. 'It is to her like worship, I think. All-consuming, all-powerful.'

He looked up, to see that Waqar was gazing at him with something like empathy in his eyes. Empathy, or pity?

For a moment after Nadeem had fallen silent, Waqar said nothing.

Then: 'Like you. You love your work with a passion. Was that why you agreed to take on her naqshas? Because you saw something of yourself in her?'

'Her work is good.'

Waqar nodded. And continued to nod, as if he was listening to something his mind was telling him. As if some thought had crossed his mind, and that it appealed to him.

'Anyhow,' he squinted up at a black kite that was circling high above, riding the thermals, 'I had thought, once, that this was going to be an unpleasant business for all of us. You, torn between duty and love. All of us trying to force you into keeping the workshop going, while all you wanted was your calligraphy.' He had been saying all of that with his face tilted up to the sky, as if he were addressing that faraway kite, not Nadeem beside him. Now, however, he turned back to Nadeem.

'I can see that you are making an effort to keep the workshop going, and I appreciate that. I appreciate, also, the fact that you just may not have an aptitude for the brocade business after all. Perhaps, no matter how hard you try, you may never be able to grasp all the nuances of managing the workshop.'

Nadeem stared, astounded at what he saw as a volte face. He opened his mouth to speak, then shut it again because Waqar had not yet finished.

'I don't want you to think me irredeemably obstinate or stuck in my ways,' he continued. 'So I have a proposition. Keep the workshop going, even if you do not supervise it. Use Zarina's naqshas, commission more naqshas, get an experienced foreman, whatever it takes to maintain the standards your great-grandmother and your grandfather had set up. Help the workshop stay profitable, and I will do all I can to help you turn your calligraphy into a profitable venture. I will recommend you to my patrons, I will show your work far and wide. I will get you custom.'

It was not until much later that it occurred to Nadeem that Waqar's generous offer was really a way of safeguarding his own interests. After all, Ismat's marriage to Nadeem had been a way of ensuring a comfortable life for Ismat: a life not far removed from the pampered childhood she had known. Now, Waqar had probably realized that with Zubair's support and Zarina's talent, Nadeem was on his way to stabilizing the workshop. Between them, over the years, Aslam, then Raheem and Mudassar had helped the workshop back into the good books of the palace. The future looked bright, even without Nadeem's reluctant supervision. To help him with his calligraphy, to get him clients who may pay handsomely, would ultimately help in bolstering Nadeem's income.

But at that moment all that Nadeem saw was generosity, benevolence. An olive branch extended, a helping hand put out.

'Thank you,' he said. 'I would be grateful.'

Things settled soon enough into a pattern, a pattern that Nadeem found very much to his liking.

Shahana, in a moment of insight, had suggested that Junaid might be sent to Kashi to be trained at the workshop there, and Nadeem, recognizing a good idea when it was presented to him, had written to Zubair. Zubair had agreed readily enough. Junaid, therefore, had gone to Kashi, and could be gone for several months. It did mean that now Nadeem was obliged to take more of an interest—even if it was a forced interest—in the work of the brocade weaving; but the thought that this was only temporary, and that Junaid would be better equipped to handle the workshop when he returned, made it an easier burden to bear.

One thing he realized soon enough: it was impossible to expect Zarina's naqshas to be put into practice without having her come to the workshop. Initially, Zarina sent detailed notes along with her naqshas, but the weavers had too many questions. Nadeem painstakingly wrote out the questions and sent them to Zarina; she wrote back with her answers, which he then had to read out to the weavers. Who, of course, in the way of most workers, had further questions. Also, until their questions had all been answered, they found it difficult to even begin work on the pattern.

Eventually, Nadeem threw in the towel. It was getting increasingly frustrating, both for him as well as for the weavers. There was only one thing to do: Zarina must come to the workshop every time she handed in a naqsha, so that she could meet the weavers and discuss it with them. She may bring whoever she wished, a maid, her mother, a chaperone, and of course she would be veiled throughout. But come she must; they could not go on thus.

To his relief, Zarina agreed. Perhaps she too had found this endless correspondence a futile and tiring exercise.

The weavers were excited, though doubtful. That she was Raheem's offspring counted for a lot; and they had already seen her naqshas. But a woman? In the faces ranged around the workshop, in the eyes that watched as she stepped over the threshold, there was amazement. Some of these men, of course, must think her forward for stepping out of her home; others might be more forgiving. But all of them, to a man, doubted her ability—in spite of those naqshas—to take the place even of a stripling like Junaid, let alone her own father.

It took Zarina no more than a few hours to break down their resistance. She was, in some ways, like Raheem: she had that same ability to talk to the weavers in their own language, to make them feel she was one of them. And yet not: also someone to be respected. Nadeem, standing on one side as she talked to a small group of weavers, found himself marvelling at the flexible way in which she was able to change her style, her way of speaking. Now gentle, appreciative of the experience and wisdom of those who had been working at the looms for far longer than she had been alive. Now authoritative, a skilled naqshband who knew her craft and all it entailed. She chuckled softly at a joke made by one of the weavers; she was clear-voiced and sharp in disagreeing with someone who tried to push forward an opinion on a subject he knew little about.

'They're not eating out of your hand yet,' Nadeem said in a murmur when he saw Zarina and her maid out to the bullock cart that stood outside. 'But they are far more amenable than I thought they would be.'

'It's all because of Abba. He was very popular among the weavers; all of them came to offer condolences, you know. And you could see how deeply affected they were by his death.'

'I could also see that they appreciated you for yourself. Not in the beginning, no; but you endeared yourself to them.'

And she had, not just with the weavers, but with Nadeem as well.

Interlude

'A woman,' breathes Gokul, his eyes full of wonder. 'I did not know women worked. I mean,' he adds after a moment, probably realizing that the world is full of women who cook and clean and sow and look after children and more. 'I mean, not this sort of work,' he says. 'Work of the mind.' His eyes narrow as he mulls over this, the thought that men are more often privileged to work with their minds, not their hands. It is a new thought, I can see. Is he perhaps also a little taken aback that women have minds that work?

He is a bright boy; it is a pity that poverty—of finances, yes; but more of mentality—has meant that his father had not seen fit to let Gokul have any form of schooling. Of course, he knows all there is to know of keeping cattle, but what earthly use is that now?

I know that in the quieter part of the day, when they are not busy foraging or doing the few necessary chores about the house, Mohsin has been teaching Gokul some letters. The Arabic script, not Devnagari, naturally, since that is the only script Mohsin knows. It confused Gokul at first, but my grandson is like me: he can be a formidable force and well-nigh impossible to resist when he has set his mind to something. And he has taken it upon himself to educate Gokul.

'There are few women who will do work like that,' I admit, 'but that is more because they have never been encouraged to do so. From the time they are little girls, they are taught that they must grow up to be good wives and mothers, and that their place is in the home. Few of them dare to imagine they could do any work such as this, but it does not mean that women are incapable of it.'

It is an audacious thought, and Gokul looks appalled. I am quite certain even I would not have accepted a woman working for the workshop if it hadn't been that my great grandmother Aabida had been the one to set up that workshop in the first place. Aabida had been an audacious woman; and her audacity allowed me to accept that trait in another woman. Not just accept, welcome. I welcomed Zarina's forwardness, as Ismat labelled it.

The more I saw her, the more I heard her voice, watched her as she discussed the naqshas with the men, I could not help but admire her. So young, but so poised, so self-assured. So free of the wiles and overdone coyness many other women affected. No, I should correct myself: not many other women. Ismat. Ismat had once been like that, her femininity so cloyingly artificial that it set my teeth on edge—until, years later, she had shed every last vestige of it and become a shrew, harsh and critical at all times.

Zarina was utterly unlike Ismat. It did not take me long to realize that, and it took me even less time to find that I had fallen in love with her.

Every year, when the winter takes Dilli in its grip, I forget just how murderous the city's summers can be. The cold wipes away my memories of the heat.

Now, with the sun scorching the earth, burning the grass and turning the leaves brittle and coarse, I remember, and my heart clenches with fear at the memory of it. The heat always mounts, inexorably and unbearably, until the rains come. But who knows whether the rains will come or not? These past two summers, whatever rain we have had has been so meagre, it has barely moistened the dust.

Will there be rain this year? Abundant rain, of the kind that fills the baolis and the wells, the kind that washes away the dust of the past months and brings the earth alive?

I fear it will be, again, a waterless summer.

Meanwhile, rumours are rife that Hemu is heading westward. He was in Bengal when the Baadshah died, and they say that over the past several months he has moved relentlessly west towards Dilli. Kalpi, Etawah, Sambhal: all have fallen before him, and after capturing Gwalior, he is now moving his armies north to Agra. Agra is not so very far from Dilli; he is, to all intents and purposes, knocking at our door.

But we need not worry, I think. It is true that the young emperor is far away, in Jalandhar, in the province of Lahore; but Agra is held for him by the able Iskandar Khan Uzbeg. There are seasoned troops aplenty to guard the city, the fort, and the throne. We need not fear Hemu getting a foothold there.

'But I wonder,' says Mohsin, as the two boys later hunker down beside my bed, 'how does Hemu feed his armies? We are hardly able to find enough to keep us alive; where do his soldiers get enough to not just stay alive, but march on, fight?'

'Such are the ways of the wealthy and powerful.' I sigh. 'Emperors, governors, mighty men: they do not worry about matters such as this. Perhaps Hemu has cartloads of food being brought every day to his encampment from the east, where this famine does not extend.'

'Can we not go east?' Gokul pipes up. 'If we travel far enough, will we not also reach a land where we will get enough to eat?' He glances toward Mohsin, and then at me. 'Some of your family is there too, isn't it? Why have you not gone, then?'

'Mohsin's mother,' I agree. 'And her youngest child. She is at her parents' home, yes; but that was because she had already travelled there when the famine hit. She had gone to bear her child in her mother's home, and all of us thought it was best for them to stay on there.' I swallow. The dryness scratches at my throat, making it difficult to speak. 'But we cannot go there, not in these circumstances. It requires many weeks of travel, even in the best of times. Now, with no food, no horses, no bullock carts—' I shake my head.

'Let us get back to work,' Mohsin says, as he reaches for the stack of pages in the wall niche nearby. From the niche beside it, he takes down the qalamdaan and the dawaat. 'We're wasting time,' he says in a brusque voice. I wonder at the sudden change in his mood, the gruffness: is he missing his mother, and the sibling he has never seen? Or is he envying them, their obliviousness to our plight?

There is nothing anybody can do about it, so there is little point in fretting. We get back to work.

As I had guessed, Zarina's mother did not approve of her daughter making naqshas for us. When Zarina began coming to the workshop to talk to the workers, her Ammi was no longer merely disapproving: she was downright angry. Zarina did not say this to me at the time; I only learnt of it much later.

Zarina's Ammi might have eventually forgiven her daughter for what she saw as hugely improper, simply because on some level she considered the weavers as part of an extended clan. Somewhat like blood brothers to her late husband, and therefore not utter strangers. But to have Zarina interact with men who were indeed strangers would put her beyond the pale. There was not the slightest chance that Zarina, despite all her knowledge, might ever be allowed to talk to our customers. I would have to wait for Junaid to return from Kashi; till then, I would blunder along as best as I could manage.

The months went by.

Two years after my father came on that visit to Dilli where he and I met for the first time after years, Sikandar Lodhi died. In the winter of that year, the Sultan, then planning a campaign to seize Malwa, was struck down by a high fever. It proved fatal, and with his death, his son Ibrahim came to power.

Sikandar Lodhi's chief queen and Ibrahim Lodhi's mother, Dilawar Begum, had already shown that she was willing to let bygones be bygones: she was the one who had accepted our workshop back as purveyors to the palace. Even if we were not yet officially designated as such, even if we never would be: the very fact that our brocades were once again being bought by the palace was enough.

Dilawar Begum, having mourned one Sultan, set herself to celebrating the ascension of another. Ibrahim Lodhi's coronation was a low-key affair, with little pomp and show: it was not seemly, after all, to rejoice too openly so soon after the death of his father. But Dilawar Begum was devoted to her son, and decided that the first anniversary of his coronation, at least, would be marked by enough jubilation to compensate for the lacklustre coronation. It would be grand, with the most talented musicians and entertainers, the most lavish gifts bestowed on the faithful, the most largesse distributed to the public.

Of course she wanted brocades. Luxurious, fine brocades of the kind that would stand out, be remembered for years after. She had decided, too, that she, Dilawar Begum, would personally decide on the patterns, the colours, everything. She would not entrust any of these important matters to underlings who might not match up to her standards.

By that time, Mirza Yasin Mohammad Khan was long retired. His place had been taken by an overwrought and nervous man, a courtier whose name I now forget. Raheem, and then Mudassar, had been meeting him periodically during their visits to Agra, and he was satisfied with their work. Then Raheem died. And Mudassar, having collapsed so sadly, lingered on for the next three months or so, getting increasingly more emaciated, until the Almighty was merciful and put an end to his sufferings.

Junaid was in Kashi, so, since there was no alternative, I had made the trip to Agra—twice. This had been before Sikandar Lodhi's death, and both times, it was Yasin Mohammad Khan's successor I met and talked with. He had been unimpressed with me. There were many questions to which I had no answers, many problems I could not solve.

The courtier had said, in dignified tones, that he hoped I would soon get someone who could handle things as well as Raheem or Mudassar had. His sniff of disdain, the lowered brows and the quiver in his wispy grey beard had shown his disapproval in no uncertain terms.

Now, with Dilawar Begum summoning a representative of the workshop to Agra for a private discussion with her, the man could no longer afford to hide his contempt for me. Or, really, what had become outright fear: he was terrified (he admitted as much in his letter, sent through an imperial mail-runner) that I would make a fool of myself. Those were his words.

Do you know that old saying about it never rains, but it pours? Well, that was what happened then. I wrote hurriedly to Kashi, begging for Junaid to be sent back post-haste: half-baked though his knowledge and competence, it was far better than mine. But no; Junaid was in no condition to travel. He had had an attack of malaria, which had been compounded by a stomach infection. For several weeks, he had swung between life and death. Only now had the fever subsided somewhat, but he could not yet even get out of bed. Any travel was out of the question. It would kill him.

There was nothing else I could do. I asked Zarina. After all, the customer was no less than Dilawar Begum. The Dowager Empress. We could hire guards to accompany Zarina, and she could take along as many maids, servants, and even perhaps a trusted apprentice or weaver to help her. If she so wished, I might go with her too.

'To supervise?'

'To protect,' I said. I had lost my heart to this woman early on, and early on, too, I had let her know how I felt. She had been shocked at first, and had been withdrawn, reticent, for a while. It had taken apologies and assurances that I would never behave in a way that might come across as predatory, before she felt secure enough to resume even the most professionally distant of relations. Now she was

back to being comfortable, even relaxed, in my presence. She teased me, in a subtle way, now and then about my feelings, but made it amply clear that she could not return them.

It allowed me to be honest with her. I was ready to escort her and her entourage to Agra, just to make sure she remained safe and well through her journey.

I did not go, after all. Zarina's Ammi, when told about the impending trip, realized that she could not oppose the trip, not when it meant angering the Dowager Empress. But she insisted that it was she who would accompany Zarina to Agra. Maids, servants, and guards were all very well: her daughter would not go ten yards from her house without her.

Who was I to quibble? All I knew was that Zarina would be able to handle Dilawar Begum. On her slender shoulders rested the honour of our workshop, and I, biased though I was, felt that she would do justice to this responsibility.

What I did not realize then was that this would be a turning point in Zarina's life, and it would eventually affect me too.

19
Dilli

Eight years later
931 Hijri (1525 CE)

'Ameen,' said the bent old cleric who had been leading the prayers.

'Ameen,' echoed the men congregated in the paved space in front of the wall mosque. From behind a heavy portable screen that had been set up on one side, there came the indistinct murmur of feminine voices repeating the word.

So be it. So may Allah will it, that the soul of the late Emperor, Sikandar Khan Lodhi, may rest in peace.

They unbent, straightening their backs. Began to move away, the solemnity of the occasion—the eighth anniversary of the death of Sikandar Lodhi—exercising a sobering effect on them. Men, all, who were in some way connected to the court. A few were courtiers who had travelled all the way from Agra to Dilli to be present at this occasion; most of the others, like Nadeem, were residents of Dilli.

'Nadeem Sahib.' A girl, her hair covered but her small, round face unveiled, had come hurrying from behind the screen. A maid, too lowly to need to hide her face and form from strange men. 'Her Highness the Dowager Empress wishes to speak to you.'

Nadeem was not surprised. Two weeks earlier, the letter had arrived at the workshop, a summons to the tomb of Sikandar Lodhi on the occasion of the death anniversary of the late ruler. Nadeem was expected to attend. There were further instructions in the letter. An imperial palanquin would be sent to the home of Zarina Begum, who would be taken to the Dowager Empress's palace in Dilli. From there, Zarina would accompany Dilawar Begum to the tomb for the prayers.

Nadeem walked the few steps to the mausoleum, its octagonal bulk sitting solid in the middle of an enclosed garden, high walls surrounding the space and separating it from the other tombs of the Bagh-e-Jud. This was a tomb markedly distinct from the imposing height and impressive proportions of that of Sikandar's father, Bahlol Lodhi, where Nadeem had once sat and had that conversation with Waqar. Sikandar Lodhi's tomb was smaller, its dome more restrained: but it was still a beautiful, carefully crafted structure. Not striking from the outside, but once you stepped in, you could not help but marvel at the exquisite ornamentation: the incised plaster, the bands of tiny tiles, yellow and green and turquoise and deep blue, arranged in geometric patterns around the arched windows that pierced the walls below the dome.

But Nadeem was not thinking of Sikandar Lodhi or of his tomb right now; all his thoughts were centred on Sikandar Lodhi's widow, who had summoned him here and wished to speak to him.

'It pleases us that you came for these prayers,' Dilawar Begum said, from behind the heavy screen where she sat. The maid who had been sent to fetch Nadeem had positioned herself in front of the screen, and from the corner of his eye, Nadeem saw the gleam of steel as a woman, dressed all in sombre brown, straightened beside the screen. A female guard, making certain he knew she was there, and ready.

He murmured a few words by way of greeting, and offered commiseration for the Dowager Empress's widowhood.

'It has been many years,' Dilawar Begum said dismissively. Yes, of course; she had once been an Emperor's consort; now she was an Emperor's mother, and a woman who held her own. Ibrahim Lodhi had been the ruler these past seven years, but it was not his wife who held sway in the palace at Agra. It was Dilawar Begum: powerful and formidable, perhaps even more so than her weak-willed son. Nadeem had wondered, many times over these past years, how it might have been if she, rather than Ibrahim, had been the Sultan.

'We had thought, when we came to Dilli for this occasion, that we would make it a point to get Zarina Begum to spend some time with us at the palace,' Dilawar Begum said. 'We had assumed that we would spend at least a few weeks in Dilli.' She cleared her throat, and murmured something to one of her ladies. There was a pause; Nadeem heard a muffled clank, the rustle of cloth, and the sound of liquid being poured. A soothing drink, perhaps, was being offered to the Dowager Empress. Behind that screen, she had probably been made as comfortable as she would have been in her own palace.

'But circumstances call us back to Agra immediately,' Dilawar Begum resumed. 'And we would wish to take Zarina Begum with us.' She paused. 'To be part of the imperial household.'

It was not a request, and Dilawar Begum neither sought Nadeem's permission nor gave him any room to deny her. 'We of course are well aware of how vital Zarina Begum is to the success of your workshop, and we would not wish your business to fail. Zarina Begum, therefore, is allowed to stay on in Dilli till the end of this week. That should be sufficient, we assume, for her to make all the arrangements needed for work to proceed without let or hindrance.'

Nadeem bowed his head. 'It shall be as you wish, Your Highness,' he replied, voice deferentially low.

There was a murmur of voices from behind the screen. He recognized Zarina's voice. Surely she was not countering Dilawar Begum's order? Even Zarina, strong-willed as she was, would not dare to do something so suicidal.

'Zarina Begum has requested that she be allowed to stay behind for a while here, to speak with you.' There was a note of reprieve in Dilawar Begum's voice, a peevishness that put Nadeem in mind of his son, when thwarted as an infant. That same childish petulance, that same annoyance at not having had one's way.

But Dilawar Begum was also an empress, and aware that granting minor favours was all part of the aura of dignity and grace surrounding the office. 'You may stay behind, and once we and our ladies have departed, you may speak to Zarina Begum.'

ଓ

'I had not thought she would ask for me to go to Agra,' Zarina said. She was walking beside Nadeem, veiled as usual, but matching him step for step.

'She did not ask.'

'And we did not have the option of saying nay.' Zarina agreed. She turned suddenly, away from him and through the arched doorway which led into the tomb chamber. Sikandar Lodhi's cenotaph stood in the centre, washed in the surreal light that filtered in, leaf-tinted, through the canopies of the trees outside the arched windows.

Zarina drew in a deep breath. 'I shall miss Dilli,' she said. 'I shall miss these trees, and the river. The buildings, the birds.' Her voice caught, choked.

'There will be birds in Agra. And trees. Even the river, the same one at that.'

'But it will not be Dilli.' Zarina shook her head. 'I have lived all my life in Dilli; how will I survive in Agra?'

'You will,' said Nadeem. 'If there is anyone capable of adapting to the situation and making the best of it, it is you. You will manage, you will make friends—you already have made friends, have you not? From what I have heard you say, you have endeared yourself to Dilawar Begum's ladies in the course of your visits to the court in Agra. Not just she, they too will welcome you into their midst.' He paused, uncertain. If he were to say what was in his heart, would she take offence? Would she baulk, flee? Or would she laugh it off? In all these years he had not repeated his confession of love; that long-ago admission had been all. His feelings, however, had not changed, and he had a suspicion Zarina knew it.

It had been enough to see her now and then. Even, when she was not there at the workshop, he had contented himself with looking through her naqshas, breathing in the beauty of what she created. In them was her beauty too, sufficient to keep Nadeem satiated.

But now she would be going away to Agra, and who knew when—if—she would ever be back again? He could not let her go thus. At least once, he had to ask her again.

'Zarina,' he said gently, 'Have you thought about what I asked, several years ago? I haven't spoken of it again, but that does not mean I haven't thought of it.'

She said nothing for a few moments. Then, carefully, as if she measured every word, she said, 'I had hoped you had forgotten it. Can you not? I do not wish it. I did not wish it then, and nothing has changed since.'

'Much has changed,' Nadeem contradicted her. 'You are older now, wiser. It was because of you that we were able to turn the workshop around. Dilawar Begum's fondness for you, the impression you made on her from the very beginning: that is what helped us get back the palace business we had once lost. You are an asset to our workshop.' That sounded terribly mercenary, he realized, even as he fell silent. If you are proposing marriage, if you are making assertions of love, you do not tell a woman how competent she is. The mind must step back; the heart must dominate the conversation.

But it was too late; it was already said. And Zarina was already shaking her head.

'That was not what I meant when I said nothing had changed. And you know it. My feelings have not changed, Nadeem Sahib. I do not wish to marry you.'

A thought occurred to him. It had not crossed his mind before, but perhaps he knew what made her refuse to marry. Him, or anyone else, for that matter.

'Is there another you love, but cannot have?'

'Of course not. I do not want to marry. Not you, not anyone. Not now, at any rate.'

A flicker of hope ignited within him. 'Someday, then? May I ask—may I ask why you wait? If you do not completely deny the likelihood of your getting married, then why not now?'

Zarina heaved a sigh. Exasperation, he thought, and perhaps fatigue. Anxiety? He did not know. But this he did realize: that it made him feel guilty about having caused her distress. 'I am sorry,' he said, before she could reply. 'I take back that question. Let it be.' He turned back towards the arched doorway, and took a step forward. 'Let us go back out, shall we? And perhaps we should go to the workshop, to discuss what needs to be done, now that you will go away to Agra?'

cs

Junaid had returned from Kashi a few months after Zarina had made her first trip to Agra. His months in Kashi had made him far more adept, more confident and knowledgeable than he had been. It would take years of experience, and maturity, for him to attain the standards of Raheem and Mudassar; but he was headed there. He could, at least, now handle the workshop with close to consummate ease. Nadeem found, finally, that he could concentrate wholly on his calligraphy. There was no cause to worry for the workshop any more.

Waqar too proved true to his word. He had made introductions, he had shown off some of Nadeem's finest work to those who might have the interest and the wherewithal to purchase it. It was thanks to him that Nadeem's career as a qaatib began to gather momentum. Better, grander commissions began to come his way, and more frequently: an illuminated manuscript here, an inscription for a mosque or a tomb there. A wealthy nobleman, for the wedding of his only son, commissioned a large piece of stone inlay on the wall of the bridegroom's bedchamber. A love poem by the Persian poet Jalaluddin Mohammad Rumi, surrounded by a scene from a garden. The inscription of the poem was done by Nadeem; the garden scene was drawn by Zarina.

It had been a spectacular work, a masterpiece in every sense of the word. Nadeem's letters, rendered into black marble, swirled and danced as if in joy. Zarina's art surrounded them: full-blown lotuses, their petals hiding carpenter bees, their wavy-edged circular leaves rising towards a full moon. A shimmer of moonlight in a pond, the glimmer of fireflies in the dark. It was meant only for the eyes of the newlywed couple, and yet Nadeem could not help but think that the piece somehow embodied his love for Zarina. Here they came together, his letters and her art, combined, each setting off the beauty of the other.

It was not to happen in real life. He did not even know if he would ever see Zarina again.

Irony, he thought, that he had actually never seen her. If he should see her someday, unveiled, he would not know who she was unless she, at least, spoke.

He should try to put her out of his mind, Nadeem decided. It would be best for him, for his peace of mind.

Three bullock carts stood one behind the other outside the house, the last of them packed high with an assortment of items: boxes, chests, bundles of various sizes. Heavy ropes bound the objects securely, both to each other and to the sides and floor of the cart.

'You're taking all that to Agra? So much?' Nadeem asked as a maid emerged from the house, going carefully down the steps, her vision obscured by the bulky quilts, folded into quarters, that she carried in her arms.

Zarina chuckled. 'Men are so completely oblivious of what goes into a household. This is nothing. We are taking only the things we absolutely cannot leave behind. Heirlooms, mostly. Or things of sentimental value.'

'I hadn't known,' Nadeem remarked, 'that your mother would be accompanying you to Agra. I had thought the Dowager Empress only wanted you.'

'She did. But where would Ammi go? Excuse me'—she hurried to the second cart, where two maids were arranging the quilts, cushions, bolsters and all that must travel with the ladies, to make their journey comfortable. 'Here,' Nadeem heard her say. 'Place the bolsters here, along the sides, so that they can cushion us. No, no; don't put the quilts here in front; we don't want the dust blowing in on them. Put them there, at the back, like that; yes. And cover them with those sheets, please.'

When she returned to his side after satisfying herself about the arrangement in the cart, Zarina continued. 'I could not leave Ammi behind here in Dilli. What would she do, stuck in this house with only the servants for company? She would be miserable. I would worry incessantly about her, as well.'

'Could she not stay with either of your sisters?'

Zarina shook her head. 'No.'

She did not explain. Were her sisters not especially filial? Were they married to men who did not welcome a mother-in-law into their homes? Were there financial considerations?

It was a sensitive topic, and Nadeem had already approached too close for comfort. He let it be.

'I spoke to the Dowager Empress,' Zarina said, 'and told her that I could not possibly leave Ammi behind. She agreed to let Ammi accompany me to Agra.'

'It would hardly make a difference, I suppose, to Dilawar Begum. Among so many ladies, one more.'

A maid had come out of the house, beside her a young boy, carrying between them a basket from which wafted the aroma of food. 'Begum Sahiba sends word that she is ready to go,' the maid told Zarina.

The maid and the boy placed the basket in the first cart, and Zarina turned to Nadeem. 'I must go,' she said. 'The sun will be rising soon, and we have been told we need to be at the city gates when they open for the day. A contingent of imperial soldiers is to escort us to Agra, and I fear what will befall me should I arrive late.' She chuckled, as if reinforcing the fact that she was joking. The soldiers no doubt knew who she was; perhaps some of them had been part of escorts to and from Dilli for Zarina in the years past.

'May Allah protect you and be with you,' Nadeem said formally, but sincerely. 'And you will write, please, as you had promised?'

'Of course.' She paused, already turning towards the entrance to the house. 'Take care of yourself.'

Nadeem nodded and smiled. 'I will. Go now; your mother will be waiting.'

When she had vanished into the house, he turned around and walked till the end of the lane, then up a short rise to the top of a low hillock, its crest crowned with an outcrop shrouded by dense scrub. Nadeem climbed to the top, and found himself a place under a ber tree with drooping branches. It offered a view of the road the little cavalcade would traverse, while making him unobtrusive.

He watched, a silent figure half-hidden by the bushes and the ber, as the three carts made their way along the road a while later. The first cart now bore the few servants who were accompanying Zarina and her mother to Agra; he could see the boy and the maid, sitting at the back, the boy talking so animatedly that his voice carried to where Nadeem stood.

Right at the back was the cart that carried their belongings, and in the middle was the cart in which sat Zarina and her mother. Nadeem, looking on, caught a glimpse of the pale turquoise cloth of Zarina's dupatta. He watched, wondering if she was looking back. Not at him, no; but at the home that had been hers all these years. At the Dilli she was leaving behind. At the life she was leaving behind.

Or had she already turned her face away from all of this? Was Zarina already lost to him, even before she had left Dilli?

He waited until the dust raised by the three carts had settled; then, with heavy steps, he descended the hillock and headed home.

20

Ismat, tight-lipped and cold-eyed, was waiting in the main courtyard of the zenana when he got home. Ostensibly, she was there to attend to work. A row of large heavy glass jars of pickles was sitting in the weak winter sunlight, and a maid was going slowly down the row, using a ladle to stir the contents of each jar. Off to one side, a sheet had been spread, on which was drying freshly-washed wheat. One maid, down on her haunches, was raking the wheat with her fingers, making sure all of it soaked up the sun.

Nadeem had left home so early, he had not had a chance to go into the women's quarters to ask about his mother. Shahana had been ill with a cold and a bad cough; nothing serious, she had insisted, but Nadeem was worried nevertheless. She was not young any more, and with increasing age she was growing more and more fragile.

He had stepped into the courtyard to make his way to Shahana's chamber, but Ismat intercepted him.

'Have you no shame?' she hissed. 'Your daughter is going to be a mother for the second time, and you cannot give up your philandering?!' She glanced over her shoulder to ensure no one was eavesdropping, and satisfied that the maids were engrossed in their respective tasks, she carried on. 'Do you not have a single thought for propriety? What will people say?'

'People have better things to do than spend their time poking their noses into other people's business,' Nadeem snapped back. It was a foolish rejoinder, he knew; there were plenty who really did have nothing better to do. 'And in any case, there was nothing clandestine or underhand about my going to Zarina Begum's home. She was leaving for Agra with her mother; I stood outside and said my farewells, that was all.'

Ismat looked briefly flustered; whoever had given her the information that Nadeem had gone to visit Zarina had not also told her the reason for his visit. Or that the woman she had regarded as a rival all these years was gone, possibly for good. As that fact dawned on her, Ismat smiled: a wide smile, her eyes shining and her face so radiant, she looked beautiful.

'She is gone,' she whispered. 'Really gone?' Her joy was palpable, the relief in her voice and in her expression so great that Nadeem felt momentarily guilty. No, he told himself, brushing that thought away. There was nothing for him to feel guilty about. His relationship with Zarina had been purely platonic, even one-sided. He had never wished for an illicit relationship, either: it was marriage he had offered. He had done no wrong.

'Yes,' he said. 'Yes, she's gone. From the city.'

Not from my heart, was the unspoken message, and from the pinched look that came into Ismat's face, he knew it had hit home. Without another word, he turned away to go inside.

'May she rot in Agra,' Ismat called after him, no longer caring who was listening. 'May she never know peace, the home-breaker!'

Zubair was in town, and had sent a note to Nadeem to meet him at the sarai where he was staying. Since Sikandar Lodhi's death, Zubair had become bolder about visiting Dilli: with Ibrahim Lodhi now firmly entrenched in Agra, there seemed little danger to Zubair if he were seen in Dilli. Besides, the young man from over twenty years ago was gone; Zubair had changed a good deal in the years since.

He still did not visit the workshop, though, or even home. At the workshop, except for Nadeem and Junaid, no one knew he was still alive. At home, too, there were the servants to be considered. The more who knew of Zubair's being alive, the more to gossip. It was best, Zubair had decided, that he confine himself to the sarai where he stayed during his sojourn in Dilli.

This time, he was not too well. A thunderstorm on the road from Kashi to Dilli had churned up the dirt road, and the cart he was travelling in had overturned. Zubair had suffered no broken bones, but he was wracked by pains and aches, and a prolonged drenching had resulted in a bad cold.

He clutched a piece of soft muslin, holding it to his mouth as he coughed, his shoulders shaking, the sweat beading on his forehead. His servant had brewed him a cup of hot honeyed water with ginger crushed into it, and from this he took the occasional sip. To Nadeem's worried questions about his health, he shook his head. His voice was hoarse, and so soft that Nadeem had to strain to hear him. 'It is a result of that mishap along the way; I will be fine.'

Nadeem lifted an eyebrow. 'Must you travel so much? You told me you have barely been in Kashi this past year? At your age, surely you can afford to take it easy.'

'It's not my usual work,' Zubair said. 'This is different.'

It came spilling out, the exciting news Zubair had to share. Some fifteen months earlier, he had gone to Lahore, taking with him a consignment of brocades. It was a valuable consignment, too valuable to be entrusted to a merchant. 'And,' Zubair added, 'I have always wanted to travel to that part of the empire. This was my chance to make the journey.' En route to Lahore, Zubair's caravan had caught up with another group of travellers: an important personage, a man on a mission. This was Ghazi Khan, the son of Daulat Khan Lodhi, the governor of the Punjab.

'You know, of course, what has happened,' Zubair said. 'There had been rumours, whispered even in Lahore, that Ibrahim Lodhi is meaning to deprive Daulat Khan Lodhi of the governorship of Lahore.'

'There has been little love lost between the two of them,' Nadeem agreed. 'And who would be loyal to one like the

Sultan?' he added, his voice lowered to a discreet murmur. 'It astounds me that he is the son of Sikandar Lodhi and the grandson of Bahlol. I have never seen such an incompetent ruler.'

Zubair's mouth curled up at the corners. 'You speak like one of those stuffy old statesmen at court,' he said. 'Too fond of sweeping statements.' Before an indignant Nadeem could counter that, Zubair patted him on the shoulder. 'I know what you mean, though I doubt you have seen, at close quarters, too many other rulers you could compare with Ibrahim Lodhi.' He cleared his throat. At the door, Zubair's servant drew the curtain aside and came in with a salver of food: kebabs, rotis, fruit, and more of the honeyed drink that Zubair needed.

The food was placed before the two men, the servant retreated, and Zubair, having taken a long, grateful sip from his replenished cup, sat back. 'Ghazi Khan was sent to Dilli by his father to find out if there was any truth to the rumours that Ibrahim Lodhi was meaning to dismiss Daulat Khan Lodhi. When I met Ghazi Khan, he was returning to Lahore to warn his father that Ibrahim Lodhi was, in fact, getting ready to depose him.'

'And so Daulat Khan Lodhi went scurrying to Kabul, to invite Zahiruddin Mohammad Babar to try his hand at deposing Ibrahim Lodhi instead.' Nadeem nodded as he began to eat. 'We know that, and we know what came of it. Babar first attacked Lahore and then Dibalpur, after Ibrahim Lodhi had already ousted Daulat Khan. Babar got both Lahore and Dibalpur, but how has that affected anything else? True, Babar's men now govern that area, but everywhere else, it is still Ibrahim Lodhi who is Sultan. In Agra, and here in Dilli.'

'Yes,' Zubair conceded. 'Babar went back then, to his stronghold in Kabul. But do you know why?' A gleam had come into his eyes, and his voice—now a conspiratorial whisper—brimmed with excitement. 'He went back to consolidate his army. To gather more troops, a more robust force.'

Nadeem stared, the food before him forgotten for the moment. It was common knowledge that the Timurid Babar—he traced his ancestry to the conqueror who had invaded Dilli a little over a hundred years ago—had made an attempt to invade the Lodhi's empire, but that he had been beaten back. That he was instead planning another attack had come as news to Nadeem. Worrying news.

'You think Babar is headed here, to Dilli?' he finally said. 'To Agra?'

Zubair nodded. 'I do not merely think so; I know it. That foray into Lahore and Dibalpur was no jaunt, just for the sake of it; Babar was setting up bases for a deeper incursion into this land.' Zubair set his empty cup down. 'He will be back. When, I do not know; but this is not the last we will see of him.'

As he made his way home, Nadeem pondered over what he had been told. Agra would be Babar's target; Dilli, while it was located en route to the capital, might escape a sack, or worse. Even in Agra, there were unlikely to be any very serious repercussions for the common people. Babar, in his conquest of Kabul, Lahore and Dibalpur, had shown no inclination to loot and plunder, let alone massacre.

But Zarina. Zarina was headed for Agra. Not just Agra, but the imperial palace, where she would be a court lady to Dilawar Begum. At the heart of the most vulnerable place in all of the empire. If Babar, all puffed up by a victory and eager to establish his power, did what all conquerors do—ravage and rape, destroy, pulverize, leave no shred of dignity to those he vanquished—Dilawar Begum's household would be the worst hit.

Perhaps, earlier that week, when Zarina was still in town, if he had heard this news, he would have done whatever it took to stop her from going. He might have pleaded with her—but no, as both he and Zarina knew, the decision was not Zarina's. It had been Dilawar Begum who had decided she wanted Zarina in Agra, and what would Nadeem or Zarina say to dissuade Dilawar Begum at this stage? That he had inside information about an impending invasion, which was why he wanted to keep Zarina out of harm's way?

Foolish thought. That would only have had him clapped into prison. It would be utterly futile, even suicidal.

In any case, there was always a chance that Babar might not succeed. He was little more than an upstart, a man who had not even been able to hold on to the throne, at Ferghana, which he had inherited. The man, too, who had lost Samarqand: not once, but a humiliating three times. Even if he gathered a large army, could he really hope to stand up to the might of the Lodhi armies? Ibrahim Lodhi may be a useless ruler, but he had a formidable army, and generals who were seasoned warriors.

There was little chance, really, that Babar would gain another victory after Dibalpur. Before the year was out, he would be heading back to Kabul, tail between his legs, and Agra would be safe. Zarina would be safe.

All he could do was hope.

The days went by, winter gently giving way to spring. The days grew warmer, the leaves on the trees turned brown and were shed. A froth of white flowers, each a tiny but perfectly shaped star, appeared on the chamrod trees.

Two months after Zarina had left Dilli, a letter arrived from her for Nadeem. It was delivered to the workshop and was all too brief, a mere reassurance that they had arrived safely in the city and were now a part of Dilawar Begum's household. She said little of what her duties entailed; just that it was exhausting to be attendant on the Dowager Empress from dawn to late at night. There was a single sentence about the beauty of the palace, followed by a barrage of questions about the workshop and the work she had left behind. How was Junaid coping? Had they found a naqshband to replace her? There was that young cousin of Junaid's; he had shown great promise. They must encourage him. Also, of all the naqshas she had left behind, there was one she had been in a hurry to finish before she left for Agra, and thus had no time to talk to the weavers about it. She was enclosing a note, which included instructions—

Nadeem sighed and set the letter aside. He should have been happy that Zarina had kept her promise of writing to him; it irritated him, though, that her letter was not what he had hoped for. It was too little, and it was not about her. It left him dissatisfied.

But at least she was safe.

There was still no sign of Babar on the horizon. Perhaps he had decided not to attempt an invasion; perhaps he had realized he was ill-equipped to take on an empire so massive.

'This Zahiruddin Babar is an adventurer,' said Mir Kaamil, an elderly gentleman who had been a courtier of Sikandar Lodhi's, but had retired before a capricious Ibrahim Lodhi had ascended the throne. Mir Sahib, white-bearded and frail, but with his wits as sharp as in his heyday, was a patron of Nadeem's calligraphy. Nadeem had come visiting to deliver an inscription, a rendering of the Bismillah, in deep blue and gold. Mir Sahib, having lavished due admiration on the piece, had finally settled back and was ready to chat.

His conversations invariably consisted of him talking and the other listening. Today was no different. 'How many men can he possibly muster?' Mir Sahib said. 'The last time he came up against the Sultan, it was with thirty thousand men, most of them those of his ally, Daulat Khan Lodhi. Daulat Khan Lodhi is a spent force now,' he added dismissively. 'He won't be able to offer much help to Babar. How many men will Babar be able to cobble together? Ten thousand?

Fifteeen? Twenty, even? I doubt if there are so many fighting men in those high mountains around Kabul!' A sharp bark of laughter underlined the contempt in that pronouncement.

'And,' added Mir Kaamil, before Nadeem could say yea or nay, 'there is the terrain. These mountain warriors, I admit, are fierce men, good fighters—but are they equally good here, in the heat of the plains? In a city like Dilli? I doubt if Babar will go as far as Agra, to assault the fort there, or that Ibrahim Lodhi will allow him to venture so far. But Dilli? Our fortifications are too sturdy, our army too huge. Babar will be like a handful of gravel tossed at a stone wall.' He shook his head. 'He will be a fool to try.'

'Will you write me another of these Bismillahs?' Mir Kaamil said, as he was seeing Nadeem out a short while later. 'The same blue, but perhaps something more muted than the gold? My cousin, I think, will appreciate it.' He smiled, his eyes twinkling happily. 'Perhaps I will commission you to make me something more elaborate, eh, once you're a little free? We'll talk about that later, yes?' His smile was benevolent, his anticipation flattering.

A man without worries, thought Nadeem as he headed home. A man who had no reason to be especially fond of Ibrahim Lodhi, given that many of his old friends and colleagues had been summarily dismissed when the Lodhi became Sultan; and therefore a man unlikely to indulge in what might have been considered wishful thinking in a sycophant.

Perhaps he was right. Babar might never make it to Dilli.

Summer came and went. The monsoon washed away the heat and the dust, and brought in its wake mud and flies and sickness. The rains, in their turn, went the way of summer, fading away into a memory even as Eid-i-Milaad-un-Nabi and Diwali came around once more and the city decked itself out anew. If Babar was gathering his forces for an attack on Dilli or Agra, if Ibrahim Lodhi was preparing to counter a possible invasion, the city did not know, and did not care. The people of Dilli went about as usual, decorating their houses, lighting lamps, stitching new clothes, feasting. Celebrating.

From Zarina came another letter, this time with greetings on the occasion of the Prophet's birthday. She mentioned the preparations for the festival at the palace: the many foods being prepared in the palace kitchens, the bolts of cloth and sacks of grain to be given away to the poor. Like many others keenly aware of their power and pelf, Dilawar Begum too believed in using festivals such as this to show off her benevolence.

Of course, when I look at it from the point of view of the poor, I cannot help but be grateful, Zarina wrote. *It is a mere drop in the ocean for the imperial household; but a godsend for the poor.* She wrote of the weather in Agra—a little cooler than it had been in Dilli last winter, around the same time—and a pretty parakeet, rose-ringed and garrulous, which someone had gifted her.

I hate to cage birds, so I let this one go as soon as I had brought it into my chamber. But to my surprise the parakeet refused to fly away. It fluttered back in and settled down. Again and again, until finally I gave up. It is now my pet, and dare I say my friend? Ammi disapproves, but since she also suspects that the person who gifted me the bird is an ardent admirer, she is torn between disapproval and hope!

Nadeem did not know what to make of that. The admirer, obviously, was a man, and possibly an eligible one, whom Zarina's mother regarded as a potential son-in-law. But did Zarina think of him, that unnamed admirer, in the same way? Had her resistance to marriage finally crumbled? He felt jealous, annoyed with her for having turned him down, only to so quickly change her mind about being married.

How ironic, he thought, that he should have ended up thus, his heart and his body going two ways. Ismat, his in the eyes of the world, had never been and never could be his at all, not in mind and not in spirit. Yet Zarina, whom he ached for, refused to be his. It was a pitiable situation to be in.

Nadeem shook his head. No; he would not let himself go down that road. Self-pity got one nowhere. He folded the letter and put it away.

A few days later, he wrote a reply, a staid and conventional letter that enquired about Zarina's health and that of her mother. He wrote a few lines about business at the workshop. He expressed a cautious hope that the Dowager Empress would order some more brocades, so that Nadeem and Junaid may have the opportunity of going to Agra.

He made only one concession, which allowed some of his true feelings to be glimpsed. He mentioned a couplet by the weaver Kabirdas, of whom Zubair spoke often in his letters, even though Kabirdas had been dead some seven years now. *Pehle agan birha ki,* he wrote. *Pachhe prem ki pyaas. Kahe Kabir tab jaaniye, naam milan ki aas.* First, there is the agony of separation; that is followed by the thirst for love. Only after this, says Kabir, can there be hope of a union with the loved one.

Who would imagine he was a simple weaver, Nadeem added. *That is mysticism, I think, of the order of one of the great Sufi saints: a Qutb Sahib or a Hazrat Nizamuddin.*

She was not stupid; she would read between the lines and know that he was trying to disguise his pain under that cloak of Kabir's couplet. Would it encourage her to write more warmly the next time? Or would it have the opposite effect, and put her off? Nadeem did not know.

It was only after he had sent the letter off that he wished he could have erased those lines. That couplet of Kabir's, and his reference to them. It struck him, belatedly, as silly. Flogging a dead horse. Even all those weeks back, when they had been talking in the garden of Sikandar Lodhi's tomb, she had turned him down. What hope was there for him?

Did he really even want that hope? If he were completely honest with himself, Nadeem realized that it was not so any longer. He loved Zarina still—perhaps he always would, in a spiritual, platonic sort of way—but he did not want her any more. That desire to lift that veil and finally see her face, he now knew as nothing more than idle curiosity. The memory of her voice, the shape of her hands, the fragrance of jasmine that wafted from her—or was it lotus? He did not remember, any more—all of that was sliding away, vanishing from his mind and his heart. He was beginning to forget Zarina as she was.

☙

Winter came, and brought with it long nights of bitter cold and days not much warmer. The trees drooped, their leaves dripping moisture long after a weak sun had dissipated the fog that blanketed them through the night. The Yamuna, shrouded by mist, saw the arrival of great flocks of migrating birds. Ducks, geese, gulls, and more, a great honking, chittering, quacking conglomeration that cloaked the sluggish waters of the river and provided a rich hunting ground for the noblemen of the city.

Waqar stopped by at their home on his way back from a hunting expedition on the banks of the Yamuna. He had bagged a dozen or so birds, plump and sleek from the bounty of the river. 'It's been many months since you visited,' he told Nadeem in an accusing but not unkind voice. 'Mir Kaamil Sahib was telling me just the other day about the latest piece you have made for him. He was all praise.' He handed over a brace of ducks to the servant who had come forward, and followed Nadeem into the dalaan of the men's quarters.

They talked briefly of the weather, and of the news from Nadeem's daughter, who was now expecting her third child. She lived in faraway Multan, and news from her came sporadically and too infrequently for Ismat's liking. 'And your son,' said Waqar. 'What about him? He is fifteen now; are you looking for a bride for him?'

Nadeem nodded, not sure what to say. Ismat, he knew, was making enquiries, searching for a suitable bride. The problem was that their son showed even less inclination to join the workshop than Nadeem had exhibited. Worse still, it was not even as if he was interested in any other profession, in anything else that might be turned into a worthy occupation. Nadeem and Waqar had tried to interest him in calligraphy, but his penmanship was hopeless. At the workshop—where he spent most of the day—he pottered about, doing little. He looked bored when called in on discussions about suppliers and customers, naqshas, and progress.

'I am worried about him,' Nadeem admitted, when Waqar continued to look at him with enquiring eyes. 'The workshop is doing well, and I earn a comfortable income from my calligraphy. But the combined wealth is by no means enough that he can live off it for the rest of his life. He must work, he must make his own way through life.'

'He isn't a child any more,' Waqar agreed. 'Do you think, if he were married off, that might help him acquire a sense of responsibility? It happens to some men, you know. They find themselves having to look after a wife, and then children. And suddenly, they grasp the gravity of the situation. It might be that way for him.'

Nadeem could do nothing except nod in a half-hearted way. It sounded like a gamble, a wild and unreliable stab in the dark.

'Don't worry,' Waqar said, patting Nadeem on the shoulder. 'It will all come around, you'll see. Allah is merciful.'

But the Almighty, it appeared, was intent on testing the family.

A few months later, when spring was warming into summer, Waqar suddenly died, felled by a fever that had ravaged a once-sturdy man, reducing him to a mere shell in a matter of hours. Nadeem was sincerely sorry: not just because Waqar had been his first tutor, but also because of that long-ago day in the Bagh-e-Jud, when Waqar had offered a truce. It was because of Waqar's willingness to let bygones be bygones that Nadeem was now able to concentrate on his calligraphy, and make a decent living from it.

Nadeem wrote to Zubair, now in faraway Lahore, to tell him of Waqar's death, and to enquire after Zubair's own health. It was getting hotter by the day; never, thought Nadeem, had he seen a summer so scorching. He wondered how Zubair was keeping.

Before Zubair's response could arrive, however, the political situation in Dilli took a turn that even Nadeem, forewarned by his father, had not imagined.

Babar, impatient to take the throne, had been moving inexorably forward and might have been expected to make his way to the imperial capital. Or, if not Agra, then Dilli. Dilli, not so long ago the capital, and never really diminished in importance, even if Sikandar Lodhi and Ibrahim had both preferred to have Agra as their seat.

Perhaps Ibrahim Lodhi did not wish the battle to come anywhere close to either of these two most vital cities. Perhaps, too, he was already nervous, and feared that Babar's army, coming all the way up to Dilli—let alone Agra—might wreak too much havoc. Babar, on his part, may have thought it would suit him to face his enemy well away from the Lodhi's own strongholds.

At any rate, it was Panipat, about forty kos from Dilli, which Babar chose as a battlefield.

And, arriving at Panipat a week before Ibrahim Lodhi could make his way to the battlefield, Babar carefully arranged his meagre army, positioning one flank along the town of Panipat, and another along the bank of the Yamuna that flowed nearby. His men dug trenches on the bank of the river, and piled up tree trunks to form an embankment.

Ibrahim Lodhi, at the head of a hundred-thousand-strong

army, faced Babar's paltry eight thousand with confidence, certain that the Lodhi army's superior numbers would carry the day. But Babar was too wily an opponent: he had planned well, and his battle tactics came as a bolt out of the blue for the Lodhi. Babar's cannon fire sent Ibrahim Lodhi's elephants stampeding off the battlefield, causing havoc in the ranks of his own army. But worse was to come: Babar's mounted archers, forming the two flanks of his army, attacked, firing fusillades of arrows while their steeds raced to and fro. The Lodhi army scattered, bunched, drew together, and turned this way and that, thrown into utter confusion.

It was then that Babar unleashed his heavy cavalry. Matchlocks, flintlocks, and camel-mounted guns were turned on the Lodhi army as it huddled, befuddled and directionless, in the centre.

By noon on that blistering hot day, 9 Rajab, 934 Hijri, known to the Western world as April 21, 1526 Anno Domini, Zahiruddin Mohammad Babar, once lord of Ferghana and of Samarqand, conquered the Empire of the Lodhis. Within the course of a few hours, the fate of the empire, and of Dilli, had changed.

Ibrahim Lodhi, trying to flee the battlefield with some five thousand trusted bodyguards, had also been killed, along with many of his men. While Babar's men examined one corpse after the other, trying to identify that of the erstwhile ruler, Babar sent his commanders off on urgent missions. His son and heir, Humayun, not yet eighteen years old but already in command, headed for Agra with a handful of generals, to seize the throne and the palace there, and to let Agra know that Babar was now its lord. Mahdi Khwaja, the husband of Babar's sister Khanzada Begum, was given the equally important task of hurrying to Dilli with an armed retinue to take hold of the treasury at Dilli.

Amidst the heaps of bloodied bodies littering the battlefield, that of Ibrahim Lodhi was finally found. Babar gave orders for its ritual bathing and burial, and once the vanquished ruler was formally interred, Babar began to get ready for his own departure for Dilli.

Three days after his victory at Panipat, Babar arrived in Dilli. In his wake came Zubair, tired and worn, but excited. As was usual, Nadeem went to meet him at the sarai where Zubair was staying, only to find his father itching to go out and about. Barely had Nadeem arrived at the sarai than Zubair had bundled him into a bullock cart and given the cart-driver instructions to take them to the Jami Masjid beside the Qutb Minar.

'It's so hot,' Nadeem said when they reached their destination, 'and you don't look at all well. Surely it would have been wiser to stay indoors?'

'And miss a spectacle such as this?' Zubair said, grinning at him. 'History is being made here, Nadeem, history. You will tell your grandchildren about this someday.'

Nadeem snorted. 'You are just over-excited, because the Lodhis have been defeated. It's not as if this is Sikandar Lodhi, either, with whom you were at daggers drawn; and it's not as if you had a hand in defeating Ibrahim Lodhi.'

'I may not have had a direct hand in the business, but I certainly did help Ghazi Khan Lodhi get back to Lahore,' Zubair remarked. 'He and his father Daulat Khan had my support, and Babar had their support.' He grinned at Nadeem before turning back, to crane his neck above the ranks of men milling about the huge courtyard of the mosque.

Nadeem too had turned, his gaze going to the minbar, the low flight of stone steps off to one side of the carved arch that signified west, the direction of prayer. The Jami Masjid, built by Qutbuddin Aibak nearly four centuries earlier, had been added to, rejuvenated, and revered long enough for it to still be as beautiful, perhaps, as in its heyday. The mosaic of coloured sandstone, honeyed, greenish-grey, flame-red, that had been carved to create its towering screens was still exquisite. The iron pillar, symbol of a long-ago ruler, still stood tall among the flagstones of the courtyard, without a spot of rust to mar it.

On the second step of the minbar, having left the topmost step vacant in deference to the Prophet, stood a sharp-nosed man: Maulana Mahmood, one of Babar's men. Along with him, now standing beside the minbar with his head bowed as if deep in prayer, was another of Babar's confidants, Sheikh Zain. Placed strategically along the periphery of the vast courtyard were men who, though they bore no visible weapons, were too alert, too stern-faced to be anything but soldiers. Babar, though he was not present, meant to assert himself here today, in the largest congregational mosque of the land he had conquered. His religious men were here to proclaim him Emperor, and his soldiers, hidden though they may be, were here to ensure that none opposed them.

'In the name of Allah, the Gracious, the Merciful,' began Maulana Mahmood. 'All praise is due to Allah; we praise Him, we seek His help.' His voice was sonorous, booming out across the flagstones.

Nadeem, the words of the sermon swirling about him, heard but did not pay heed. His mind was far away, worrying. Not about himself or his family, but about Zarina. Zarina, who was part of the imperial household in Agra. A household that must have been shattered by the defeat and death of Ibrahim Lodhi, and above which now loomed the spectre of the approaching victor.

'I do not claim to know the man, at all,' Zubair had admitted, when he had dragged Nadeem along with him to the mosque. 'I have seen him from a distance, that is all. But he treated Ibrahim Lodhi's body with respect. Had it washed and buried with all the right prayers and ceremonies. I don't think he is the type who will vent his anger on the women of the man he defeated. He does not seem the vindictive kind.'

The words had been cold comfort for Nadeem. Humayun and his entourage might be nearing Agra, if they were not already there. Once they took over the palace, what would be the plight of Dilawar Begum and her ladies? Sickening visions of rape and pillage filled his imagination.

He came back to the present with a start as he heard the Maulana invoke blessings on the name of the ruler. Zahiruddin Babar Mohammad, Baadshah.

And it was done. With the Friday sermon, the khutba, having been read in his name, Babar was formally named the lord of the empire he had fought so hard and so long to acquire.

Interlude

'We are to have a new king,' Mohsin says. He and Gokul have just come back from a trip to the local market. It is not as if there is much to be bought; the rains have been poor this past monsoon too, but what little there has been has helped produce something. A little millet, some lentils, even some of the pods and wild melons that grow in the west, in the desert lands: all are now sporadically available, even though at prices that make them unaffordable for most people. Nevertheless, there are those who can buy them, and many who will be digging into their savings to celebrate the coming festivities. Diwali is around the corner; I must think, too, of how we will celebrate it, given that Gokul is now part of our household.

For now, we are trying to come to terms with what has happened in a realm from which we are far removed. Back in the summer, when Hemu was nearing Agra with his armies, we had been secure in the belief that Iskandar Khan Uzbeg held Agra for Akbar; we believed the capital city would be safe. But Iskandar Khan Uzbeg crumbled, and that in so ignominious a manner, it embarrasses me to have to recount it. He fled Agra, leaving everything for the oncoming army. Hemu took over Agra, and having left some of his men in charge, proceeded to pursue Iskandar Khan Uzbeg and his men, who were headed for Dilli.

Hemu is now very close to Dilli, and rumour has it that Tardi Beg Khan, the governor of Dilli, is getting ready to decamp, just as Iskandar Khan Uzbeg did from Agra.

'No,' says Mohsin, when I mention this, 'that's not correct. In the bazaar, they were saying that the Baadshah has sent word that Tardi Beg Khan is to face Hemu. The troops here will be joined by those of others; neighbouring governors and commanders will send reinforcements.'

'But Hemu too is gathering allies as he advances,' I say. I may be housebound, unable to move much, but I have eyes and ears. I just need to sit on the charpai outside, under the tree in our courtyard, and I can hear voices drifting in from the lane on the other side of the wall. Occasionally, visitors come by too, now that this drought seems to be easing. 'All the way, as he's moved towards Agra and now beyond, he has been joined by others.'

Gokul, who has just stepped in, adds in a tone of near-ebullience, 'Panditji says it has been more than three hundred years since a Hindu ruled Dilli. Now Hemu will become the maharaja and bring Ram Rajya to this city.'

That, I fear, is wishful thinking on the part of the Panditji, the priest at the small temple in the lane behind ours. Panditji has long been critical of our rulers: first Humayun, then Sher Shah Suri, and then Humayun again; he must be hoping that a Hindu ruler might not be guilty of the many failings he attributes to the Muslim rulers so far. Who knows. In any case, this idea of Hemu wanting to set up a Hindu dynasty, or whatever Panditji fondly hopes for, may not be quite accurate.

Before I can say anything, though, Mohsin utters a snort, a sound part derision and part amusement.

'Panditji is just saying what he hopes for,' he says. 'Hemu is no enemy of Muslims. Didn't he serve under Islam Shah Suri, as his chief of intelligence? And he did so well there that Islam Shah's successor, Adil Shah, made him wazir as well as commander! If Hemu was so very antagonistic to Muslims, why would he have served Adil Shah?' He is looking belligerent now, and Gokul—I feel sorry for him, poor child—is bewildered.

'But I'—he begins to say, only to be cut off by Mohsin.

'Hemu won more than twenty battles for Adil Shah Suri,' he says, and he is now beginning to sound obnoxiously pedantic. 'Many have said he is the greatest military leader the Afghans have ever had here in Dilli and in Agra. If he wanted to establish a Hindu dynasty, why did he wait so long? Don't tell me he was scared of Humayun?' He chortles, and I have had enough.

'Stop,' I say. 'Go and say all of this to the pandit, if you feel so strongly about it. Gokul is just telling us what the pandit said; there is no need to spout all this at him.' Gokul looks at me with deep gratitude, and I, somewhat soothed by that look, nod at Mohsin, who has been startled by the admonition. 'It is all right, child,' I murmur. 'It is all right. There is no need to be so agitated; it serves nothing. If Hemu defeats Tardi Beg Khan and comes to power, how will it affect us? I cannot say, and nobody, not even Panditji, can be certain.'

We cannot be certain of anything anymore. Not even, really, if we will see the next dawn.

Mohsin is annoyed with me, affronted at my admonition. He sulks for a few hours, taking himself off into the courtyard and pottering about by himself. Gokul, realizing that he is the unwitting, indirect cause of this petulance, wanders around with a hangdog expression until I take pity on him and call him to my side. We practice some Persian, and I am astonished as well as pleased to find that the boy has made a lot of progress. He is bright indeed. If he goes on this way, it may well be him to whom I will be dictating my memoirs, not my own grandson.

In the meantime, though, I must make my peace with Mohsin. All said and done, he is a wise boy; he will realize, on his own, that I was right. A few hours, some reflection, some time to get over his anger, and he will be back. Then we will talk, and I will tell him what I feel.

He does come to me, later that evening. Gokul and I are sitting together, Gokul reading his letters to himself under his breath, memorizing each nuance, each sound, each curve. Mohsin glances at him, his gaze guarded: he is wondering, of course, if Gokul holds his earlier fit of temper against him. But Gokul looks up, and after a moment of consideration, gives Mohsin a small, tentative smile. Mohsin smiles back, and they are friends again. A little awkward, perhaps, for the moment, but that hesitancy will evaporate soon enough.

'It does not do for us commoners to worry ourselves over what the high and mighty will do,' I say, once we have settled down. 'You and I, we might think religion is important, that decisions are taken and allies forged to further the cause of one religion over another. Perhaps to convert, perhaps to show that one god is mightier than another.' The boys, sitting cross-legged on the floor, turn their faces up to me, their expressions identical: attentive, interested.

'That is not true,' I say, hoping my voice conveys the emphasis I want it to. 'Remember, those in power invariably want more power. And more power comes not through religion, but through strategy. You must ally with the right people, you must say the right things, you must make the right decisions, in order to hold onto that power and acquire more power. Religion can be the means to get more power, it is rarely the end.

'If Hemu's aim was to set up a so-called Hindu dynasty, opposed to the Muslims, why would he seek the help of the Afghans?' I ask. I am careful not to look at Gokul; I do not want him to think this a renewal of Mohsin's tirade. I just want to make a point. 'And, more importantly, why would the Afghans help him? Some say, in fact, that Hemu still regards Adil Shah Suri as his master; that when he comes to the throne—if that happens, and no one can be sure of that—it will be as a vassal of Adil Shah Suri.'

'Adil Shah is in Chunar, isn't he?' Mohsin says. 'That's a long way away.'

'The realms of emperors can stretch many kos north and south, east and west,' I reply. And in people's hearts, their minds. The greatest rulers, the ones with the most influence, are not the ones with the most fearsome weapons or the biggest armies; they are the ones who know how to rule people's hearts. Babar was one such. He won that decisive battle at Panipat, against what had seemed overwhelming odds, not only because he was a strategist, but because he knew how to keep his soldiers loyal. They would have laid down their lives for their emperor.

'We waited and watched,' I tell the boys, once we have settled down again and Mohsin has his paper and pens out, busy inscribing all that I am saying. 'We watched as Babar stopped in Dilli, en route to Agra. He spent several days here, visiting the important sites. The Hauz Khaas, and the dargahs of Hazrat Nizamuddin Auliya and Qutbuddin Bakhtiar Kaki. I remember some people saying that Babar made it a point to go to Qutb Sahib's dargah, because it was Qutb Sahib whose blessings won him this Empire. Qutb Sahib was also from Ferghana, you know, which was Babar's fiefdom before he lost it.'

I recall that time, those few days when Babar and his retinue moved around Dilli. There were many in Dilli who, perhaps tired of the incompetence and self-serving nature of Ibrahim Lodhi, looked on Babar as a saviour. They lined the streets to welcome him as he rode into the city on his stallion. Perhaps they cheered, as some later said; I don't recall such an outbreak of emotion. I, at least, was apprehensive. Even if Babar did nothing more here in Dilli than let his new subjects acknowledge him, would it be the same in Agra? There was the palace in Agra, and in it was Zarina. Despite my father's assurances, I could not help but worry. Even though I knew now that I was no longer in love with her as I once had been, I was worried, as one would worry for a friend or a member of one's family.

But the days went by. Babar reached Agra, and there was no sudden conflagration, no flurry of terrified fugitives fleeing the city to take refuge in Dilli. There was quiet, a quiet which made me impatient and tense. Was all well, or was it the silence of the tomb?

Then word began to spread in the bazaars of how Babar had treated Ibrahim Lodhi's household, his women and relatives: with extreme courtesy and consideration. Dilawar Begum and her ladies had been allowed to retain their palaces and their slaves. None of them had been imprisoned, no children separated from their mothers, no widows or unmarried women summarily handed over to Babar's soldiers.

I had breathed a sigh of relief, a relief so complete and utter that it left me exhausted.

'You must have really loved Zarina Begum a lot,' Mohsin says. His voice is grave, but there is a teasing twinkle in his eye.

'A wise man does not go around offering marriage to just any woman,' I say, in as austere a tone as I can manage. But even I can appreciate the playfulness in Mohsin's words, and I cannot help but add: 'besides which, I was worried about that parakeet-gifting admirer, you know. What if the strain of the invasion had driven her into his arms, eh? What then?'

Mohsin bursts out laughing at that, and even Gokul cannot suppress a giggle. I smile back at them, and for a brief while, the space of a few minutes, we are happy. Two boys and an old man, amused at the plight of a man from long ago.

'Actually, though,' I admit, 'by then, it was worry for an old friend, not much more. Your grandmother,' I tell Mohsin, 'was jealous for no reason; by then, she need not have regarded Zarina as a rival. But I never told her that; her anger amused me.' That last sentence comes out unbidden. It strikes me, even as I blurt it out, that it was the truth: Ismat's fury, her jealous rages—even though she denied that jealousy—had made me feel strangely delighted.

The boys are looking blank now, unable to comprehend the puzzling depths of an adult's heart.

We hear Mohsin's father at the door, calling to his son. Mohsin goes to open the door, and my son comes in, taking off his turban as he enters the room. His face is strained, his eyes troubled.

'Abba,' he says, coming to me and sitting down, his turban still clasped loosely in one hand. 'Hemu has arrived in Dilli. At Tughlaqabad. He is getting ready to fight.'

☙

Iskandar Khan Uzbeg, fleeing to Dilli from Agra, had been closely followed by Hemu and his troops. Hemu, along with his four commanders (two of them, I point out to Gokul, are Afghans), gathered his army into formation on the plains beside the village of Tughlaqabad, not even two kos from the Jami Masjid where I had long ago heard the khutba read in Babar's name.

Iskandar Khan Uzbeg tried to redeem himself by joining hands with Dilli's governor, Tardi Beg Khan, and various commanders who had come to their aid from nearby. The battle, on the plains of Tughlaqabad, with the massive stone fortress of Ghiyasuddin Tughlaq looming beyond, was dusty and bloody, from all we heard later. But when is battle not bloody, not dusty?

Howbeit, Tardi Beg Khan and his allies managed to deploy their forces effectively enough to capture several hundred of Hemu's elephants, and to kill several thousand of his Afghan soldiers. It looked a sure victory for the Baadshah's side, even if the Baadshah was not on hand to see it.

Which, in hindsight, was probably all for the best; the Baadshah might have been distressed to see what happened next. For Tardi Beg Khan's men, assuming that the battle was theirs, broke ranks and set out to loot and plunder Hemu's side—not realizing that Hemu was far from being a spent force. He still had many men and many elephants in reserve, and he used these to charge forward at what was now a poorly manned enemy front.

And thus it was that Hemu won. Tardi Beg Khan and

his allies have fled westwards, no doubt to report to the Baadshah and his regent Bairam Khan.

These past couple of days, the bazaars have been full of what is happening in Dilli. At the citadel of Din Panah, which Humayun had begun building and Sher Shah Suri had taken over, Hemu has now had himself crowned king. A rajyabhishek, I am told, is what it is called. There was a grand durbar at the palace, and Hemu—who has styled himself Raja Hemchandra Vikramaditya—was ceremonially anointed with sacred water from the Ganga, blessed by the chanting of many priests, and then presented to the populace with an ornate brocade parasol held above his head.

It all sounds very exotic to me; in my nearly sixty years, I have been used to a new ruler being announced by way of a khutba in the mosque. This is new to me, and I wish I was strong enough to have gone there, to witness the ceremony.

At this rajyabhishek of his, our new king also rewarded his many allies, both Hindu as well as Afghan. Fine robes, Arabian horses, and grants of fertile land have been given out to hundreds of military men who have proved faithful.

'Panditji is not pleased,' Gokul reports. Of course, if Panditji has been looking forward to the dawn of a Ram Rajya, as he has fondly believed Hemu capable of heralding, then this bestowal of largesse on Muslim Afghan allies—indeed, the very fact of Muslim allies—will have come as a bad blow.

'Perhaps we simply need to wait and see what happens,' I say. Yes, that should be it: to see what Hemu will do. How he will bring about this Ram Rajya. If he will.

And, of course, to see what Jalaluddin Mohammad Akbar, erstwhile Baadshah, is now going to do. Or rather, what his advisors are going to do.

'How is it,' says Mohsin, 'that in all this chronicling of yours, you never refer to Abbu by name? Everywhere, you call him “my son”, or “the boy”. Never “Shaadaab”; you never call him by his name.’ He is bent over a pen, which he is busy cleaning with a bit of old silk cotton.

What do I tell him? That this son was borne to me by a wife I never loved, and for whom I felt nothing? That Ismat, bitter and distant, had become for me a symbol of my own neglect, and that I felt both guilty about not loving her, and also unable to do anything about it. No matter how hard I tried, I could summon up no feeling for Ismat. Or, I admit to myself, for the son she bore me. I do not hate him; I never have, and I confess that, as the years have passed, I have begun to like him, a good deal more than I ever liked his mother. But I have never felt for him the way I should feel for an offspring.

I cannot say that to Mohsin.

‘Is that so?’ I say, frowning in puzzlement. ‘I had not noticed. That won’t do. When you have some time, will you go back over the manuscript and put his name in, wherever it’s mentioned?’

Mohsin nods, but he says nothing. He is hard at work cleaning the pen. Too hard. I suspect he guesses something of how it was between me and Ismat. I did blurt out that stupid confession the other day, after all, of how it pleased me to see Ismat fret over my love for Zarina, even when that love had died. Mohsin can see into my soul, I sometimes think, when I catch him staring at me with that look of close concentration. He can see me for the often selfish, hurtful man that I was for so many years: a man too flawed to be perfect, and now too old to change.

But Mohsin is old enough now to appreciate that even those nearest to us, and dearest, are not without their flaws. And that flaws and all, we go on loving them. Or, virtues and all, we go on being indifferent to them.

I am not given the luxury—or the pain—of pondering this matter, because Gokul comes in. He has been helping my son clean a small, long-neglected shed at one end of the courtyard. I am not sure what my son has in mind, whether he intends to put it to some use, or he is cleaning it simply to keep himself occupied.

But now Gokul is here, and we can go back to our work. We can go back to that day, deep in the heart of summer thirty years ago, when I went home from the workshop to hear news that made my heart leap to my throat.

21

There was not a cloud to dim the brightness of the sun, or soften the edges of its searing harshness. The monsoon should have arrived a few weeks ago, but a parched Dilli still waited. A torpidity, a lethargy of movement and thought, seemed to swamp everything, from the weavers in the workshop to the birds in the trees: all, it appeared, waited, thirsty and hot and desperate for the rains.

Babar, having left one of his trusted men in charge of Dilli, had carried on towards Agra nearly two months earlier. Little had changed in Dilli; it was as if Ibrahim Lodhi had never been defeated and Babar had never come to the throne. It would take time, thought Nadeem, as he entered his home at the end of the day: time for Babar to assess the domain he had won, time to understand its people. Unlike invaders such as his own ancestor Taimur, Babar did not seem inclined to ravage the land and take the spoils back to his own capital; no, this man intended to rule, and time would tell how he would rule.

Ordinarily, it would have been a servant who would have met Nadeem at the door, welcoming him back home. This time, even before the door-keeper had shut the main gate of the house, a veiled figure had appeared at the doorway at the end of the path and was beckoning to him. Shahana, her gestures almost frantic. Excited.

'You will not believe what has happened,' she said in an urgent whisper as soon as he had reached her.

'What is it, Amma? At least let me have some water to drink—'

Shahana stopped just long enough to call out, over her shoulder, for water and refreshments to be brought for Nadeem; then she hustled him on, towards her room in the zenana.

'You know our former cook, Ataullah?' she said, as soon as they were inside the room. 'He of the malpuas? He made excellent malpuas.'

She was too excited, too eager to spill her news, to be making sense. Nadeem contained his impatience as best as he could, and with gentle probing, wormed it out of her.

It emerged, still in somewhat incoherent sentences. This was momentous news, after all, and for a household accustomed to a mundane everyday routine where little of note ever occurred, it was especially so. Ataullah, though now retired, had kept in touch with the household—one of his sons had succeeded him in service at Nadeem's home—and every now and then he would come by, mostly just to gossip. He had come earlier that day, and he had brought a piece of news that had sent the kitchen, and consequently the household, into a tizzy.

Ataullah's cousin, a cook named Ahmed, had been working in the kitchens of the imperial palace in Agra these past six years. Ataullah did not hold him in great esteem as a cook; but there was obviously something in Ahmed that compensated: a deep and unerring sense of loyalty, perhaps. For, a couple of years ago, Ahmed had been elevated to the position of a food taster, a chashnagir. He had been chashnagir in Ibrahim Lodhi's service, and when Babar took over the palace in Agra, along with all who served in it, Ahmed became part of Babar's entourage.

Ibrahim Lodhi's mother Dilawar Begum, intent on avenging the death and defeat of her son, had succeeded in getting a message through to Ahmed. It came along with a screw of paper enclosing a potent poison: Ahmed was to pass it on to one of the Hindustani cooks who had now, like Ahmed, become one of Babar's household. That poison was served up to Babar, in a meal that included fried carrots, hare, and bread. Babar had been curious about Hindustani food, and had allowed himself to be persuaded to try some of the food cooked by the Hindustanis; little had he realized that the local dishes he was going to taste, so much more heavily spiced than those of his native Ferghana, would mask, by virtue of that spice, the flavour of poison.

But Babar was lucky; he began feeling ill soon after, and instantly suspected poisoning. He soon began to retch, and within a few minutes had vomited up his meal. The same food had also been consumed by two of Babar's men, and they too had a terrible time, throwing up their food and feeling very ill. It was poisoning, there was no doubt about that; and an investigation was immediately underway. The web of intrigue was revealed, and punishment followed swiftly.

'Poor Ahmed,' said Shahana, in a dramatic whisper, 'has been cut to pieces, and the cooks who consented to add the poison to the food have been flayed alive! Can you imagine? One maid who helped at the meal was shot dead with a matchlock, and the Dowager Empress's lady, the trusted one who brought Ahmed the poison—she has been trampled to death by an elephant. But do you know, the Dowager Empress herself, though she is the actual culprit, escapes punishment! She has merely been sent off, exiled to Kabul. Now where is the justice in that, I ask you?'

But Nadeem was not listening any more.

Dilawar Begum must have many trusted ladies, he told himself. A task as delicate as the proposed poisoning of the conqueror, would not be entrusted to one who had been in her service a relatively short while. Logically, it could not be Zarina.

And yet there was that niggle of doubt, the fear that would not go away, no matter how hard he tried.

❧

Junaid had been to Agra just the previous month, and in the course of his visit, had tried to gauge if the palace might be interested in the brocades he had taken along. Babar's womenfolk, however, were still away in Kabul. And Babar, disgusted with the heat and dust of Agra, was in no mood to buy brocades and other fripperies.

But Junaid, because he had visited the palace, had made it a point to ask after Zarina, and had met her briefly.

'She seemed content,' Junaid recalled. 'The Dowager Empress had been frantic back then. Grieving, of course, for her son, but unable to decide whether she should kill herself, or Babar.' A small, sarcastic smile flickered on his lips. 'She chose to try killing him instead, eh? The old lady is certainly courageous.' He shook his head. 'No, I doubt if the Dowager Empress would have chosen Zarina Begum. She likes her well enough, but for a job such as this, Dilawar Begum would have chosen someone she had known long and well.'

He sounded confident, and it bolstered Nadeem's flagging spirits.

'Anyhow,' Nadeem said, 'when you travel next to Agra to meet our clients there, I will accompany you.'

That did not happen. Now that Babar had installed himself firmly in Agra and there appeared to be some hope of stability, both in governance and in the state of the economy, those with wealth to spend began to open up their purses again. The slackness and caution that had taken hold of trade began to dissipate. The workshop's business increased. Nadeem's calligraphy, ironically enough boosted by the death of Waqar—many of his uncle's clients shifted their allegiance to him—made Nadeem the most sought-after qaatib in Dilli.

At home, things had settled down somewhat. Ismat, along with Shahana, was so involved in finding a bride for her son that she no longer had any time to fret over Nadeem's lack of interest. Of the many girls the two women had seen, they were partial to three, and it would take perhaps another few meetings with the girls and their families to decide which would be the boy's bride. He would be married before the year was out.

There was so much happening, such frenetic activity,

that Nadeem forgot his worry for Zarina. In any case, after Junaid had reassured him, he had written to Zarina, wishing her well and hoping she was safe. No reply had come, but there could be many, all perfectly plausible, reasons for that. The household at the imperial palace might be in turmoil, now that Dilawar Begum had been exiled. It would be stressful anyway, given that Babar and all his men would now be suspicious of Ibrahim Lodhi's womenfolk and servants.

The weeks passed. News arrived that Dilawar Begum, travelling to Kabul with the contingent of soldiers who had been deputed to accompany her into exile, had committed suicide by throwing herself into the Indus. She had no doubt realized what might happen to her when she reached Babar's harem in that mountain town. The Baadshah's ladies, feisty warrior women that they were, would not spare her. Death at her own hands was far preferable.

Shahana was not keeping good health; age was catching up with her, and life was a series of aches and pains. Her joints were knotted and stiff with arthritis, her body so frail that it looked as if a sharp gust of breeze would take her away. But her mind was sharp as ever, and she liked to talk of the years gone by, the sorrows and the joys of long ago. Nadeem rarely had time to sit beside her for long, but Ismat and her son were more patient, more accommodating.

On this day, though, Nadeem had come home early, and had decided to spend some time with his mother. When she began reminiscing about the long-ago wedding of one of Zubair's sisters, he humoured her.

'Do you know, there were so many guests from out of town, we had to prepare the entire field behind our house,' Shahana said. 'The servants were busy night and day. They cleaned and levelled the field, and set up a thorn fence around it. Then they spread reed mats all over, so that there was no dust. Charpais were brought, and laid out for all the menfolk there. We women were all inside, we had the entire house to ourselves.'

She rambled on, describing the feast, the decorations. The celebrations at the workshop, and the singing and dancing when the weavers came to offer their congratulations—along with a specially woven brocade—to the newlyweds. And, priceless: the groom's face when he saw the beauty of his new bride. Shahana chuckled. 'Oh, you should have seen Abbas Miyan. His jaw dropped and we thought his eyes would pop! He was her devoted slave from that day on. Shamsher goes after his father, in his devotion to his wife. He is just like Abbas Miyan, his wife is his all.'

Nadeem sat up straight, a thought coming to him. His cousin Shamsher lived in Agra.

Later that day, he wrote a letter to Shamsher. In it, he reminded Shamsher of Raheem, who had taken his little boys around the workshop that day, many years back, when Shamsher had come to Dilli. Raheem was no more, but his daughter Zarina Begum was in the imperial palace, formerly one of the ladies of Ibrahim Lodhi's household. They had had no news of her and were worried. Would it be possible for Shamsher to find out if all was well with her?

Shamsher did reply, after nearly a month, and with his letter was enclosed another, from Zarina.

Ammi has been unwell, wrote Zarina after a brief salutation and an assurance that she was safe. *The turmoil and anxiety of the past several months have taken their toll on her. We were not sure how the new Baadshah might treat us, and after that incident—of which you no doubt know—we were very worried indeed. The two maids involved in the attempted poisoning of the Baadshah were known slightly to both Ammi and me, and it was dreadful to hear of what happened.*

I try to keep my spirits up, but truth to tell, it is difficult. We are now part of the Baadshah's household, though his womenfolk are yet to arrive from Kabul. We, those who were spared, keep to ourselves and are treated with dignity, but still. Ammi is failing, and the hakims say that nothing can be done but to keep her comfortable.

It was reassuring to learn that Zarina was safe, but the letter left him feeling restless. His heart went out to Zarina, having to look after an ailing parent at a time like this, when she must be adjusting, too, to living in an unfamiliar household.

There was nothing he could do about it, though, except to offer commiserations and to assure Zarina that Allah would be merciful, as he had been all along. Shamsher, in his letter, had assured Nadeem that he, being in Agra, would be happy to be of service to Zarina and her Ammi, and this message Nadeem passed on in his letter to Zarina. *My cousin is a good man, and even though he had met your father only briefly, I know he held him in great regard. Please feel free to ask him for any help you may need.*

ɞ

Nadeem's son was married a few weeks after the monsoon had receded. His bride was the eldest daughter of a man who traded in cloth. The father had a respectable business, his trade links reaching across the length of the land, all the way from Bengal to Sindh. His daughters, of whom there were four, had been brought up mostly in Bengal, which was their natal home. They had only recently come to Dilli, where their father had bought a house. Not really to live in permanently; they would miss the east too much—but at least during the months when Dilli's weather made it liveable.

Shahana and Ismat had gone to meet the womenfolk of the family, and had unanimously approved of the eldest daughter.

'Well-bred girls,' Shahana said with a contented smile. 'And our Shaadaab's bride is the most beautiful, the sweetest of them all. He will be a very happy man.'

Shaadaab, of course, had no say in any of it. He would see her for the first time only after they were married.

For several weeks, the house was in a whirl. Dozens of

servants—or so they seemed, the house was swarming with them—were everywhere, cleaning and washing and sweeping and mopping. Rugs were dusted out, sheets washed, new drapes stitched. Precious old ceramic bowls and cups were retrieved from where they had been kept for safekeeping, washed and carefully dried. Metal platters and dishes were polished, many new sets of clothing, all very fine, made for the bridegroom. A week before the wedding, additional cooks and helpers arrived to start making sweetmeats, grinding spices, and cleaning rice and wheat for the wedding feast.

It was a joyous occasion, and for a few weeks before and after, the household was in a blur of festivities. Zubair, though he dared not come to participate in the rejoicing, sent many gifts and a letter of congratulation to his grandson. *May all the blessings I have coming to me be yours instead,* he wrote. *May your days be long, your happiness untold. May your match prosper and be blessed.*

Winter that year took its time settling in. For many days after Diwali, there was nothing more than a mild coolness in the air. It was pleasant, gentle weather: good weather for sitting under the trees, watching the birds flying in, skeins of them rippling across a clear blue sky, headed for the abundant waters of the monsoon-filled Yamuna. Weather for breathing in deep of the clean, cool air; of looking back at a year that had started off in turmoil but seemed to be ending on a note of hope. Babar was settling in, far away in Agra, and the news was that he had already sent for his ladies to travel to Agra from Kabul. Surely, if that was the case, it meant he intended to make this land his home.

Dilli rejoiced, if only in a subdued, controlled way. Rulers who thought of the land as their own were apt to invest in it, not to simply use it and vanish. Of course, given that Babar had spent most of his nearly forty years outside Hindustan, it was hard to believe he would feel any very powerful love for Hindustan. It was said that he spoke in disparaging terms of the summer heat, the dryness, the poor horses, the dreadful meat and the charmless people. He complained about the lack of everything from candles to grapes, cold water to good bread: nothing, except perhaps the cooling breeze in the monsoon, was to his liking.

But he was settling in, planning gardens and palaces along the Yamuna in Agra. His ladies were coming, and what further proof was there that Babar did not intend to be another Taimur?

When winter came—suddenly, one morning, it was colder, and mist blanketed the ground—it came with a vengeance. Swiftly the nights grew so cold that it was impossible to get warm enough to be comfortable. Braziers were lit, more quilts pulled out, and warming infusions brewed to deal with colds and fevers.

Shahana, already so frail, caught a chill. It settled in her chest, and soon she was coughing late into the night, the phlegm erupting from her in great, obscene gouts. They did what they could, but it was no use. She was too old, too fragile, and too easy a prey for the cold. That very night, Shahana coughed one last time, and then her eyelids fluttered shut forever.

Nadeem mourned her, of course. He had loved her dearly; she had been ever his confidant, both loving as well as wise. What surprised him, however, was the intensity with which his wife mourned the death of her mother-in-law. Ismat's howls were over-dramatic and her tears copious; she wept through the night. Her daughter-in-law, Shaadaab's timid bride, fluttered helplessly about, finally sitting down on the threshold of Shahana's room, where Ismat kept a vigil beside the old matriarch's body. The next morning, Ismat consented to wash her face and compose herself just before the arrival of the women summoned to ceremonially wash and lay out the dead body.

By the time Nadeem returned from the graveyard, it was to be greeted with the news that Ismat had taken to her bed. Shaadaab's wife was sitting at the sufferer's bedside when Nadeem entered the room; she quickly veiled herself and shrank back into a corner of the room. But Ismat, hauling herself up on her elbows and giving Nadeem a long, lugubrious look, decided she needed privacy. The young woman was sent off on an errand, and Ismat lay back, her eyes closed, her mouth turned down into a scowl.

Nadeem seated himself beside her. He thought, briefly, of offering some sort of comfort—perhaps taking her hand, or patting her—then set it aside. He did not really wish it, and he doubted Ismat wanted it. Not from him, at any rate.

He was tired, he realized. Tired from all these years of domestic rancour. Even when there had been no arguments, there had been little of the peace, the sense of sanctuary, of calm and belonging one might expect of a home.

Ismat was not the only one to blame; he knew that. Had known it for a long time, even if he had not admitted it. Neither of them had made an effort, neither of them had wanted to make anything of their marriage.

He did not even want anything from it now.

'Ismat,' he said softly. 'I know I have caused you much suffering. I am sorry.' She opened her mouth to speak, but the expression on her face was enough for him: this would only be a repetition of all that had gone before. The same complaints, the old bitterness.

'No,' he said, stopping her before she could even utter a word. 'No, Ismat; please. Let us not argue. I have no strength for it, and no will. If we cannot live in peace, at least let us not be constantly railing at each other.' He drew in a deep breath. 'I bear you no ill-will, you should know that. If you can live, and let live, without arguments and anger, it would make life easier for all of us.'

He rose to his feet, gathering the ends of his long coat close to him, and left the room without another word.

Behind him, he heard a snarl of impotent rage. Then Ismat began calling for her daughter-in-law, a maid, someone. She needed water to drink. Her head hurt. She needed it massaged. She wanted something to soothe her aching throat. *Where was everyone?!*

ღ

The months went by, the winter warming into spring and then summer. Life went its way. In Nadeem's household, though her daughter-in-law was now there too, Ismat reigned supreme. During Shahana's lifetime, Ismat had found herself having to defer to her mother-in-law. She had had to hold her tongue when Shahana pronounced this dish too spicy for her taste, or relegated this favourite bolster to the rubbish heap. She had been obliged to say no when every pore of her body screamed yes, and yes when, deep in her heart, she opposed what was being said.

Now there was nobody to lord it over her.

Ismat's newfound sense of power seemed to, gradually, mellow her. The pinched look, the suspicious gaze and the irritability slowly diminished. She was a happier woman than she had been just a few months earlier, and because of it, the entire household breathed a sigh of relief.

In summer, one of Zarina's now sporadic and rare letters arrived at the workshop for Nadeem. It was brief, stilted. Her Ammi, ailing these past many months, had died. It seemed, from the cursory way in which she spoke of it, that it had been several weeks, perhaps even months, since the old lady's death. Nadeem wrote her a letter of condolence, assuring Zarina of his prayers and hoping that she was safe and well. If there was anything he or Shamsher could do for her, she must not hesitate. He could not, alas, come to Agra at this time; matters were too fragile, life too hectic and uncertain, for him to leave Dilli.

Still, he did not tell her the truth: that his heart had changed. Surely it would hurt her, to know that the man who had professed to love her so many years, now felt nothing of that long-lost emotion for her? It would be an affront, would it not?

On second thought, perhaps not. Zarina had turned him down twice, and had made it amply clear on both occasions that she had no wish to marry him. She would probably be relieved if she knew he was no longer in love with her.

After much deliberation, Nadeem said nothing. He was still her friend, and he would remain so. There was no real need to tell her that she need not fear any further attempts to turn that friendship into anything more.

Less than a week after Zarina's letter came another letter, this one from Zubair, who had been living in Lahore this past year and more. One of Faisal's sons was now handling the workshop in Kashi, and Zubair had decided he was no longer needed there. Instead, having fallen in love with Lahore on an earlier visit—the same one, when he had been a travelling companion to Daulat Khan Lodhi's son—he had moved to that city. *It reminds me of Dilli*, he wrote. *The same searing summers, the same monsoon. The same trees. The neem and the palash, the bakain and the gular. Here, every similarity with the city of my birth makes me yearn for Dilli; but at the same time, that yearning is somewhat satisfied by this sister of Dilli. That is what they are: sister cities, each beautiful, each intoxicating in its own way.*

Zubair was very ill; a bad cough had worsened until he could barely breathe. The hakims said it was consumption, and that too in an advanced stage: they could do nothing for him. Zubair wished dearly to meet Nadeem before he died, but the precarious condition of his health forbade him from even attempting the journey from Lahore to Dilli. Would Nadeem come, to meet him one last time?

You are all that remains of what and whom I have held dear, he wrote. *Come, my child. Come, so that I may close my eyes to a loved face.*

22
Lahore
935 Hijri (1529 CE)

Two of the Baadshah's aunts had travelled to Agra all the way from Kabul the year following his victory. They had brought with them all the paraphernalia without which royalty would not dream of moving: many chests full of clothing and jewellery; carpets; curtains; wall hangings; musical instruments; games; and much more to keep them somewhat comfortable along the way.

And they brought one musk melon, as a gift for Babar. That fruit, fragrant and redolent with the scent of his faraway Kabul, brought tears to Babar's eyes as he cut it. It was common knowledge by then that Babar had not quite been able to fall in love with this land he had won. For a mountain man, used to snows and cool weather through the year, the dust and torrid heat of these vast plains was unbearable.

The sight, the weight, the scent and the taste of that melon took him back to the land he loved, the people he loved. It intensified the homesickness, and it made him wish that his family—wives, children, aunts, cousins—were with him again.

The two aunts and their entourage stayed in Agra for nearly a year, and when they made the journey back to Kabul, they took with them the Baadshah's orders: his womenfolk were to come to him, without further delay.

It took them time, of course; time to prepare, time to gather all they needed—from the many things they feared they might not find easily in Agra, to the determination to make the long journey—and when they finally set off from Kabul, it was on an arduous five-month long trail, in horse-litters and occasionally in palanquins, to Agra.

It was in Lahore, where he had just buried his father, that Nadeem happened to cross paths with the caravan that carried the Baadshah's womenfolk to Agra.

Zubair had taken a long time dying; though he had been very ill, there had been, too, a restlessness about him, a sense of work left unfinished, of promises unfulfilled and words left unsaid. For weeks, with Nadeem by his side, he lingered on. Between bouts of coughing, he dictated long letters, to be sent to this man and that. He wanted to close his affairs, bid farewell to the world. The house he had inhabited in Kashi had to be sold, now that there was no chance of his returning. Faisal's son had to be sent various papers to prove that neither Zubair nor his descendants would stake a claim in the Kashi workshop. It had been a refuge to Zubair in his time of need; he had worked hard for it, and had contributed to its success. His debt to Faisal, long departed from this world, had been paid.

It took many months for Nadeem to do all that Zubair asked of him. He needed to travel, and to send several letters. Finally, when all was done, Nadeem came back to his father's side in Lahore.

Zubair stayed alive less than a day after Nadeem returned. Within a few hours, his condition had begun to worsen, and in the hour just before dawn, when birdsong was already beginning to fill the air, he had breathed his last, his hand clasped in Nadeem's.

Now, with Zubair buried, Nadeem was making the rounds of Lahore, tying up all the loose ends of Zubair's life. The small house where he had lived was sold. Of Zubair's possessions, Nadeem had retained a few, the odds and ends that evoked for him the memory of the father he had not known through much of his life, but to whom he had grown increasingly close over these last years.

To dispose of the rest—the clothing, the household goods,

the remnants of a life—took a few days. There were men to be paid, others from whom payments had to be collected.

Some of the people Nadeem had to meet were hard to pin down. A merchant from whom he had to collect a payment for some brocades Zubair had supplied, was proving difficult to get hold of. His clerk had told Nadeem that Sethji was travelling and would return that evening. He would probably be at his shop the following day; Nadeem could come there.

But when Nadeem arrived at the shop, a harried-looking shop assistant informed Nadeem that Sethji had been unexpectedly called away by a neighbour. It was unavoidable, but Sethji had left word that he would be back within the hour. Nadeem was to be entertained, to be offered refreshments and made comfortable. Would he sit?

The man, his attention divided between a customer, a servant who was stacking bales of cloth, and two porters who were unloading a consignment from a bullock cart, looked overwhelmed. 'I'll wait outside,' Nadeem said. He took up a position in the shade of a maulsari tree, its glossy green canopy hung here and there with tiny bright orange fruit.

It was still early, and the bazaar around him was not as crowded as it would become later in the day. Stalls and shops were being swept, their wares dusted and put out. A bhishti, his leather water skin swollen, was wandering along the stretch of dusty road in front of the shops, sprinkling water and exchanging greetings with the shopkeepers: they must pay him a weekly wage, perhaps, to do this task for them. From somewhere farther along, hidden from sight, came the strident twanging of an iktara, with a reedy male voice singing to its accompaniment. A mendicant, seeking alms.

'Oh, look at this! What is this?' Nadeem's reverie was broken by a high-pitched, excited voice: a child. 'I have never seen anything like this. It's not'—the unseen child hesitated briefly before adding, 'a green almond? It looks the same shape, but it's so big! A giant green almond,' the child concluded, with a little gurgle, amused at its own silliness.

The child's accent was unfamiliar to Nadeem; he could not place it. Perhaps she was from somewhere far to the northwest. Qandahar? Kabul? Perhaps even farther west?

'It's a mango,' said a male voice. The vendor of the fruit, his voice oddly deferential.

'A mango! I have never eaten a mango,' said the child. 'Bibi, let us buy some, shall we? Please?' A wheedling tone had crept into the child's voice.

'My Lady,' came the voice of a woman—a mellifluous voice, somewhat deep for a woman, but the more attractive for its raw earthiness—'we should be getting back to the camp. We will have been missed by now, and you know what will happen. No one will say a word to you, but I—'

The mendicant had stepped into view, and with that, his tuneless song had become suddenly louder. The fascinating conversation Nadeem had been overhearing became inaudible. For a moment, he held back, telling himself that he should wait outside Sethji's shop for his return, not go wandering off. But it was an interesting conversation, and he was curious. Who was this little girl who had never seen a mango before, and whom a woman addressed with such deference? A little girl, too, who seemed to have absconded from some camp, but would not be scolded for this misdemeanour.

Nobility, thought Nadeem. High nobility.

Captivated in spite of himself, he moved forward towards the row of stalls where vendors of fruit and vegetables peddled their wares.

He found them just beyond, standing at a small stall which, as he had expected, was dominated by a large heap of mangoes, green-gold and orange. It towered, bountiful and glorious, behind carefully arranged pyramids of other, lesser fruit: purple-maroon falsas, glossy jaamuns, guavas.

Small and intensely fragrant musk melons. The mangoes were obviously the centerpiece here, the fruit-seller's prize wares.

In front of the vendor, facing him across the heap of mangoes, stood a small but splendid figure. The little girl wore a long dress in pale cream, its fitted sleeves reaching till her wrists and its calf-length skirt brushing the tops of fine boots made of soft brown leather. On top of the dress, she wore a waistcoat, richly embroidered with flowers in silk thread: pink, lilac, green, purple and white, colours that were echoed in the cap she wore. The woman beside her was dressed in a similar style of garment, a long dress with boots; but instead of a waistcoat, she wore a long thin robe; instead of a cap, on her head was a headdress with a veil that hung down her back and around her head, concealing her hair; and her clothes, while well-made and obviously expensive, lacked the richness of her little companion's attire.

Right now, the woman was looking very harassed. She had given in to pressure and bought a few mangoes for her charge, but for lack of anything to carry them in, she had been obliged to convert the long skirt of her robe into a makeshift sack. She held it in front of her, bunched up in both hands, bulging with a dozen or so mangoes that threatened to spill over the hem at any moment. On her face was an expression of patient long-suffering.

The child was looking up at the woman, and from where he stood, Nadeem got a good view of the little girl's face: her cheeks rosy and dimpled, two thick glossy black plaits falling on either side of her face down to her shoulders, her large eyes solemn.

He had not expected solemn eyes; from the brief conversation he had overheard, Nadeem had expected a little imp, pushing and bullying to get her own way. If she had indeed badgered her companion to buy the mangoes, the little girl now looked repentant about it.

She held an intact mango, slim and green, in her hands,

and was looking up at the woman. 'Bibi Sarv-Qad,' she said, 'I'm sorry. Your pretty mursak will get stained,' she mumbled, nodding at the woman's robe. 'Let us return them; I don't want them.'

For a moment, the woman looked as if she would happily acquiesce with the suggestion; but she sighed and shook her head. 'No, My Lady; after having paid this poor man, it would be ungenerous to return them. And besides, you did want to take some back to the camp, didn't you?'

The little girl nodded, though with reluctance, as she scrutinized the mango in her hands. 'But I wouldn't want to take something bad. What if it tastes bad? My Lady would not be happy.'

'Her Highness,' pointed out Bibi Sarv-Qad, 'will not be happy if we stay away from the camp much longer. As it is, she will be wondering where we have got to.'

Her Highness? Nadeem pursed his lips, frowning in puzzlement before he realized who these people were: the women of Babar's family, on their way from Kabul to Agra. Of course; there had been talk in Lahore that they would be passing through, and preparations had been made for them to halt at the old mud fort, some five hundred years old, that stood on the east bank of the Ravi. He had heard that a huge entourage had arrived, many hundreds of people, including slaves and soldiers, but he had not expected to run into any of them thus, wandering about the marketplace.

He wondered who the child was. Royalty, definitely; a minor princess, perhaps.

Whoever she was, she was right now a little distressed. She had no idea how to go about eating the mango, and tasting it, it appeared, was an essential prerequisite of taking the mangoes back to the camp. The fruit-seller, distracted by some newly arrived customers, had turned away and was too busy to offer advice. Bibi Sarv-Qad, busy juggling the mangoes in her mursak, had no advice to offer. Nadeem doubted that she, whoever she was, had ever seen a mango either.

The two of them looked lost.

Nadeem moved forward. 'My Lady,' he said softly, bowing to the little girl, and nodding briefly at Bibi Sarv-Qad. 'My name is Nadeem. Can I help you? You seem to be in distress.' He had deliberately lowered his voice, trying not to come across as intimidating or encroaching.

The little girl blinked, taken aback. Bibi Sarv-Qad looked momentarily startled, but her gaze turned level the next moment. She subjected him to a long, critical look, then nodded, as if to say he had her permission to proceed. Her charge, too, had turned to the woman, as if seeking direction on how to behave. On seeing the woman's nod, she too nodded, a sweet mirroring of the gesture, made all the more charming by the grave innocence of the little girl.

Nadeem held out his hand. 'Let me show you how to eat a mango,' he said. When the little girl looked confused, and a little affronted, he could not resist adding, with a twinkle in his eye, 'I will not eat your mango, My Lady. I will just show you what you have to do.' He took the fruit now proffered, and rolled it between his palms. 'The mango, you see, is best sucked, not cut into pieces.' He grinned, satisfied at the way he had managed to knead the flesh beneath the thick green skin into submissive softness. 'And to suck it, you must soften it first, the way I have done.'

He held it out to her, the mango upright, so that the small black nubbin where the fruit had been attached to its stalk was uppermost. 'Here,' he said, indicating it, 'pinch that off, and then you can suck the flesh from there.'

But she was a small child, after all, and this was all new to her. She still looked puzzled. Bibi Sarv-Qad was no help; she was far too busy trying to hold the mangoes in that improvised apron of hers.

There was no help for it; she may be an aristocrat, but she was, all said and done, a child. Younger than his own grandchildren, his daughter's sons. 'See, this way,' Nadeem said, reaching out and moulding the girl's little fingers around the mango. Once she was holding it, he pinched off the top of the mango, exposing a coin-size portion of the vibrant orange flesh within.

'Lift,' he murmured, suiting the word to his actions, as, his hand cupping her smaller one, he raised the mango to her mouth. 'And suck.' He mimed the action. He was vaguely aware of a scandalized gasp from Bibi Sarv-Qad: perhaps she thought this too audacious, that he should not have presumed to treat her charge like any other little child.

The child seemed to harbour no such inhibitions. She was not shocked; merely cautious, suspicious of this strange fruit she was about to taste.

But she obeyed, tentatively. The next moment her eyes lit up with glee.

'I have never tasted any fruit better than this!' she squealed, and before Nadeem could react, she had lowered her head and was back to sucking.

Nadeem moved back a step. His glance, triumphant, went to Bibi Sarv-Qad. For a moment, she looked as if she was going to rebuke him for his effrontery; then, she merely shook her head and turned to look at the little girl. The child, oblivious to the unspoken dialogue between the two adults, continued to enjoy her mango with all the relish of one living in the moment. This, thought Nadeem as he watched her, had been serendipity for this child. She had insisted, perhaps, on the mangoes being bought because they were a novelty; now, she might just plead for even more to be bought.

'Oh,' the little girl said in a tone of deep disappointment. She had sucked all the pulp out of the mango; all that was left in her hands was the green skin, now squeezed tight and folded round the thin hard length of the pit inside.

'Now,' said Nadeem, with a smile, 'if you were at home, and there was clean water and a napkin to spread over your clothes, you could have pulled up your cuffs and dived in further.' He held out a hand, and the child placed the remains of the mango in his palm with some reluctance. 'You have to peel back the skin, and then scrape the flesh off the seed. It is delicious, but it is messy.'

The child looked wistful. 'My Lady would not approve,' she agreed.

'Indeed,' said Bibi Sarv-Qad, in a sharp voice. 'And she will not approve of you having been gone so long! Please, My Lady,' she added, her tone now placatory. 'We have been gone far too long. Her Highness will be furious. Please, let us go. I can send a maid to buy more mangoes for you. Would you like that?'

The little girl nodded, a dimple flashing in one rosy cheek as she did so. Then, as if remembering her manners, she turned to Nadeem and looked up at him. 'You have been very kind,' she said, in a tone so formal, it made her appear years older than she was. 'Had it not been for the help you offered, I might not have known what to do. Thank you.'

Nadeem blinked, caught off-guard by the very grown-up way in which the child had spoken. Beyond the girl, he saw Bibi Sarv-Qad staring pointedly at him. Her hands, of course, were occupied in holding on to the mangoes, but she was trying to gesture with her chin and shoulders. She waggled her chin at him, and then dipped her head in a deep bow that almost sent the mangoes spilling out of her robe.

She was encouraging him to bow, and deeply. Nadeem complied. 'My Lady,' he said, addressing the little girl, 'I am glad to have been of service.'

The little girl gave him a quick smile, and then, turning back to Bibi Sarv-Qad, she said, 'Come, Bibi; let us go.'

They had gone only a few paces before the woman stopped and turned. With a murmured word to the child, who continued to stand where she was, the woman hurried back to Nadeem.

'She is "My Lady" to me, sir,' she said, in a low voice. 'To all others, especially to those not of the imperial family, she is "Your Highness".' She smiled a small smile of satisfaction, well aware that she had caught Nadeem by surprise. 'That is Gulbadan Begum, the favourite daughter of his Imperial Highness, the Baadshah.'

As the two of them walked away, Nadeem heard the little princess say, 'Bibi Sarv-Qad, do you not know any songs about mangoes? Sing me something, please.'

There was a pause, while Bibi Sarv-Qad thought. 'Mangoes?' Nadeem heard her say, in her rich, resonant voice. 'Where are there mangoes back home? But I do know verses about other fruit. Have you heard about Mirza Jaami, Nur-ud-Din Abdur-Rahman of Jaam? He wrote a poem about an orchard—'

The two figures turned a corner and vanished from sight. Faintly, from a distance, Nadeem heard Bibi Sarv-Qad's voice as she began singing, but she was too far for him to distinguish the words.

Babar's daughter, he thought, shaking his head in wonder. He had met the Baadshah's daughter, and he had treated her like any other child.

Nadeem returned to Dilli, tired and still grieving for Zubair. It would be good, he thought, to be back in familiar surroundings, to the quiet and predictable routine of home. With Ismat now calmer and less liable to fly into a rage at the very sight of him, home was a better place to be than it had been before.

But Ismat was angry. Not at him: that, at least, was something to be grateful for; but at their son, Shaadaab, who had announced that he did not want to continue at the workshop. He had tried hard, these many years, and none of it made sense to him. 'He hasn't tried hard!' Ismat insisted. 'If he had really worked hard enough, would he not have succeeded? It is not as if he is being told to make naqshas or do calligraphy: talent is needed for that. To understand brocade, to sell it, to talk to a customer: where is the talent in that? All it needs is hard work.'

Nadeem privately thought: *and an ability to bear with the mundane, the soul-sapping boredom of pure commerce*. He, with the naqshas that called to the artist in him, had at least had that aspect of the business to interest him. It had not been only a trade for him. It was likely different for Shaadaab; the man was not artistically inclined.

He also disliked conflict, and so when Ismat railed at him, he simply kept quiet and let her words wash over him. It only served to infuriate his mother further; and when she could not contain herself any more, she turned on Nadeem.

'This is because of you,' she hissed. 'You, who put ideas into his head with your own behaviour. If you had stuck with the workshop and not given it up for calligraphy, he would not have thought he could do it too. Why could you not have set a good example?' Tears of rage sprang up in her eyes; she blinked them away. 'You have brought this on with your behaviour, you set it right.'

Nadeem tried talking to the boy, but Ismat had been right in this instance: he had no footing. The father had chosen his own path in preference to the workshop, and so the son saw nothing wrong in following in the father's footsteps. Shaadaab did not even need to say anything: he merely looked at Nadeem with his steady, solemn gaze, and Nadeem flinched. His words died on his lips, half unspoken.

'What will you do, then?' he finally asked. 'You do not have the luxury of sitting around at home, doing nothing. It is not as if we have a good deal of inherited wealth, which will give you and your family a comfortable home for the rest of your lives. Whether you like it or not, you will have to earn.

'You are a married man now,' Nadeem added, when his son did not answer. 'You have a responsibility towards your wife. Soon, perhaps, there will be children. If there is something you would rather do, if not the workshop, tell me. We will find a way.'

Finally, pushed, Shaadaab murmured, in a stifled voice: 'She is missing her home. She's very homesick.'

Nadeem blinked, caught off-guard. 'Who—oh, your wife? Is her family not in Dilli anymore?'

No, they were not. The previous month, Shaadaab's father-in-law had decided that the family had had enough of Dilli. They did not like the city's dryness, they missed all their friends and neighbours. They missed their ancestral home in Tanda, in Bengal. The father's business in Dilli could always be carried out by his agents. It was not imperative for the family to stay in a city they did not feel comfortable in.

They had packed up and left Dilli, while Nadeem had been away in Lahore by the deathbed of Zubair. Now Shaadaab's wife was pining too, not just for her siblings and her parents, but for Tanda too. Tanda, at the point where the Ganga split into the Bhagirathi and the Padma, was, according to Shaadaab's wife, far more beautiful than Dilli could ever hope to be. Green, cool. Surrounded by dense forests and emerald fields of gently waving rice.

'She is sickening here, from yearning for Tanda.'

'Then?' Nadeem could sense what was coming, but he wanted to hear his son say the words.

'We will go,' Shaadaab said. 'Her father has offered me a position in his trade. He will teach me.'

Nadeem swallowed. 'Your mother will not like this.'

His son looked up then, into Nadeem's eyes. His own were clear, fearless. 'It doesn't matter to you, that I don't stay with the workshop?'

Nadeem shrugged. 'I have no right to stop you, and you know that. Besides,' he added, 'Junaid is there, and he has apprentices he is training to handle the work. We will manage. In any case, having someone around who does not understand the work and finds it tedious is more a burden than anything else.

'Your mother will find the house empty when you're gone,' he said, in a softer voice. 'She may be lonely. That is all.'

'Then you might start spending more time at home. If

Junaid and the others are running the workshop, why must you go there every day too? Especially if all you do is to work on your calligraphy. You can work on that here, at home.'

Nadeem did not think it would be his company Ismat would wish at home, but he said nothing about that.

'When will you tell her?' he asked. 'You need to steel yourself.'

To his surprise, his usually quiet, soft-spoken son gave a small smile. 'I will manage. I'm not scared of Ammi.'

And indeed he did manage. Within a month of Nadeem's return to Dilli from Lahore, Shaadaab and his young wife had set off on the long journey east to Tanda.

Interlude

All these days, I have been wondering what must be going through the mind of that boy, Jalaluddin Mohammad Akbar, who has so suddenly found himself pushed off the throne he had assumed was his. He is merely thirteen, no more than a boy. These Gurkanis, of course, as they call themselves, initiate their sons into the art and craft of war early on: this boy's father, Humayun, had been given charge of an entire province when he was just twelve years old. Babar had appointed his son governor of Badakhshan before he had set off to conquer Hindustan.

But I am meandering; I meant to talk of Akbar, not of Humayun. I wonder how he feels, how he thinks. At his age, I would not have known how to cope with a setback like this. I might have retreated, found a safe and obscure place in which to take refuge, and hidden myself away.

But Akbar has more steel in him than I did. There is of course also the consideration that he is—or was—a ruler; rulers do not have a choice the way we commoners do. Perhaps, too, Akbar's advisers—experienced and competent men like Bairam Khan, who served under Humayun and is reputed to be one of the finest generals this land has ever seen—have been bolstering his spirits. Perhaps it is Bairam Khan who is behind this latest development.

Because, less than a month after Hemu ascended the throne of Dilli, we have heard that Akbar's armies are preparing to reclaim the throne for their lord and master. News has come that the army is heading towards Dilli, and in order to counter it, Hemu has gathered his own troops and is setting out. Of course he will wish to take the battle away from the city so as not to cause harm to Dilli; he will march forward and meet the boy-king's men on some plain far away. What will be the outcome? I fear for Akbar.

Hemu is eager to win, and confident; his victory at the Battle of Tughlaqabad has emboldened him. His armies, too, outnumber those of Akbar.

When Babar had first arrived in Hindustan and crowned himself Baadshah, I had thought it heralded the start of a new dynasty; the Lodhis giving way to the Gurkanis. With the coronation of Humayun, that belief had been strengthened, only to be dashed when Humayun had shown himself unworthy of holding onto his inheritance. And now—

Mohsin, who has been sitting with me and to whom I have been addressing the odd remark now and then, holds up a hand, interrupting me.

'Let us proceed in chronological order, if you please,' he says. 'You are rushing ahead, and you will leave your readers utterly baffled.'

'My readers, surely, will know this much basic history,' I reply. 'The loss of the throne for Humayun was an important event in the history of Dilli. As was its recovery, so many years later.'

'Important in a span of thirty years,' Mohsin concedes. 'But who knows how history will remember these years? What if, two hundred years from now, no one even remembers Humayun? Or even Babar, for that matter? Babar could just be another invader who came, ruled for four years, and then, when he died, that was the end. Like Sher Shah Suri and his successors, the Gurkanis too will have been a short-lived dynasty.'

'Who knows,' I say, 'it may be that Akbar's generals will win this battle for him.'

'With Hemu's forces far outnumbering them? And Hemu so confident, so certain of victory?' Mohsin looks sceptical, and I shrug. He's right; in the days of yore, a stripling Dawood might have brought down the giant Jalut with a slingshot, but in today's day and age, it is highly unlikely that the outcome will favour Dawood. This David will be crushed by a Goliath hundreds of times more powerful than him.

'We should write about how Humayun became Emperor,' Mohsin says, with an air of finality. 'After all, that is what should logically follow after your mention of Babar becoming Baadshah, isn't it? Should I get out the paper and pens? Should I call Gokul so that he too can hear?'

I have no choice but to agree. And he makes a pertinent point; after all, we do not know what will happen. Perhaps, a hundred years from now, no one will even remember the name of Jalaluddin Mohammad Akbar, the boy who was briefly Baadshah. We should document what happened, even if it is only from my point of view.

Four years after he had defeated Ibrahim Lodhi at Panipat, Babar was well-settled on the throne. His womenfolk had joined him the previous year; his favourite daughter Gulbadan Begum had arrived, and he had been enchanted to see that the toddler he had left in Kabul a few years earlier was growing into a poised little girl. She was his daughter by his wife Dildar Begum, but when Babar's favourite wife Maham Begum—mother to Humayun—had asked to be allowed to bring up Gulbadan, Babar had handed the baby over to Maham. It was with Maham Begum, whom Gulbadan referred to as 'My Lady', that the little princess had travelled to Agra. There had been many more women, hundreds of them, stepmothers and stepsisters, aunts, grand-aunts, and other noblewomen in the entourage, including Gulbadan's real mother, Dildar Begum; but it was to Maham Begum that Gulbadan deferred.

Babar's obvious love for Maham Begum was possibly also the reason he loved her son Humayun so much. For Humayun, even when he disobeyed his father and drew his ire, was forgiven quickly enough; and it was for Humayun that Babar was willing to give up his life.

'That happens only in stories,' Gokul blurts out. 'Who gives up their life for another?' When I look at him, I see the pain lurking in his eyes. He is remembering his mother, who gave him up and married that money-lender. He feels betrayed, of course, and I am tempted to explain that perhaps his mother has sacrificed herself to keep him safe and alive. But that is a revelation that must come with age, or someday when and if his mother decides he is old enough to confide in. It is not my place to tell him. In any case, it may be that I am wrong.

'True,' I say, 'But when it came to Babar and Humayun, they say that it did happen.'

Babar had left Humayun in Badakhshan when he, Babar, set forth to conquer Hindustan. However, shortly after, Humayun handed over Badakhshan to his younger brother Hindal and came eastward into Hindustan. Babar chastised him for what he regarded as dereliction of duty, and then proceeded to forgive Humayun by bestowing on him, his favourite son, the governorship of Sambhal.

A few months later, Babar received news that Humayun had fallen ill. A fever, and one that would not subside, no matter what. The hakims did all they could, to no avail; and finally, when there was no hope left, Babar said that he would offer himself up instead of his son. Those around him tried to dissuade the Baadshah. Their combined prayers, they said, may still work; but the doting father was not persuaded. Babar, it is said, made circumambulations around Humayun's sickbed, offering prayers every step of the way. Hour after hour, unceasingly. If a life must be taken, he begged Allah, let it be mine. Let my son live.

His prayers must have pleased the Almighty, for Humayun began to mend soon after. The fever broke, the young man recovered—and Babar fell ill. Some, the more sceptical, whispered that it was part of the effect of that poison Dilawar Begum had had fed to him several years earlier; that it had harmed him irrevocably, and the strain of these past few days had been all too much. The more devout believed that his prayers had been accepted, and that Babar's life had been exchanged for Humayun's.

That winter, four and a half years after he conquered Hindustan, Babar died. Humayun, twenty-two years of age, became Baadshah.

'He was Baadshah all these years?' asks Gokul. 'Twenty-five years?' Of course, this child does not know of the ups and downs of Humayun's career. He may not even be aware of Sher Shah Suri being ruler, till nearly two years ago; he is a child, after all, and one of a poor family. The poor have enough to do keeping body and soul together to bother about who sits on the throne. Two poor people, when they get together, talk about where they might find their next meal; they do not discuss superfluous things like politics. Politics is for the privileged.

'No, you ignoramus,' Mohsin says affectionately, cuffing Gokul gently on the head. 'He got back his throne only a little while back.'

Gokul is looking bemused, so I step in. In any case, we have to write about this: about those ten years before Humayun lost his throne, seemingly irrevocably, to Sher Shah Suri. Ten years, in which much changed for me and my family.

23

Agra

Five years later

940 Hijri (1533 CE)

Shamsher's sons, whom Nadeem had last seen on that long-ago trip they had made to Dilli, were now strapping men, fathers of sons older than they had been when they had followed Raheem around the workshop. Confident, self-assured men, cheerful men. Nadeem felt a twinge of envy watching them joke easily with their father, or when their children came by, to say their salaams, the youngest ones tumbling joyfully in Shamsher's lap and pulling his beard. A happy family, comfortable with each other, so obviously loving each other.

Shamsher's wife had passed away a couple of years earlier. 'I miss her desperately,' Shamsher confided in his cousin. 'Everybody told me time would dull the ache, that I would forget. But the only thing that has happened is that I have got used to living with the pain. I don't tell everyone how lonely I feel without her, but there is a gaping hole within me.'

What a far cry from how it was with him and Ismat, thought Nadeem. He did not know whether to feel regret, or anger, or indifference. Perhaps a bit of all of that, and more.

'But tell me about yourself,' Shamsher said, brushing aside his own woes. 'I was very surprised when I heard you were coming to Agra. For the brocade business, is it? You were supplying to the palace, weren't you?'

But the workshop had lost that business, several years earlier. While Dilawar Begum and some of the more important ladies of Ibrahim Lodhi's zenana had been alive and at least somewhat able to control their own finances, brocades were ordered for the palace. Not a fraction of what they had once been, and now only small, personal things: a piece of clothing for someone who was going to be married, a gift for a new mother, even—a tentative attempt at diplomacy—a gift for Babar's favourite wife, Maham Begum, on her arrival in Agra.

Even that was gone now. There had been no orders from the palace for the past few years. Ibrahim Lodhi's household was gone, extinguished in name, absorbed by that of Babar, and later, Humayun. The Gurkani women did not seem to care for these brocades. Perhaps they were too new, too strange. Perhaps it was a matter of anger: these very brocades had been beloved of that treacherous Dilawar Begum, who had tried to kill Babar.

With the collapse of the palace business, the workshop had suffered the loss of much of its income. When Zubair had given up his stake in the Kashi workshop, it had not initially made much difference to the relationship between the two establishments. They had continued to exchange naqshas and brocades for a few years, but then, slowly, that too had tapered off. Once in a blue moon, now, a request would come for a new naqsha, but that was all.

'Junaid does what he can, but the spark is gone,' Nadeem said. 'In Abbu's time, or in Grandfather's days, there was an energy about the place. Everybody seemed to want to do well, to give of their best. That's no longer the case. We're carrying on, but there's no momentum.

'But, to compensate,' he added, with a smile, 'my calligraphy is a success. In Dilli, I have many patrons, some of the wealthiest people in the city, and the more discerning—not that they are necessarily the same,' he clarified, with a laugh. 'And now in Agra too. One of my Dilli clients recommended me to his brother-in-law who lives here, and I have been summoned to create a piece of calligraphy that will be inscribed on a mosque he is building.'

They had gone on to talk of other matters. Of Nadeem's

children. The fact that Shaadaab had gone away to Bengal with his wife, and was, till then, not yet a father. Of Shamsher's grandchildren, each more intelligent and beautiful and charming than the other.

Of how Dilli compared to Agra; of how Humayun compared to Babar, and to Ibrahim Lodhi before him.

'Oh,' Shamsher said, a thought suddenly occurring to him. 'Do you remember, you had asked me to check on that lady, Raheem's daughter, when Dilawar Begum was exiled? Zarina Begum? She is still at the palace, and has settled in quite well, I think, as part of the household. You should go and meet her, perhaps she might be able to put in a word for the Gurkani ladies to look at your brocades.'

Nadeem was not carrying any brocades with him, so that might be futile. But he might show them some samples of his calligraphy, he thought. And, it would be good to talk to Zarina again, to find out how she was, whether she was happy.

He would not have recognized her, Nadeem thought. At one time—it seemed a lifetime ago—he could have recognized Zarina despite the veil that always hid her face. The shape of her, the way she held her head, her posture: he knew them all so well that he had not needed to hear her speak to know that it was her.

No longer. She still held her head high and kept her shoulders straight, but there was a gravity, a maturity about her now. She was not the slim, girlish figure she had been, but she moved in a more assured way too: as if she knew exactly where she was going, and was confident about getting there. The feistiness had given way to a calm, a serenity that did not fit with the impatient young Zarina he had known.

'It has been so long,' she said, seating herself on the stone bench opposite him, in the outdoor pavilion where he had been escorted. It had not been easy for Nadeem to gain entry to the imperial palace; Shamsher had contacts among the minor courtiers, and knew a man who had in turn approached a court lady who was a distant relative—and so on and so forth, but it had still taken time and effort. The wheels of the court turned slowly, over several days, before Nadeem had finally received news that Zarina Begum would be pleased to meet him.

Now she sat here, with other people around. A maid stood beside the bench, another at the entrance to the garden. A pair of soldiers, sharp-eyed and stolid, were also stationed at the entrance. Zarina was no longer a mere naqshband; she was a court lady, a woman of consequence.

She laughed when he mentioned it by way of compliment. 'Oh, I assure you, no. This is the palace, after all, and all the women are well-guarded.' She paused. 'Also, because of my husband.' Her voice dipped at that, as if she felt awkward about mentioning the fact that she was now married.

It came as a surprise, and a younger Nadeem, passionately in love with Zarina, might have been shattered at those words. Now he did feel hurt, but not at the knowledge that she had married another; it hurt that she had not bothered to let him know. But perhaps that had been because she had thought him still deeply in love with her, and had hoped to spare him the pain of knowing that she could now never be his.

'Zarina Begum,' Nadeem said formally, in a level voice, 'please accept my sincerest congratulations on your wedding.' He hoped he had emphasized the sincerity sufficiently; enough to convince her that he did not hold it against her that she had married another, and yet not so much that she would feel affronted at his having not been more shaken by the fact. What a tightrope love had to walk, he thought, even when it was not love any more.

She seemed to be relieved, though, and Nadeem breathed a silent sigh of relief. Yes; married or no, Zarina had proven herself to be, yet again, the woman he had known: not overly sentimental, not given to the airs and high emotions of several of the women of his own family.

Her husband, it emerged, was a courtier; he had come to Hindustan as one of the entourage of Babar. 'After Ammi passed away,' Zarina explained, 'the court ladies and the others'—she did not explain who these 'others' might be—'said that it was not seemly for me to be on my own, especially given my age.' She laughed, in a self-conscious way. 'Ammi I could persuade that I did not need to marry; I think she also realized why I could not marry then. But when she was gone, my only reason for not marrying was also gone.' The embarrassment, the momentary awkwardness of that inadvertent confession vanished as suddenly as it had appeared. 'I was left without any responsibilities, without any real direction to my life,' she added, in a small, desolate voice.

'I agreed, therefore. I had met him a few times, and he seemed a personable man. I had been told by others that he had been very good to his first wife, who had died a few years ago in Kabul. We have been married four years now.'

And is he good to you, Nadeem wanted to ask. This man, whom you do not name, but whom you married because you no longer had to look after your mother? Would it have been so very difficult, he wondered, to have told him, years ago when he had asked her to marry him, that she felt it her responsibility to live with her mother and look after her? Had she trusted him so little that she had thought he might insist on separating her from her beloved Ammi?

But that was all water under the bridge. A life that might have been another's, for all the connection Nadeem felt to it.

He found himself unable to tell her why he had come to meet her. He talked to her, told her about the deaths in his family over the past several years. He asked her about herself, her husband—how was it that she was still living in the imperial palace if she was married?—and about life in Agra.

Her husband was a distant relative of the imperial family, a member of the household, Zarina explained. The late Baadshah had had a lot of faith in him, and had entrusted him with the financial matters of the household. That was why, perhaps, all the ladies, from the Baadshah Humayun's wives to his aunt Khanzada Begum—now the matriarch at the head of the zenana—had trusted him too. 'It is good for me that we live within the palace grounds,' she said. 'I am in familiar surroundings, among people who have now known me for years. I am home.'

'Till when are you in Agra?' she asked, when it was time for him to leave, a mere quarter of an hour since they had begun their conversation. 'There is someone I want you to meet, but he is not here right now; if you are in town tomorrow, I would be grateful if you could come again. Yes? You will be able to? Thank you; I think you will not be disappointed.'

The following day, as he made his way once again to the riverside palace, Nadeem wondered who it was Zarina wanted him to meet. An old acquaintance? But then she might have mentioned who it might be; and anyway, he could not think of anyone he knew who might plausibly be part of the imperial household.

The palace was part of an old fort, the citadel of Badalgarh, which had been built by Sikandar Lodhi when he had shifted his capital to Agra. Babar, perhaps because of his distaste for the land he had conquered, had shown no inclination to build a sprawling citadel for himself; he had simply occupied Badalgarh and made it his own palace. This, too, was where Humayun had been crowned Emperor three years earlier.

Today, Nadeem did not have to wait to be allowed into the palace. At the gates, he was met by a soldier who held the bridle of Nadeem's horse to enable him to dismount.

While the horse was taken away to the stables, the soldier escorted Nadeem to the same gardens he had been led to the previous day: not part of the zenana—since Nadeem, as a male and an outsider would never have been permitted into the zenana—but near enough.

The stone bench to which he was led was not bare today; a fine white sheet had been spread on it, and brocaded bolsters set at the ends. A sailabchi, an ewer and basin for him to wash his hands, was brought forward shortly after he had been seated, and a soft, perfumed towel offered for him to wipe with. A soft-spoken maid informed him that someone had gone to let Zarina Begum know her guest had arrived. She would be here soon; meanwhile, would he like something to eat and drink? Some kebabs? Some sherbet? Fresh fruit?

And here she was. Nadeem rose, expectantly, at the sight of the entourage that had arrived at the entrance to the garden which abutted the zenana. But instead of the woman, decorously veiled, whom he had expected, there came running down the path towards him a small figure. A girl, about ten years of age, richly clad in silks and velvet, the gleam of pearls and silver thread enriching her robes. Behind her, breaking loose of the knot of maids and court ladies and urdubegis—the female soldiers who guarded the zenana—came a woman who, because she was unveiled, Nadeem recognized immediately. She was not a woman it was easy to forget: Bibi Sarv-Qad, whom he had last seen in the marketplace at Lahore.

The girl, of course, was the Princess Gulbadan. Taller than before, and grown out of the chubbiness of her younger self, but otherwise recognizably the same. She came to a stop a yard away from him, and there flickered in her fine features an expression of indecision: as if she was suddenly aware of the dignity she should be preserving, the office to which she was born. Princess, not commoner.

Nadeem bowed low. 'Your Highness,' he said gently. 'I am glad to see you well. Do you still enjoy mangoes?'

A small gurgle of laughter bubbled up from Gulbadan. 'Master Mango Tutor!' she said, her voice low but full of mirth. 'That is what I told Bibi Sarv-Qad when we noticed you yesterday.' She glanced at her companion. 'I did not recognize you,' she admitted artlessly, 'but Bibi Sarv-Qad did, and she reminded me that you had taught me to eat mangoes, in Lahore. Thank you.' She beamed at him.

'It was my pleasure, Your Highness.' He paused. 'You noticed me yesterday?'

'Yes, we were returning from a visit to the riverside gardens, and we saw you leaving. You were deep in thought, you didn't see us.'

'You should have sent someone to stop me, Your Highness. I would have been honoured to know that you remembered me.'

'It is not difficult for us to find out who has been visiting whom.' It was Bibi Sarv-Qad who answered instead of the princess. There was in her voice a faint smugness: she was showing Nadeem his place, reminding him that the princess was no ordinary girl. 'A slave sent to the gates, then to Zarina Begum's apartments, when we learnt that it was she you had come to visit.' She looked around. 'Zarina Begum should be here soon,' she murmured. 'We had better finish our conversation, so that we do not intrude on yours,' she said.

'I am certain Zarina Begum would not mind,' Nadeem replied. He turned back to Gulbadan. 'How have you been, Your Highness? Are you liking Hindustan?'

For the first question, she simply nodded her head. For the second, she considered, nibbling on her lower lip as she did so. 'I think I do,' she said, after a few moments. 'Baba did not. I am told that was because he had lived all his life in the mountains; he could not adapt to the heat of the plains. But I don't mind it,' she shook her head, changing her mind the next moment, 'I mean, I do, but it is not without its pleasures.'

'Such as mangoes?' Nadeem suggested with a smile.

'Yes.' Gulbadan dimpled. 'Mangoes are the best thing about the plains. But I also like the river,' she added. 'And the flowers in spring. And how green it all becomes when the monsoon arrives. I love the smell of the new grass when it comes up after the rain.' She glanced up into Bibi Sarv-Qad's face. 'What did you say we used to go out to see when we lived in Kabul? All the ladies, mounted up, going to see something that came up?'

'Riwaaj, My Lady?' Bibi Sarv-Qad said. 'Wild rhubarb. It grows in the mountains around Kabul, and when it blossoms, the slopes are covered with clumps of pinkish-red flowers.' Her voice had fallen to a low murmur. Homesickness, thought Nadeem; a common malaise among the ladies of the zenana? Gulbadan was too young to remember all she had been made to leave behind; but the others, the older women, would remember and must ache for it all.

'Yes, riwaaj,' Gulbadan looked up into Bibi Sarv-Qad's face, her own now clouded. 'I am sorry, Bibi, I reminded you of it. I know you miss it; I should have remembered.' She took Bibi Sarv-Qad's hand in her own, even as the woman assured her that it was all well. 'I wondered if the riwaaj in bloom looked as beautiful as the new grass after the rain.'

'They each look beautiful in their own way,' Bibi Sarv-Qad said softly. 'Oh, look; Zarina Begum is here. Shall we go, then, and leave them to their talk?'

'She is easy to like,' Zarina said, as Gulbadan went down the path to the zenana, followed by her retinue. 'She was the late Baadshah's favourite daughter, you know; I had feared she would have all the airs of the princess she is.'

'I had not imagined her a princess, when I first met her in Lahore,' Nadeem agreed. 'She is very kind.'

'Her father was like that too,' Zarina said. 'And generous. Her half-brother is the same. Generous, large-hearted.'

'To a fault,' Nadeem agreed, with a rueful laugh. 'The Baadshah Humayun has I think been far too generous to people who would gladly stab him in the back for the throne. His brothers—'

Zarina stopped him with a sharp hiss. 'Do not,' she whispered. 'Do not say just what you will. Remember where you are.'

Feeling like a fool, Nadeem changed the topic. Whom had Zarina wanted him to meet, that she had called him here today? Was it the princess, Gulbadan?

No, of course not. It just happened that the princess and Bibi Sarv-Qad, having noticed Nadeem the previous day, had had enquiries made. When they had discovered whom Nadeem had come to meet at the palace, they had called on Zarina. She had been told all about that fortuitous meeting in Lahore, and how kind and good Nadeem had been to Gulbadan. 'She is kindly disposed towards you, because of that long-ago encounter in Lahore.'

Nadeem could not help a chuckle. 'Of which she remembers nothing! She admitted it; that lady, Bibi Sarv-Qad, was the one who told her who I was.'

'What difference does it make? The point is, that you are a fortunate man, to be in her good books.'

Nadeem was to realize only later just how fortunate he was, and how generous Gulbadan was.

'I wanted you to meet my son,' Zarina said. Then, as if realizing that more clarification was needed, she added, 'My stepson, I should say. He is thirteen years old, and calligraphy is his great passion. Not,' she added with an embarrassed laugh, 'that he is very good at it, but he wishes he were.' She hesitated. 'I think he would benefit from meeting you. I told him yesterday about you, and about how wonderful your work was. He was very excited at the prospect of being introduced to you.'

Nadeem expressed his gratitude, and Zarina added, 'I was speaking to him while the Princess Gulbadan was visiting me. When she heard that you were a skilled calligrapher, she was quite fascinated too. I do not know about the hand she writes, but it is well-known that, child though she is, she loves her letters. Perhaps someday, like her father before her, she too will write about her life.' Zarina chuckled, a small sound of happy affection. 'I showed her the few pieces of your work that I have with me, and she liked them so much, she said she would be grateful if you would make something for her too.'

Nadeem nodded, privately offering up a prayer of thanks to a divinity that had done for him, all unasked, what he had been hoping for. 'It would be an honour.'

'I hope I have not caused distress to you,' Zarina said, her voice awkward, formal. 'You are busy enough as it is, and this would only impinge on your time. I am sorry if I acted, and spoke, when it was not my place to do so.'

Nadeem was then forced to tell her that the brocade workshop was faring poorly, and that he had decided to let it die its own death. 'Everything is slowly falling apart,' he admitted. 'The business cannot keep going much longer, no matter how hard any of us try. And nobody, really, not even Junaid, has the will any more to keep going. Perhaps I will sell it off, to whoever might wish to buy it.' He paused, then added, as kindly as he could, 'I am sorry, Zarina'—he had not addressed her by her name for many years now, though it came unbidden now—'you invested so much of your life in the workshop, and I am going to let it go, just like that.'

'Not without trying,' Zarina said consolingly.

She did not sit in judgement or berate him for the step he was about to take. 'How can I not be?' she said, when Nadeem thanked her for being considerate. 'You allowed me to work at what I loved; who am I to come in the way of you doing what you love?'

There was the sound of footsteps approaching on the flagstones of the path, and when Nadeem turned to look, it was to see a boy, in his early teens, stepping forward. A slim, slight boy, rather pale and with eyes wide and nervous.

Zarina got to her feet. 'Ah, here he is. Come.' She held out a hand, and the boy came obediently forward, to stand beside her.

'This is my son, Nadeem Sahib,' Zarina said. 'His name is Suleiman, and he would very much like to be able to learn something of the craft of fine writing from you.'

Zarina was not being overly modest when she had told Nadeem that her stepson Suleiman had little talent for calligraphy. In that very first meeting, even though it had been brief, Nadeem had realized as much; but the boy was earnest and eager to learn. Nadeem had promised to call on him and spend time with him the next time he was in Agra, but when that next visit might happen was something he could not foretell with any certainty. Once he got back to Dilli, he would have to begin the search for someone who might wish to buy the workshop. It was best sold while it was still profitable: and, somewhat neglected and deteriorating though it was, it was still a good buy for a brocade manufacturer looking to expand. A little investment, and it could soon be turned around and returned to its former glory.

Junaid, when informed of Nadeem's decision, did not look surprised. 'I will look around for someone,' he said, of his own accord. 'I know others in the trade, both in Dilli and elsewhere. I am certain a good price will be offered for this place.'

Nadeem bit his lip. 'I am sorry, Junaid,' he said, remembering a similar conversation with Zarina more than a week earlier in Agra. 'You have invested so much in this workshop, and to sell it off.'

Junaid smiled a rare smile, his eyes crinkling up. 'I will be fine,' he said. 'I will make it a part of the contract that I and my descendants remain part of the workshop. You need not worry about me.'

Nadeem heaved a private sigh of relief, glad that the conversation with Junaid had been a relaxed one. As it was, it was not Junaid he had really been worried about. The other, inevitable confrontation was what he dreaded.

Ismat's happiness and mellow nature had proved short-lived. It had begun to crumble when her son had decided to forge his own path; it had been utterly destroyed when he and his wife left Dilli and went away to Bengal. With their departure, Ismat had found herself suddenly very lonely. To combat that loneliness, she had packed her days full of frenetic activity: spring cleaning, long visits to relatives and friends, pilgrimages to all the shrines in and around Dilli. The ceaseless bustling about could only last so long: when an exhausted Ismat finally collapsed, it was to take refuge in anger and self-pity. She had wept over her condition, she had blamed Nadeem and Shaadaab for not caring a whit about her. She had wished, loudly and repeatedly, that she had never married the father, never birthed the son.

Then, news had come from Bengal: Shaadaab's wife had died in childbirth, and her baby with her. It was yet another straw on the camel's back: Ismat went into hysterics and could not leave her room for a week.

Now she received the news of the impending sale of the workshop with poor grace, as Nadeem had feared she would. 'You took this decision after going to Agra, isn't it?' she asked.

Nadeem explained that he had long had it in mind; for several years now, in fact. She looked at him with disbelief written all over her face.

'That woman convinced you to sell it off,' she said. 'That Raheem's daughter. She must have told you to get rid of it. What? Does she want you to sell it off and go to live with her?'

No matter what he said, no matter how patient he was, Ismat had her suspicions firmly entrenched in her mind. After a while, Nadeem gave up trying to reason with her.

24

Dilli

Six years later

946 Hijri (1339 CE)

That day, six years back, when Nadeem had met Gulbadan Begum again, had proved the beginning of a long and fruitful association with the princess. Zarina had been right when she had said that the princess was fond of her letters; not only was she an avid reader and a seeker of knowledge, she was also an aesthete. The beauty of well-formed letters was something she appreciated, and shortly after Nadeem had returned to Dilli, she had written to him, praising his calligraphy, which Zarina Begum had shown her. That first letter, a self-conscious child's letter, had been artless, but earnest. She wished to commission a piece. A gift that she wished to give to her foster mother, Maham Begum, on the occasion of her birthday: a verse from the Al-Baqarah, the second chapter of the Quran. She was not quite sure how she wanted it done. What size, what colours. But she would trust him to do what was best.

That had been the start of Nadeem's association with the princess. As the years passed and Gulbadan had grown up, her letters had become more assured, more certain. She was now precise, organized, and very punctual. Every six months, she would write to him with a list of people on whom she wished to bestow presents. Nadeem would be required to write back, with the details of what he proposed to do: what he would write, how he would style it. What paper he would use, and how large. Whether, for an especially favoured recipient, he might also employ an artist to illuminate the calligraphy. Only when the princess was satisfied would he proceed, and the work would take him most of the following six months to complete. He was busier now than ever before, so busy that he barely realized how quickly time went by.

ଔ

'It is exquisite,' said Suleiman, speaking in an awed whisper, as if he feared his very breath would taint the Quranic verse he was looking at. 'How do you manage to bring in these shades of ink? It is almost like a fine painting, as if all the beauty of Allah's creation had been poured into your calligraphy.' He had come to Dilli for a few days, and—as always, when he came to Dilli—he had come visiting. Nadeem, of course, had shown him what he was working on, and Suleiman's interest in the work had been flattering.

Nadeem laughed as he took back the piece. 'You are biased,' he said, chuckling still. 'But thank you; I am grateful for your appreciation, and I am glad you enjoyed it.'

'Who would not?' Suleiman leaned back and reached for the goblet of sherbet that had been placed well away, so as not to accidentally tumble on to the precious pieces of calligraphy he had been shown. 'And Gulbadan Begum, I am sure, will show them around to all in the zenana. Ammi says the princess is very proud of her Master Mango Tutor,' he said, with a mischievous grin.

'How is she?' Nadeem asked with a smile, as he carefully folded the cloth covering over the sheaf of papers.

'Ammi? She is well. Abba has been ailing of late, so she spends most of her time by his bedside, looking after him.'

Nadeem did not have the heart to correct Suleiman, to say that he had been asking after Princess Gulbadan, his patroness, and not Zarina.

Suleiman, reminded, by his own remark, of his father, began to reminisce about him. The many years of hard work in the service of the court, the careful balancing of expectations with resources, of personal with professional. 'Abba has had a long and hard life, and he says he is tired now. That it is time for him to go. Do you think, Nadeem Sahib, that a man can see death approaching?'

The conversation wound around, as it is wont to do between friends who have not met for a while, to all that had happened in the space between their last meeting and now. Much of it was already known to Nadeem; Suleiman was diligent and detailed in his correspondence, and left little out. Even so, he had news to share; his wife, whom he had married a few years earlier, had gone to Kabul to attend the wedding of her younger sister. She had taken her two children with her, and Suleiman, doting father that he was, was missing his daughters.

'But by being in Dilli, I feel oddly closer to them,' he said, with an embarrassed chuckle. 'Agra is too far from Kabul.'

Nadeem smiled indulgently. 'Can you not be spared for a while from your duties?' he asked. 'It would take only a few weeks to travel to Kabul from here.'

Suleiman shook his head. 'As it is, those in charge were not eager to have me come to Dilli. I was told it would be a waste of resources; since it was only a question of documenting the progress at the construction site, that could be done by any scribe in Dilli.'

Earlier this year, Humayun had decided to build a citadel in Dilli. Had he tired of Agra? Had he felt, like Suleiman did, that Agra was too far from Kabul—which, for Humayun, had once been home—and that Dilli, by virtue of being a few hundred kos closer to Kabul, was more home? Or was it simply a manifestation of the same ambition, to hold sway in Dilli, that had driven many men before him to build their own citadels and cities here in this plain between the easternmost edge of the Aravalis and the course of the Yamuna?

Whatever his motivation, Humayun had chosen a spot beside that very river, north of Ghiyaspur, for the laying of the foundation stone of his citadel, Din Panah, the 'refuge of the faith'. Construction had already begun on what was probably going to be a grander, more beautiful structure than Firuz Shah's kotla, a hundred and fifty years old and a little north of Din Panah.

'You have been to the site, then?' Nadeem asked, interested. 'I have heard that there is hectic activity on there, that they have nearly completed the work. Some say the Baadshah and the court will be here before winter sets in.'

Suleiman shook his head. 'No, there's still time before that can happen. I went the day after I arrived, and every day since then. A good deal of construction has been completed; the surrounding walls and the ramparts are all done, the bastions are ready, and the gates nearly so. But inside? There is perhaps a year's work, maybe more.' He shook his head again. 'No, the Baadshah will not be able to settle in Din Panah any time soon.'

Nadeem nodded, his expression grave. 'I thought it sounded too fanciful. In any case,' he added, 'with the way things are right now, I doubt if the Baadshah even remembers he has a citadel being built here in Dilli. He is plagued by too many troubles at the moment.'

Indeed, in the few years he had been ruler, Humayun had faced more than his fair share of enemies, both internal and not. For one, there were his nearest kinsmen, his brothers and half-brothers, nearly all of them with their eyes on Humayun's crown. Adjured by his father to treat his brothers with love and respect, Humayun had forgiven these rivals for his throne even when they had openly defied him. His well-wishers had repeatedly warned the Baadshah, telling him to be less forgiving, to remember that he was responsible for an empire, no less. But could Humayun go against his basic nature?

And there were others: the enemies pressing in on every side, the most ambitious of them the fierce Sher Khan. An Afghan warlord with his base at Sasaram, in eastern India, Sher Khan had been born Farid Khan; the epithet 'Sher Khan', it was said, became his after he killed a tiger that had attacked his overlord, Bahar Khan Lohani, the governor of Bihar. Under Bahar Khan Lohani, Sher Khan was a tiger tamed and shackled; under his son and successor, the boy Jalal Khan whom Sher Khan served as regent, he began breaking out of those shackles. Turbulence had gripped Bengal and Bihar, with Sher Khan eventually finding himself ranged against various alliances, small and large. And, in what now seemed a portent of things to come, he swept them all aside. Having taken over Bengal and Bihar, Sher Khan was now gathering his forces again. Looking towards Agra and Dilli, eyeing the throne.

With such a formidable foe on the horizon, it was hardly surprising that Humayun was in no hurry to have Din Panah completed and readied for a grand entry. That could wait for happier times; meanwhile, he was preparing to counter Sher Khan and the others who threatened his realm.

Right now, Humayun was in Gaur, in Bengal. He had led a campaign to that area to expand his empire, and after his victory, had settled in at Gaur and was busy enjoying the fruits of that victory.

'The Baadshah might do well to cut short the celebrations and get back to his duties as Emperor,' Nadeem said with a sigh of exasperation. 'They say he is sunk deep in opium and food and dancing girls all day long these past many months, ever since he won Gaur.' His mind went briefly to his son, resident now in Tanda, close to Gaur. Shaadaab had not written for a long time now; Nadeem wondered if he was still mourning his dead wife and child. Or busy with his father-in-law's trade. Or could it be, as a fretting and anxious Ismat prophesied, that he had decided to part ways forever with his parents?

But he had been talking about Gaur, and what Humayun might be doing there.

Suleiman was looking mortified. He murmured something about the Baadshah having a right to his rest, as did everybody else; but Nadeem waved him into silence.

'So many months of rest? No, Suleiman. You may be loyal to him, but to deny his failings is to distort your own loyalty. If all those truly loyal to him wished to show their faithfulness, they would jolt him out of this laziness. I have heard that Gulbadan Begum's full brother, Hindal, is getting ready to have the khutba read in his own name. If the Baadshah does not want to be left without a throne, he had better look sharp.'

Later that day, as he was leaving, Suleiman said, 'Ammi and I were wondering, when I met her last, how the workshop was faring, with its new owner. Have you visited? Is Junaid still there? And any of the others—Ammi named so many of the old weavers, but I remember not a single name!' he finished with a sheepish laugh.

Nadeem, startled by the unexpected barrage of questions, was quiet for a few moments. Then, with a shrug and a self-conscious laugh, he said, 'It is doing well, and Junaid is still there. As also most of the weavers Zarina Begum might know, though some have retired. And there would be new ones.' He shook his head after a moment. 'But I have not visited. I could not summon up the courage. Or,' he looked down, away from Suleiman's level gaze, 'let us say I was too awkward to do so.'

Suleiman did not say anything then; it was only as they reached the gate and Suleiman's servant, waiting for him there, went to fetch his master's horse that Suleiman turned back to Nadeem. 'You should not blame yourself,' he said. 'If your passion tugs you down one path, it is useless to force yourself down another path. You would have been miserable devoting your life to something you felt nothing for. And you would have been no good at it, either.'

Nadeem gave him a fleeting smile, of gratitude and affection. 'Not always. Look at you. You wanted to do calligraphy, but you work as a scribe. And you are good at it.'

Suleiman laughed. 'That is because I had no real talent

for calligraphy. And it isn't as if I hate the work I do. It is interesting enough. I try to make it look beautiful.' He grinned.

'Why did you ask about the workshop, though?' Nadeem said, as the servant arrived, leading Suleiman's horse.

Suleiman looked pensive, as if unsure what to say. 'You might think me mercenary,' he said, 'but I wondered if Ammi might someday want to take it over. I fear Abba will not be with us much longer; and when he is gone, Ammi will only have my little sister to look after. It is not enough for Ammi; she is not the maternal type.' He said it in a bald, matter-of-fact way that softened the adjective, making it merely another descriptor of Zarina. 'You know Ammi better than most,' he added, 'and you can imagine how frustrated she will be if all she must do is sit around and be the doting mother. She could never do it.'

'We need not worry about Zarina Begum,' Nadeem said comfortably. 'She lives in the Baadshah's palace, she is part of the court. Even if, Allah forbid, she is left a widow, she will have the entire household still around her, still upholding her. She will not need to find another means of income.'

'Oh, of course, she will not need for money,' Suleiman agreed. 'While I am alive, I will look after her and my sister; they need never fear destitution. But I feel Ammi might find the zenana begin to pall. I think she already does; has done so, for several years, though she usually hides it well.' He took the bridle from the waiting servant. 'We shall see. It is early days yet.'

Within a month of Suleiman's visit to Dilli, his father had breathed his last, leaving Zarina a widow. Within another week, the Baadshah had suffered a humiliating debacle, which would pave the way for his ultimate exile from Hindustan.

As many had already begun to fear, Humayun's half-brother, Gulbadan Begum's full brother Abul Nasir Mohammad 'Hindal' had taken advantage of Humayun's absence. He had pounced on the empty throne in Agra and proclaimed himself Emperor. Humayun, languishing in Gaur with his womenfolk and their children, had realized then, too late, that he could not afford to be negligent about the throne he had inherited: it needed constant guarding. He started back for Agra, but his harem now proved an encumbrance. The imperial ladies, pampered and unused to the rigors of the march, could not move fast enough. Their many cartloads of luxuries, their carpets and lamps and vases and musical instruments and whatnot; their hundreds of servants; their demands for frequent halts; their constant complaints about the summer heat and the humidity—all combined to slow Humayun down just when it was imperative that he get back to Agra quickly.

Sher Khan, waiting for just such an opportunity, pounced on the trapped Humayun at Chausa, near the town of Baksar. Within a matter of a few hours, the Baadshah's forces had suffered a humiliating, crushing defeat. His army was routed, of course; but worse than that, many from his harem—including two of his wives as well as his young daughter, the six-year-old Aqiqa—were either killed or went missing in the roiling waters of the Ganga, now swollen by the monsoon. Humayun himself had a narrow escape: his horse floundered in the river and lost its footing. Humayun might have drowned, had it not been for the quick thinking of a local bhishti, a water-carrier named Nizam who flung himself into the Ganga and rescued the Baadshah.

'What will happen to all of this?' Suleiman said, his voice brimming with desperation. He had come to Dilli yet again, in connection with the building of Din Panah. Besides his work, he had other business in Dilli too: he had to find a suitable home for his stepmother and his little half-sister Asifa. Zarina had decided that she did not want to stay on in Agra any more now that her husband was dead. She had refused, outright, to let Suleiman buy the brocade workshop for her—she had no desire, she said, to go back to that, though she would continue to practice her naqshas and teach little Asifa the craft of her ancestors.

Nadeem had been roped in to help: Suleiman had pleaded for his company on an expedition across the city to see a few houses, and to offer suggestions. Now, having spent the entire day traversing the length and breadth of Dilli, they had wound up, tired and thirsty, their clothes and faces dusty and sweat-stained, on the bank of the river outside Din Panah. The high stone walls of the citadel were silent and deserted; it was as if the hectic activity of the past several months had never been. A ghost citadel.

'There is hope yet,' Nadeem said, though the listlessness in his voice belied his words. 'The Baadshah may still recover his throne.'

Suleiman shook his head, despondent. 'The Baadshah has lost heart. His wives and daughter died at Chausa, and I think he feels Sher Shah—that is what he calls himself now, you know, not Sher Khan any more—he feels Sher Shah is too powerful for him, too wily.'

Suleiman, employed at the court, was understandably anxious; his livelihood depended upon the welfare and success of the Baadshah. But for Nadeem, too, there were bound to be repercussions. If Humayun could not recover from the debacle at Chausa, if he could not retain his throne, what might become of the Princess Gulbadan? Not only was she Humayun's sister; even the man she had married, Khizr Khwaja Khan, was a courtier of the Baadshah's. Not a prominent one, it was true; but perhaps that made it worse for Gulbadan. A powerful and wealthy husband might have meant she would have something to fall back upon, a comfortable existence apart from the court, an identity beyond that of her blood. But the relatively meagre stature of Khizr Khwaja Khan meant that Gulbadan remained first and foremost a Gurkani princess. With the fall of the Gurkanis, she fell too.

'Do you know,' Nadeem murmured, 'I did not even know Gulbadan Begum had been married. She addresses her letters to Master Mango Tutor, and she didn't tell Master Mango Tutor that she had been married!' He shook his head, chuckling as he did so.

'She must have been shy,' Suleiman offered. 'But why did you think of her, suddenly?'

'Because I have not heard from her these past few months. I should have; her letters may be infrequent, but they arrive exactly when they are supposed to. She is very precise, very organized. But she has not written, and I am worried. For her, of course, but also—I know I am being selfish, Suleiman, do not blame me for looking out for my own interests—for myself. I fear what will happen if Gulbadan Begum cannot commission any more calligraphy from me. I have been spending the past few years mostly doing her work; to build up a clientele apart from her again will take a lot of time and effort.'

But Suleiman could offer no solace. He was too worried for himself.

The two men stood on an outcrop and looked out at the walls of Din Panah, gilded by the last rays of the setting sun. The Bada Darwaaza, its arched doorway of red sandstone flanked by two formidable bastions, complete with arrow slits and guard posts, looked as if it was prepared to take on anything an enemy might care to throw at it. The moat around the citadel, not yet filled with water but already excavated, was deep and broad, a good defence.

But would Humayun ever get to ward off an attack on Din Panah? Or would Sher Shah crush him before he ever got to Dilli?

Epilogue

I have been struggling these past few hours. Every breath is a battle. To open my eyes is an endeavour, to move a finger opens up a world of pain. I am lying in my bed, too weak and too ill to do anything.

This illness came on me like a bolt out of the blue. One moment, I was safe and well, eating a chapati that Mohsin had made for me—yes, there is food now, and while it is frugal and of poor quality, at least we get to eat, now and then, something we haven't foraged … as I was eating, my chest suddenly felt as it had been bound in iron bands, pressing ever closer. I broke into a cold sweat, my head spun, and darkness overwhelmed me. When I came to, I was here, covered with a thin sheet, staring death in the face.

I am not being melodramatic; the truth is that I do see death approaching. That day, many years ago, when Suleiman had asked me if a man could foretell his death, I had kept silent; I had not known what to say. Today, I know. I feel it, like the marrow deep in my bones. My body has been slowing down over the years, and the famine of these past two years has been the last straw.

The odd thing, though, is that my mind is lucid. My body is giving up, but my mind is ready to go on. Anxious to go on, too, knowing that I have not yet completed my chronicling of all that has happened to me and my family. I have fifteen years to complete; I have yet to say how Zarina returned to Dilli, and how she became acquainted with my family. How I was forced to rebuild my career as a calligrapher after Gulbadan Begum fled Hindustan, along with the rest of the imperial family, when Sher Shah defeated Humayun once and for all at Bilgram, less than a year after the battle at Chausa.

So many things I must tell, so many stories I must recount. Will they remain locked in my chest, to be interred with me? Will I ever get my breath back, will I ever be able to speak without the effort it now takes to utter every syllable?

Deep in my heart, I know it will not be. Perhaps my son and Mohsin, between them, might be able to put the pieces together. It will never be the whole, but it will be a sketch of the whole. A naqsha, as Zarina would have said: a pattern indicating the final tapestry. Unlike Raheem's or Zarina's beautifully detailed naqshas, though, this one will be sparse. No details, no nuances, just the outlines.

These thoughts swirl in my head, even as I listen to the excitement in Suleiman's voice. Yes, Suleiman, Zarina's stepson, who has come again, after a gap of more than a month, to visit us. He has brought momentous news: at Panipat, where Jalaluddin Mohammad Akbar's grandfather Babar had once defeated Ibrahim Lodhi, Akbar has defeated Hemu. Raja Hemchandra Vikramaditya, short-lived ruler of Dilli, has been crushed—like 'new grass before driving rain', as Suleiman puts it, in a burst of flowery poetry—by the Baadshah's troops.

Not, it seems, by the Baadshah himself in the vanguard. No; young as he is, his commanders and his regent, Bairam Khan, insisted on keeping Akbar a good, safe way behind the front lines. A full four kos away from the battle, in fact.

Not so Hemu. Hemu, mounted atop his elephant Hawai, led his armies into battle: fifty elephants strong, with thirty thousand of his Afghan cavalry following. They would have carried the day for Hemu, but for one of those odd coincidences that remind us, every now and then, that a power beyond human comprehension rules the universe. Even as the Baadshah's armies were floundering, a well-placed arrow struck Hemu in the eye. It felled him, and seeing him fall, Hemu's armies panicked. They fled, leaving a sixth of their men dead on the field. Many more were killed along the way.

Hawai, with the unconscious Hemu still atop the

elephant, was captured after several hours of being chased. The elephant was brought to where Akbar was encamped, and Bairam Khan advised the young Baadshah to execute the vanquished Hemu with his own hands. Akbar refused, and could be persuaded only to touch the blade of his sword to Hemu's neck. The actual decapitation was done by Bairam Khan himself.

'When I heard of that, I was reminded of what the Surah Al Imran says,' Suleiman says, his eyes aglow with a pride I have not seen in many years. 'Do you remember, Nadeem Sahib? "Allah loves the doers of good, those who restrain their anger and pardon others". Surely this young Baadshah of ours is destined for greatness; if at such a young age he is able to take the path of righteousness, we may be seeing the start of a new age.'

Mohsin, sitting on one side of me, is looking at Suleiman with disbelieving eyes, but Suleiman is oblivious. On his beaming face, radiant with excitement, is a somewhat silly smile. The relief is palpable.

I feel it too.

What a trying time this has been, these past few years. The turbulence, the instability. The famine, which reduced us to little more than animals. The pain, the sickness, the loss of dignity, of all that makes us human. How we had fallen.

But somewhere, somehow, this young man, little more than a child, has brought back hope. Not because his forces have succeeded in defeating an enemy, but because he has shown that he can rise above hatred, above the petty vindictiveness that is so intrinsic a part of the character of most men in power.

My breathing is growing laboured; the tightness in my chest, which has never quite gone away these past few days, has grown to the point where it is now not merely uncomfortable, but painful. I feel light-headed.

I close my eyes. I still feel giddy, the pain squeezing my

chest like a pair of powerful hands wringing wet cloth. Twisting, grappling, forcing every breath from me.

I am going. I must say my farewells.

Years ago, when my uncle Waqar was first teaching me the basics of calligraphy, he insisted I keep with me a small bundle, thumb-sized, of Multani mitti, fullers' earth. It is the standard eraser, if you wish to call it that, for mistakes made while practising calligraphy. Novice qaatibs cannot do without their little bundle of Multani mitti, so easily smoothing away the errors, the lines that do not flow well, the splashes here and there, the crookedness. A gentle rubbing, and it all vanishes as if it had never been. You are left with a clean page.

I gave up my bundle of Multani mitti years ago, but I wish now that I could have something like it back. Something, at any rate, that could erase the many mistakes I have made over the years. My faults. The pride, the arrogance. The selfishness.

'Abba,' I hear my son say, his voice anxious. 'Abba? Are you feeling worse?'

I open my eyes. It is an effort to do so, but it must be done.

'Shaadaab,' I whisper. 'Forgive me.'

'Abba,' I hear him say. His words blur. His face blurs.

The pain. The dizziness. Air...

From somewhere in the fog, I hear Mohsin's voice: 'But what happened to the Garden of Heaven? The frieze?' His father says something in a harsh tone. There is a brief altercation; I cannot hear. I cannot comprehend. My head is swimming. My vision is fading. My ears are full of cotton wool. My chest is going to burst.

'Just one question,' Mohsin pleads, his voice clear, bell-like. His hand is gripping mine, his fingers warm and firm against the cold, clammy skin of my hand. He is life.

And I? I am death.

My name is Mohsin. My father's name is Shaadaab. His father was Nadeem, the former qaatib who began this chronicle about our family.

My grandfather died on the ninth day of the month of Muharram, 964 Hijri, a week after the forces of the Baadshah Jalaluddin Mohammad Akbar defeated those of Raja Hemchandra Vikramaditya, at Panipat. Verily we belong to Allah, and truly to him shall we return. Om sadgati, whispers my friend Gokul, who is sitting beside me as I write these words.

The two of us have taken on the task of completing this chronicle. Gokul wants to help because my grandfather was good to him, and also because he wants to know what happened. The only person who really knows what happened is now gone, but my father knows something of it, so we have turned to him for help.

Just a little short of a year after the Battle of Chausa, the Baadshah Humayun faced Sher Shah once again, at Bilgram, less than twenty kos from Kannauj. Sher Shah was victorious, and Humayun, now with his brothers Hindal and Askari, fled towards Agra. Sher Shah pursued them, and kept on their tails all the way to Dilli. With their entire entourage, women and children included, the Gurkanis were forced to make their way to Lahore. From there, they scattered, and for the next fifteen years, Humayun became a nomad, a king without a throne. He went here, there and everywhere, with only a ragtag bunch of loyal servitors with him. On the way, he married a young woman named Hamida Bano Begum, and it was she who gave birth to our recently crowned Baadshah, Jalaluddin Mohammad Akbar. Humayun even spent many years in Persia, where the king treated him very well.

Gulbadan Begum, Nadeem's patroness in the last few years, had left Agra and gone away to Kabul even before the Battle of Bilgram. With her gone, Nadeem had to find other clients for his calligraphy. Several former clients were annoyed at him for having taken over Gulbadan Begum's work to such an extent that he had not had time for them. They had felt affronted, and they had their revenge by refusing to now give Nadeem any work. Thus Nadeem's work never quite recovered. What work came his way in the last fifteen years was sporadic.

Shaadaab's wife had died in childbirth, never having given birth to a living child, though she had been pregnant several times. After her death, Ismat persuaded Shaadaab, through a series of letters, to marry a second time. Much to Ismat's annoyance, Shaadaab chose to marry one of his wife's younger sisters; her father, who was also Shaadaab's employer, felt that would be best.

The wedding took place in Tanda. My grandmother was unhappy about that, and she began pestering her son to return to Dilli. She wanted her new daughter-in-law beside her. Eventually, my father (or my future father, I should say) discussed it all with his father-in-law, and they decided that the newly married couple could come to Dilli. Shaadaab would handle the trade here. Unlike Shaadaab's first wife, my Ammi was not quite so tied to Tanda; she had lived briefly in Dilli, years ago, and she liked it well enough.

Ismat was initially quite dazzled by her new daughter-in-law: she was beautiful and seemed gentle, docile. But Ammi began showing her true colours soon, and my grandmother did not like that. My mother, who bore me fifteen years ago, is a strong-willed woman, who knows her mind and is not shy about speaking it. She soon took her husband in hand, and let her mother-in-law know that she would brook no interference.

Ismat hated it. Given that she was the one who had insisted on Shaadaab remarrying, she could not blame the situation on anyone else. That must have frustrated her even more. She raved and ranted at Nadeem, and worked herself into a frenzy over small things. Nadeem annoyed her; her new daughter-in-law got her all worked up. Shaadaab she no longer had any patience with, because he seemed to have turned into a meek, hen-pecked husband. She also now began to hold him responsible for the loss of the workshop. She said that if he had been more alive to a sense of duty, he would have tied himself to the workshop.

She would complain to anybody who cared to listen, and to many who did not even care. She wept day and night and finally she went to Zarina Begum, who had moved to Dilli the year my parents were married.

After Humayun had fled and Sher Shah had become the Emperor, Suleiman had found himself without a job. He had therefore left Agra and come away to Dilli (where Sher Shah installed himself too, at Din Panah, where he built several beautiful buildings, including the Sher Mandal—coincidentally, the building down which Humayun later tripped and fell and subsequently died). When Suleiman moved to Dilli along with his wife and his household, Zarina Begum too shifted; Suleiman had already found a house for her and her daughter Asifa.

Zarina Begum was well-off; as the only widow of her husband, she had inherited a good deal of his wealth. It was enough for her and Asifa to live comfortably on for the rest of their lives.

Ismat was half-crazed by then, and in the dim recesses of her mind, she perhaps thought that Zarina Begum might be persuaded to help her. One day, when neither my grandfather nor my father were at home, my mother was busy with me and the servants all occupied with their chores, Ismat slipped away and went to Zarina Begum's house. There, she introduced herself to the lady and tried to cajole her to help our family. (We came to know all of this later; Zarina Begum told us). When my grandmother started to tell Zarina Begum all her woes, Zarina Begum was puzzled. She had not met my grandfather since her return to Dilli, but Suleiman, who visited us often, had kept her informed. She knew that we were not close to poverty, or in any way desperate.

So Zarina Begum asked her some probing questions (I remember Zarina Begum, from later, and she always reminded me of my mother. Kind and wise, but not so meek that one may ride roughshod over her). She was not one to easily accept the words of someone who was, all said and done, a stranger. Ismat could give no coherent answers to her questions. Finally, Zarina Begum told my grandmother, clearly and firmly, that she saw no reason to extend any monetary help unless Nadeem himself asked for it.

Ismat did not even bother to come out of Zarina Begum's house; from the zenana, she ran out into the adjacent courtyard and flung herself into the well. The household flew into a panic. In response to Zarina Begum's cry of alarm, servants came running. A rope was thrown down into the well, and a man servant went down it. But Ismat had known what she was doing, and had not tried to stay afloat. Her corpse was brought up by two men, soaked and pale and finally at peace.

Zarina Begum had my grandmother placed in a bullock cart, enshrouded and now dignified, and sitting beside her, brought her home to our family. That was the first time she visited us, and though it was an inauspicious beginning, it heralded the start of a long and fruitful relationship. Zarina Begum and my mother, perhaps because they were so alike in many ways, became fast friends despite the disparity in their ages. Zarina Begum would visit at least once a week, often more, and I am told that she played an important part in looking after me when I was small.

My father says that it never seemed to him that Nadeem felt anything for Zarina Begum. Most days when she called, he was not around, or even if he was at home, their paths would not cross. She would meet my mother, she would play with me: that was why she visited us, not to talk to my grandfather.

I remember a little of her. I was ten years old when Zarina Begum died, of a virulent fever that reduced her to a bag of bones within a matter of days. Her daughter, Asifa, who is several years older than me, had come to our house as soon as her mother had fallen ill, and Ammi had gone to their home, taking maidservants, a local physician, and many odds and ends—medicinal herbs and bark, fresh fruit, ghee, and more, all of which she believed could help restore strength and good health.

She stayed in Zarina Begum's house a week, and despite all of Ammi's best efforts, as well as those of the physician, the maids, and even a vaid whom Ammi insisted on summoning from a neighbouring village, Zarina Begum did not survive. She was lucid and even smiling till the last, but so painfully emaciated by then, it was a marvel she lived that long.

After her death, Ammi brought Asifa home to live with us. Ammi said Asifa's only other family, Suleiman and his wife and their children, would not take as good care of her. Suleiman's wife would be domineering and would make Asifa do all the housework, and Suleiman's pampered children would bully the girl.

Asifa lived with us till two years back, when Ammi, who was then expecting my little sister, went home to my maternal grandparents in Tanda, to have her baby. One of Ammi's nephews, my cousin, is a year older than Asifa, and Ammi decided that it would be a good match. So Ammi took Asifa with her when they set out. After my sister had been born, Asifa was married to my cousin, and she has settled down there with them in Tanda. Zarina Begum, very early on, had had high hopes of Asifa being a naqshband as she had been; but Asifa had no talent for the craft at all. She never even tried to excel at it, much to her mother's disappointment. I hear she is happy in Tanda, being wife and mother, no more than any other woman of her age and class.

A lot happened while Humayun was wandering, far off to the west. Sher Shah Suri became the Emperor and remained ruler for nearly eight years until his death, after being wounded in an explosion while besieging the fort at Kalinjar. His successors were not half as efficient or resourceful as Sher Shah had been, and Abba says many people thought it was high time Humayun—who was then in Persia, being pampered by the Persian ruler, Shah Tahmasp—tried to regain his kingdom. Others thought Humayun was too weak, and not ambitious enough. They thought the Gurkani rule in Hindustan had been a flash in the pan: just Babar, and that was all. The Gurkani would never return to this land, at least not as rulers.

But all of that changed. Fifteen years after he had been evicted from Hindustan, Humayun came back. Almost two years ago, he captured Lahore; then, within less than six months, he won Dilli and Agra as well, defeating Adil Shah Suri, the last of Sher Shah's short-lived dynasty.

From nothing, he came back to it all, and then, less than a year later, he was dead. His son, Akbar, too, seemed to have been deprived of it all, but like his father, he has come back. How long will he live? How many rebellions will he have to face? What sort of a ruler will he be?

We cannot say. As Abba says, who knows the path of the wind, who can tell where it intends to go?

We can only live on. Or try to live on, as best as we can.

Gokul says, 'But you haven't written what your grandfather said about the Garden of Heaven.'

I had forgotten. We had all been so confused and so distracted by our grieving, I had not stopped to think over the meaning of the one word my grandfather said to me, his last word ever.

'Metaphor,' I say, testing the word out. I have heard this word before, but I do not know what it means.

'Something that stands for something else,' Abba says, when I ask him. He wears a look of deep contentment today. His eyes are shining, and his face looks as if a weight has been lifted off his shoulders. I know why this is so: a letter has arrived yesterday from my maternal grandfather, saying that Ammi and my little sister are returning to Dilli, now that the famine has abated. My cousin, Asifa's husband, will be accompanying them.

'But what does that mean? The Garden of Heaven is a metaphor? A metaphor for what?'

Abba shrugs, shakes his head. 'His mind was wandering,' he says. 'He was very ill, Mohsin. He did not know what he was saying.'

I do not believe that. My grandfather, like Zarina Begum some years ago, was clear-headed right till the end. His body had given up, but his mind had stayed lucid.

I spend the twilight hour sitting at the edge of what used to be a pond till two years back. It has dried up, of course, but my memory of the cool water remains. I settle myself down there, staring into space, remembering the elegant black-winged stilts tip-toeing through the shallows, the herons, still and stiff as soldiers on guard duty. The sudden blue flash of a diving kingfisher, the plaintive repeating call of a lapwing.

Beyond, on the western horizon, there are clouds. Clouds unlike the light, cottony ones we have seen these last months and weeks. These are heavy, dark. Rain clouds, I think. I wonder. I hope.

If it rains, Dilli will be fertile again. A garden, burgeoning with new life, new growth.

Perhaps that was what my grandfather meant: that the Garden of Heaven was a metaphor for the city itself. Dilli is like a garden, and like a garden, it can be many things. In its spring, it can be beautiful, colourful, bright, the picture of prosperity and happiness. Even then, its surface beauty conceals danger: like the thorns and the snakes, the scorpions and the locusts, there are the corrupt, the criminal, the greedy and avaricious. The dross and the danger, which will always be there, even when spring is at its peak, even when the garden that is Dilli is at its most glorious...

I wonder, though, if that was what my grandfather meant. Was that all the Garden of Heaven was? No more than a figment of someone's imagination, a metaphor for a city? No, it cannot be, I think, because the first part of the story, the one that Shagufta told Nasiruddin, was mostly about the Garden of Heaven, and it was a real thing, a work of art. And Daanish, their son, forfeited it, only to pass on to his nephew Qasim, years later, the responsibility of bringing it back into the family.

I am convinced the Garden of Heaven really exists. Or existed; who knows if it has survived all these years? But even if it still exists, where would it be? If I were to go looking for it, where would I begin?

I am not another Qasim. These last two years have eaten a big chunk out of our lives, and I do not have any more time to waste. I have my life to live, and I will not dwell on the past any longer.

The clouds have drifted closer, now so dark that I, lost in thought as I gaze out over the barren landscape, have mistaken the gathering gloom for the coming of the night. Suddenly, the darkness is ripped apart by a flash of lightning. On its heels comes the reverberating, deep-throated rumble of thunder. I look up, and a drop of rain falls right into my eye.

By the time I've blinked it away and stood up, there are more drops, falling fast, falling thick. I think to turn and run back home—Abba and Gokul will be putting out water pots, vessels, buckets, anything that will hold the rainwater, and I must help them—but I pause. It has been so long.

I stand there, face tilted up, letting the rain wash over me. The sweat, the grime, the dust, all washed off, washed away.

When I go home, it is to find that Abba and Gokul have put out the vessels, but with that task done, they too are standing, both of them bare-chested, in the rain. The three of us stare at each other, drenched to the bone, the water mingling with the tears on our faces, and we begin laughing.

Historical Note

In 1398 CE, the Chaghtai warrior Taimur invaded India and captured Delhi. For three days, Taimur's armies plundered and ravaged the city; when they withdrew, they took with them not just what they had plundered, but also intangible wealth: thousands of skilled artisans were imprisoned and taken to Taimur's native Samarqand to help embellish the city.

Taimur's invasion dealt such a blow to Delhi that the city did not fully recover from it for nearly a century. Not only had the invading army been especially brutal; Delhi's Sultans around that time were not the most efficient, far-sighted or capable. Nasiruddin Mahmud Shah Tughlaq (r. 1394-1413), who was ruler of Delhi during Taimur's invasion, was not a patch on his more illustrious (or at least more charismatic) Tughlaq predecessors. Even before Taimur's invasion, the Delhi Sultanate had become so weak that its vassals had begun to assert themselves: Bengal had shaken off Delhi's rule in 1390, Jaunpur four years later. In the wake of the invasion, others too rebelled and broke loose: in 1402, Mewat; just five years later, in 1407, Gujarat.

Within a few years of the Timurid invasion, Nasiruddin Mahmud Shah Tughlaq was a spent force: when he died in 1413, the Tughlaq dynasty ended with him, and Khizr Khan, who had once been the Governor of Multan, became the Sultan at Delhi, establishing the Sayyid dynasty. While their antecedents have been disputed by historians, the Sayyids derived their name from their claim to have been descended from the Prophet Mohammad.

The Sayyids were no better rulers than Nasiruddin Tughlaq had been; the four Sultans that comprised this short-lived dynasty held Delhi for less than forty years. It was under the third of the Sayyid Sultans, Mohammad

Shah, that a former horse trader named Bahlol Lodhi came to prominence: first as a supplier of fine horses to the Sultan, then as a general who played an important part in defending the Sayyid domains from the attacks of Malwa. Bahlol Lodhi proved too ambitious for the good of his Sayyid masters; in 1443, while Mohammad Shah was still Sultan at Delhi, Bahlol (by now appointed Governor of Sirhind, in Punjab) made the first of three attacks on Delhi. His third assault on the city, in 1451, ended the Sayyid dynasty. Bahlol Lodhi (r. 1451-1489) became the first of the three Lodhi Sultans to rule Delhi.

Bahlol was a capable ruler, a strong-willed and ambitious man who embarked on a mission to expand the empire, reclaiming for it territories such as Jaunpur and Malwa. His equally driven son, Sikandar Lodhi, continued the expansionist agenda of Bahlol, annexing areas from Punjab through to Bengal. As part of his plan to subjugate territories in Gwalior, Malwa and Dholpur, Sikandar Lodhi shifted the imperial capital from Delhi to Agra in 1505. Agra (which he named Sikandra, after himself), being in closer proximity to Malwa and Gwalior than was Delhi, was regarded as a more suitable base for campaigns in the region.

Sikandar Lodhi was a great general and administrator, putting in place numerous land and agricultural reforms; building a network of highways across the realm; requiring jagirdars to submit auditable accounts; and promoting literature and learning. His religious bigotry (ironic, given that his mother, Bibi Ambha, was a Hindu) was however virulent enough to make him unpopular among the bulk of his subjects.

Sikandar Lodhi's son, Ibrahim Lodhi, the third (and last) of the Lodhi Sultans, ascended the throne after the death of Sikandar Lodhi in 1517—and ruled for a mere nine years. Ibrahim's high-handedness with the powerful courtiers of the land antagonized many of them, to the extent that an incensed Daulat Khan Lodhi, the Governor of Lahore, invited the ruler of Kabul, Babar, to overthrow Ibrahim Lodhi and take the throne of Delhi.

Zahiruddin Mohammad Babar (b. 1483), a descendant of both Taimur as well as Genghis Khan, was heir to the principality of Ferghana. Along with Samarqand (his father's fief) Ferghana was snatched from Babar by ambitious relatives when Babar was still in his teens. Desperate for greener (and more vulnerable?) pastures, Babar set his sights on India. Moving eastward, he captured Kabul in 1504. Over the next fifteen years, Babar consolidated his territories around Kabul, and by 1519, was making inroads into Punjab. In the landmark year of 1526, egged on by Daulat Khan Lodhi, he led his troops right up to Panipat to challenge Ibrahim Lodhi.

Despite having a far smaller fighting force than did Ibrahim Lodhi, Babar used strategy to defeat the Lodhi. Ibrahim Lodhi was killed here, at the First Battle of Panipat, and Babar, making his way to Agra to take over the throne, established a new dynasty in India: the Mughals, as they came to be known (though, since 'Mughal' implied 'barbaric', they never referred to themselves as such; instead, they called themselves the House of Taimur, or the Gurkani). Babar did not get long to enjoy his new acquisitions; four years after he had conquered India, he was dead, popular myth putting his demise down to his having sacrificed his life for that of his ailing son, Humayun.

Babar had not had the time to consolidate and strengthen the empire he had won; it fell to Humayun to do that—but Humayun was too ineffectual, too weak and far too generous for his own good. He pardoned his recalcitrant brothers their many attempts on his life and throne, was unable to tackle the financial instability of the empire, and eventually lost out to the increasingly powerful Sher Shah Suri (r. 1540-1556). Sher Shah was an Afghan who had enlisted as a soldier in Jaunpur, and had steadily made his way upwards, first becoming the regent of Bihar and then gaining control of neighbouring Bengal. In 1540, Sher Shah defeated Humayun at the Battle of Kannauj, snatching away Humayun's throne in the process and leaving him to wander, rootless, for the next decade and a half.

Sher Shah Suri's reign was beneficial for the people of the realm: he carried out administrative (especially tax) reforms, clamped down on corruption, and revamped highways—the Sadak-e-Azam, today's Grand Trunk Road, was laid out by Sher Shah along the route of Chandragupta Maurya's ancient highway, though Sher Shah extended the highway, built sarais and dug wells along its length, and erected kos minars to mark every kos. Sher Shah was a worthy administrator, doughty general, a ruler who knew his people and knew how to rule them: all that Humayun had failed at.

For fifteen years, from 1540 to 1555, Humayun remained outside India, spending most of his time in Persia, where he was treated with much generosity by Shah Tahmasp, the ruler of Persia. In 1545, Sher Shah Suri was wounded during the siege of Kalinjar, and died shortly after. His son and successor, Islam Shah Suri (also known as Salim Shah Suri) reigned for about nine years, till late 1554; like Sher Shah, Islam Shah had been a competent ruler—but his death saw the collapse of the dynasty. Within the next year or so, a series of rulers came to the throne, but none could hold it long enough to consolidate his reign. Taking advantage of the chaos, Humayun made a bid to reclaim the throne. Under the generalship of the able Bairam Khan, the Mughal armies were victorious at the Battle of Sirhind (June 1555) and Humayun once again became ruler of Delhi and of India.

Humayun was singularly unfortunate; less than a year after he re-ascended the throne, he fell down the stairs from his library in Delhi's Purana Qila, and succumbed to his injuries four days later. His thirteen-year-old son Akbar, with the faithful Bairam Khan acting as regent, was proclaimed Emperor. However, since Akbar had been appointed Governor of Punjab earlier that year, he was far away from the capital at Delhi. An ambitious general, Hemu (who had served under Adil Shah Suri, the last of the Suri dynasty) immediately took steps to lay claim to the throne. Marching westward from Bengal, where he was stationed, Hemu quickly captured the states between Bengal and Delhi, finally taking Agra and then Delhi itself. Crowned Samrat Hemchandra Vikramaditya in a grand rajyabhishek, Hemu could not rule Delhi for long: on November 5, 1556, less than a month after his coronation, Hemu's armies were defeated at the Second Battle of Panipat by Akbar's forces, led by Bairam Khan.

And thus Akbar became Emperor, the greatest of the Mughals, as he was to prove in the course of a long reign.

Given that *An Unholy Drought* is a work of fiction, I have taken certain liberties with the real-life personalities that appear in it. The interactions of fictional characters with people like Bibi Ambha, Dilawar Begum and Gulbadan Begum are obviously completely imaginary; but there are aspects of their lives that are true. Bibi Ambha was indeed the daughter of a Hindu goldsmith, and Dilawar Begum was an ambitious, strong-willed woman who was exiled to Kabul after she tried to poison Babar. Gulbadan Begum, Babar's daughter, was a child when her father conquered India, and came to Agra as a little girl, as part of a retinue that included the reciter and entertainer, Bibi Sarv-Qad, 'Mistress Tall-as-a-Cypress'. In later years, Gulbadan was requested by Akbar to write her memoirs; what resulted was the manuscript known as *Humayunnama*.

For the 150-odd years that are the focus of this novel, from just after Taimur's invasion in 1398 to the Second Battle of Panipat (1556), Delhi was mostly not the capital of the empire. With Sikandar Lodhi shifting the capital to Agra and both Ibrahim Lodhi and his nemesis Babar retaining Agra as the seat of the empire, Delhi lost, for many years, its position as the most important city of the realm. Though both Humayun and Sher Shah Suri would return to Delhi (Humayun establishing Din Panah, the citadel today known as Purana Qila, and Sher Shah adding to it), Delhi would not regain its political significance until Shahjahan returned to it almost a century later.

This did not mean, however, that the city utterly languished in the meantime. Although plagued by a succession of ineffectual rulers, and, as a result, a disturbed and unstable political scene, Delhi survived. It continued to be a centre of religious and spiritual significance; arts and crafts (carving, embroidery and brocade, jewellery and weaving among them) still continued to be created. And though neither the Sayyids nor the Lodhis were prolific builders like their predecessors, the Tughlaqs and Khaljis, they did construct some impressive tombs, especially in the area known as Bagh-e-Jud, today Lodhi Garden, where Mohammad Shah Sayyid and Sikandar Lodhi's tombs stand. According to the British historian Simon Digby (whose arguments seem very plausible to a layperson like me), the Sheesh Gumbad in Lodhi Garden is the tomb of Bahlol Lodhi.

Acknowledgements

To thank an editor in the acknowledgements is par for the course; but that is not why I begin with a grateful mention of Aruna Ghose. Aruna deserves my gratitude because without her, *An Unholy Drought* would have been an unholy mess. Her keen vision, her wisdom, and her refusal to accept anything substandard challenged me and pushed me to do better, and if you have enjoyed reading this book, it owes a huge deal to Aruna. Thank you.

Then, the people at my publishers, Speaking Tiger, along with the consultants and associates they work with. Renuka Chatterjee, whose editorial eye is, as ever, unerring, and whose insight into the (to me, puzzling) world of publishing has been an enormous help throughout, from far before this book. Ravi Singh, Dyuti Roy, and many others who worked tirelessly behind the scenes. Maithili Doshi, whose exquisitely designed cover graces this book. Tanu Dogra and Atika Gupta, of Atika Gupta PR & Communications Services, who excel at what I struggle to do: market my books. Thank you.

Several others, friends and family members, helped in ways big and small to take this book a step closer to completion. Yusuf Kar explained how the death anniversary of an elder may be observed at a graveyard; Sarabjeet Dhody Natesan, by way of reminiscences about learning calligraphy, explained the use of Multani mitti to erase mistakes. Harini Srinivasan, with whom a conversation about historical fiction led to my finally breaking through a roadblock at one point of the plot. Thank you, all.

A special word of thanks to the many readers who wrote in to tell me how much they enjoyed the prequel to this book, *The Garden of Heaven*. Among them, Rajani, Tejaswini Apte-Rahm, Nikhil Kamath, Natasha Ramarathnam, Abdullah

Khan, Anuradha Warrier, and Ava Suri: thank you. A special thanks to the friend and fellow writer to whom this book is dedicated: Dipali Taneja. May all writers be blessed with readers like you.

As always, my very learned and extremely helpful sister, Swapna Liddle, was the one I turned to when grappling with questions that no amount of (relatively limited and fumbling research) could answer. Swapna shared books, patiently answered questions, and was the perfect sounding board for ideas.

My parents, who (like all good parents everywhere!) couldn't be prouder, and have always supported my writing. And, of course, those I live with: my husband Tarun and our daughter, both of whom are patient, supportive, and generous beyond all imagining.

Thank you, everybody: without you, this book wouldn't have made it.

Selected Bibliography

Ed. Frykenberg, RE. *Delhi Through the Ages: Essays in Urban History, Culture and Society*. New Delhi: Oxford University Press, 1988

Peck, Lucy. *Delhi: A Thousand Years of Building*. New Delhi: Roli Books, 2005

Ed. Kaul, HK. *Historic Delhi: An Anthology*. New Delhi: Oxford University Press, 2000

Liddle, Swapna. *Delhi: 14 Historic Walks*. India: Westland Ltd, 2011

Eraly, Abraham. *The Last Spring: Life in India's Last Golden Age*. India: Penguin Books, 2015

Gascoigne, Bamber. *A Brief History of the Great Moghuls*. India: Robinson, 2002

Raghavan, TCA. *Attendant Lords: Bairam Khan and Abdul Rahim, Courtiers & Poets in Mughal India*. India: Harper Collins Publishers India, 2017

Mukhoty, Ira. *Akbar: The Great Mughal*. New Delhi: Aleph Book Company, 2020

Mukhoty, Ira. *Daughters of the Sun: Empresses, Queens & Begums of the Mughal Empire*. New Delhi: Aleph Book Company, 2018

Godden, Rumer. *Gulbadan: Portrait of a Princess at the Mughal Court*. New Delhi: Speaking Tiger Books, 2016

Gulbadan Begum. *Humayun-nama* (Beveridge, Annette S, Trans). London: Royal Asiatic Society, 1902

Shokoohy, M, and Shokoohy, N. *The Lady of Gold: Sikandar Lodī's mother (c. 837/1433–922/1516) and the tomb attributed to her at Dholpur, Rajasthan*. Bulletin of the School of Oriental and African Studies, Cambridge University Press, 2018

ALSO IN SPEAKING TIGER

THE GARDEN OF HEAVEN

A Novel

Madhulika Liddle

A magnificent stone frieze—built up into curves and flourishes, peacocks and curving vines and trailing leaves—runs like a thread through this gripping, sweeping saga that spans a period of two hundred years between two invasions of Dilli—that of Muhammed of Ghur in 1192 CE, and Taimur in the winter of 1398. For whom was it carved, and what happened to it as family fortunes and dynasties rose and fell?

Ten-year-old Madhav comes to Dilli after his world is torn apart by the battle in which Prithviraj Chauhan loses his throne and his life, paving the way for the Delhi Sultanate. In the teeming city, Madhav starts a career as a stone carver, and the craft becomes a manifestation of his very being. It eventually inspires him to create his masterpiece, a stone frieze that he calls the Garden of Heaven.

Running parallel to Madhav's story is that of another family of stone carvers—Nandu, his arrogant daughter Gayatri, and Gayatri's daughter, Jayshree, who befriends an unusual, headstrong young woman who wears the clothes of a man and one day leads her army into battle as Razia Sultan. A gentle courtier named Amir Khusro also plays a part in this grand drama, as does Ibrahim, whose forbidden love for Chhoti brings two families together. And then there is poor and lonely Shagufta, who rescues Nasiruddin, a wounded Timurid soldier, and to distract him from his agony, tells the story of her city and herself....

A richly human, layered and dramatic narrative about Delhi on the threshold of a new phase in its long and eventful history, *The Garden of Heaven* holds the reader in thrall till the end.

[illegible]

THE GARDEN OF HEAVEN

[illegible]